STOCKBROKING TODAY

STOCKBROKING TODAY

J. Dundas Hamilton

SECOND EDITION

M

First edition 1968
Second edition 1979

Published by
THE MACMILLAN PRESS LTD
London and Basingstoke
Associated companies in Delhi
Dublin Hong Kong Johannesburg Lagos
Melbourne New York Singapore Tokyo

Printed in Great Britain by
REDWOOD BURN LTD
Trowbridge and Esher

British Library Cataloguing in Publication Data

Hamilton, James Dundas
Stockbroking today – 2nd ed
1. Stock exchange – Great Britain
I. Title
332.6′42′0941 HG5432

ISBN 0-333-24237-8

Contents

Preface to the Second Edition

In introducing the first edition of *Stockbroking Today*, I posed three questions: what was the purpose of the book? for whom was it to be written? and what, if any, were my own qualifications for writing it?

Now, over ten years later, the answers to the first two questions at least remain the same. It is still, to my knowledge, the only book which is concerned, not about The Stock Exchange as an institution nor about investment, but about the day-to-day work in a stockbroker's office. The readership is still intended to cover almost all those intersted in investment, particularly the student considering stockbroking as a career. As for myself, I am certainly older, I hope wiser and possibly more experienced.

The need for a revised edition is much more obvious, since the speed of change in stockbroking has increased remarkably over the period. The clientele has altered, with the gradual decline of the private investor and the rapid growth of institutional funds. The membership of The Stock Exchange has passed through two periods of transition: first, the unification of all the Stock Exchanges in the United Kingdom and the Republic of Ireland into The Stock Exchange, with its centre in London and five provincial trading floors; second, the crucial aftermath of the disastrous slump of 1974/75 when, through mergers or decisions to cease trading, a fifth of the firms of stockbrokers disappeared and the employees in the stockbroking and jobbing industry declined by almost a third. No other industry, to my knowledge, has seen such massive closures and redundancies and emerged with so little adverse comment and without the need of outside assistance. Only the decline in the number of jobbing firms has attracted publicity and this, as I hope to explain in the text itself, is due to the move away from specialisation to a general spread of interest rather than to a major reduction in competition.

The computer has revolutionised the procedures of settlement, client accounting, portfolio valuation, data retrieval for research and a host of other time- and people-intensive operations. Communications have become faster and more sophisticated so that the international aspects of stockbroking have become more closely entwined with domestic activities.

And lastly, since the publication of the first edition, we have a new Stock Exchange itself; the most modern trading floor in the world; a tower block both used as a commercial property and housing the offices of the Council and its senior executives; over a thousand employees engaged in a variety of functions, regulatory, settlement, property management and also, in these hazardous days, personal security.

In the final paragraph of the introduction to the first edition, I expressed my gratitude to those who had been kind enough to assist with information, criticism and amendments to the text. In particular, I thanked all those officials of the various overseas Stock Exchanges who had provided the information on which Appendices 7–16 are based. They have once more updated this information with exemplary speed. The facts are due to their diligence. The errors and omissions are my own.

February 1978 J. D. H.

I The Industry and the Profession

A Stock Exchange exists to provide the facilities of a market-place where potential investors can put their money to work by purchasing securities and those who already own securities can equally freely and speedily turn them into cash. An effective securities market requires four qualities: liquidity, so that dealings can take place easily in large amounts; choice, so that investors have a wide spectrum both of classes of security and individual items within each class from which to choose; efficiency, so that both the proceeds of the sale and the title to the securities purchased are available on the due date; and, most important of all, regulation, so that the price is seen to be fair both to buyer and seller, stockbrokers will be known to fulfil their obligations and the public will be kept fully informed about the securities listed.

Side by side with the market in existing securities a Stock Exchange can also provide the facility whereby borrowers such as Governments, public authorities or companies, who require additional capital can be satisfied by lenders who require an outlet for their funds. Stock Exchanges also provide the principal mechanism for raising new risk capital, the equity shares of corporations, which in the United Kingdom make an important contribution to the external funds subscribed for industry and commerce.

Stockbrokers in the United Kingdom perform three separate functions. Initially, they make arrangements for the listing of the stock or shares of a company so that dealings can take place in the market. Secondly, they act as agents in the buying and selling of securities, since no outside investor can deal through the medium of The Stock Exchange without using the services of a stockbroker. And finally, they act as advisers to their clients in the selection and administration of their investments.

It is the last function, the service of the client, that turns stockbroking from being purely an industry into a profession. It is the position of trust in which stockbrokers are placed, acting as both agent and adviser, that limits their activities and oddly enough throws them open to criticism from the people whose interests they are endeavouring to protect.

But first it is important to look at the industry as one would look at any other industry in the financial sector, such as banking, hire-purchase or insurance. Stockbroking in the United Kingdom has altered materially since the first edition of this book was written. At that time there were stock exchanges in twenty-one of the major towns and cities, which had recently been linked into four main groups—London, Midland and Western, Northern and Scottish, together with about 100 firms in other provincial areas. In March 1973 these were unified into one exchange, The Stock Exchange, which also included members of the Belfast Stock Exchange and of the two Southern Irish exchanges in Dublin and Cork. The Stock Exchange can therefore boast of being the only truly international exchange in the world, with members and subsidiary markets under a different statutory and legal authority.

Just as London is the centre of this network of stockbrokers throughout the British Isles, so it is only one stock exchange in a much larger global network. Most people are familiar with the famous New York Stock Exchange on Wall Street, but this is only the largest of the two stock exchanges in New York and of the eleven stretching across the American continent to Honolulu, Los Angeles and San Francisco. At the end of 1976 there were nine stock exchanges in Australia, five in Canada, eight in Japan and twelve in Brazil. New stock exchanges are being formed as one country after another reaches a state of modern development. The latest in the list, the Kuwait Stock Exchange, has recently been established.

Stockbroking, therefore, is an international industry, and the importance of London as a financial centre is emphasised by the number of branch offices of overseas firms which are maintained there. No less than 28 firms of New York stockbrokers and 13 Canadian firms maintain London offices. In addition there are four Japanese holders of Principal's Licences and eleven from the EEC.

Membership of The Stock Exchange in the United Kingdom differs materially from that in other countries. It is limited to the individual, and there is no requirement to buy a seat. The activities of a stockbroking firm are carefully prescribed and largely restricted to dealing in stocks and shares. In America, however, stockbrokers may operate in the commodity markets. In West Germany the great majority of stock exchange transactions are carried out by the banks, who are also members of the exchanges. And in other countries stockbrokers may engage in insurance and other activities.

To write in detail of the stockbroking community in all these centres would require not only a volume many times larger than this, but also a knowledge infinitely greater than my own. Some readers may, however, be interested in dealing in foreign securities. Purchases or sales can be carried out in London of almost any security quoted on a foreign exchange, but for those who like to know the operation of foreign exchanges in more detail, appendixes have been added giving the basic information about all the principal overseas markets whose securities are quoted daily in the *Financial Times*.

Although the purpose of this book is to describe the functions and operation of a stockbroking business, rather than a stock exchange, some introduction is necessary to the systems operated in the various exchanges.

STOCK EXCHANGE SYSTEMS

Three basic systems are maintained in the world's stock exchanges: the call-over system, used in the majority of the smaller exchanges; the trading-post system, used in a number of centres including Wall Street, Sydney and Melbourne; and the jobbing system, which is peculiar to the United Kingdom.

(*a*) CALL-OVER

At fixed times, normally once in the morning and once in the afternoon, the members of the stock exchange assemble around the chairman or other official and the list of securities quoted in that centre is read out, together with the price ruling at the time. As each security is called, brokers who have buying orders will bid for stocks or shares and those with selling orders will offer them. When a buyer and seller agree on a price suitable to both, a transaction is made. If the agreed price is different from the call-over price, the latter is adjusted at the time of the next call-over.

This system would imply that shares can only be bought and sold at the fixed times of the call-over during the day, but this is not so in practice. When a broker receives an order at another time of the day he approaches those other brokers who have shown interest at the time of the previous call-over, and transacts his business.

(*b*) TRADING-POST

Under this system a given point on the floor of the stock exchange is allocated as a meeting-place for transactions in certain specified securities. Brokers with business to carry out in these stocks and shares meet at the trading-post and conclude a satisfactory bargain between themselves. In the New York Stock Exchange twenty-three trading-posts have an average of some sixty-five to seventy common stock issues each, and price indicators show the price of the last sale in each security. In addition the 'tape' gives a record of every transaction, including both the number of shares and the price, and is transmitted immediately to many brokers and investment institutions throughout the U.S.A.

If the ruling price in a security is much different from the price at which a broker has instructions to deal, or if there are no other brokers who wish to match his order with one in the opposite direction, it is obviously a waste of his time to stand around the trading-post waiting on the off-chance that he may be able to deal. Certain members, therefore, undertake this duty as 'specialists'. Each security has its own specialist and one specialist may deal in several securities. Specialists not only accept 'limit orders' (orders at fixed prices, as opposed to 'market orders' which must be executed at the best price possible at the time of dealing), but they also trade for their own account. In order to help maintain an orderly market to protect other brokers for whom the specialist may be operating on limit orders, his own trading is hedged around with a number of restrictions.

(*c*) JOBBING SYSTEM

The London Stock Exchange was founded on the jobbing system. The Stock Exchange operates as a market, very much like any other, whether in meat, fish or vegetables. The market floor contains a number of 'pitches' around the walls or in the shape of hexagonal stands (see Figure 2), and here the jobbers act as stall-holders. While the specialist in New York acts primarily as an assistant to the broker in keeping his limits under surveillance, and only acts more infrequently on his own account, the jobber always acts as a principal. Unlike the stall-holder in the vegetable market, however, who knows the identity of the growers and also of the buyers, the jobber never knows until the last moment whether a broker is going to sell shares to him or buy them from him. This factor, combined with the competition between several firms of jobbers dealing in the same securities, tends to keep the margin between selling and buying prices down to a minimum.

Each of the three systems described has its own peculiar merits and is suited to a particular financial centre. The call-over system is most suitable for the small stock exchange where the number of transactions is limited, since the activity would be insufficient to provide a reasonable livelihood for either the jobber or the specialist. The trading-post system is suitable for those centres where there is a limited number of securities and a relatively high degree of activity. The jobber is of particular value in matching substantial institutional orders with a large number of small orders in the opposite direction from other sources. As a result the leading British securities enjoy a freer market than many of their counterparts in New York. The system comes under fire from a number of sources, largely on the grounds that the expense of dealing is higher than in other centres where the trading-post system is operated, owing to the jobber's turn (the difference between the jobber's buying and selling prices), and that only a few jobbing firms are prepared to take a really substantial position and then only in a limited number of leading securities. It is not my intention to become involved in this controversy at this stage, but there is little doubt, in my own mind, that the purported cost of the jobbing intermediary appears in other markets under a different guise. Market-making is an essential part of a liquid market and the client ultimately pays for what he gets.

FUNCTIONS OF A STOCKBROKER

The three functions of the stockbroker have already been mentioned: to arrange the listing of stocks and shares; to act as an agent in buying and selling securities; and to act as adviser to his clients in the selection and management of their investments.

Listing is primarily required by either Government or quasi-Government organisations or commercial and industrial enterprises. When these concerns wish to raise funds by means of new issues, the stockbroker's function lies in submitting the necessary documents for listing, in advising on the best price which can be obtained for the issue, and in arranging that funds are available to guarantee its subscription.

The second function is relatively simple, although it covers more than just the procedures of buying and selling stocks and shares. Where securities are quoted in more than one centre, for example, the broker may check the market in both exchanges to ensure that he deals to the best advantage of his client, in some cases cabling or telephoning his agents or branch office in an overseas centre.

Although stockbrokers' charges are almost entirely derived from commission on the purchase and sale of securities, by far the greater part of their time is devoted to the third function, the advisory services in the selection and administration of investments. Valuations of clients' portfolios, written reports, attendance at meetings and a wide range of services on the telephone may all be provided free of charge. In the days before the Second World War, stockbroking was largely a matter of having the right connections and using a certain amount of common sense. But today a far more scientific approach is made to investment. The quality of a stockbroker's business is much more dependent on the service that he offers to his clients than on his social connections.

VARIETY OF BUSINESS

One of the fascinations of the stockbroker's work lies in its variety. One minute he may be recommending investments for a pension fund, running into several hundreds of thousands of pounds, and the next he may be advising an elderly widow on the investment of under a hundred. One day he may be advising on the tactics of taking over another company, and the following day discussing the plans for a listing of shares on the stock market. One month he may be visiting a textile mill in Yorkshire and the next an electronics factory in Japan. In the larger firms the duties of individual partners and executives are usually somewhat specialised, as will be seen in the following chapters, but in the smaller firms members are expected to be jacks-of-all-trades. And even in the largest organisations the personal contact, and the confidence inspired in the client by the personality of a particular individual, make it difficult to decentralise all responsibilities completely. However much, in the interests of efficiency, the work of the firm is delegated between carefully devised departments, in the end it all depends on whether the individual in the firm and the client see eye to eye and like and respect each other.

The move towards a more scientific approach to investment has produced two changes in the structure of stockbroking firms: first, it has led to a degree of specialisation by those firms who are closely connected with certain industries; and second, in order to provide the expert service demanded by the institutional investors, the smaller and medium-sized firms are tending to amalgamate into larger units.

SPECIALISATION

Specialisation in the past has largely been confined to classes of security and types of business. For instance, the bulk of the institutional business in the gilt-edged market was traditionally carried out by only half a dozen firms, although this has now spread to about twenty. The issue of stocks for water companies is still almost entirely carried out by one firm of brokers. In recent years, however, certain firms have developed a reputation in selected ordinary share markets—property, breweries, insurance and investment trust shares being well-known examples. This degree of specialisation demands a high quality in the service which is offered to investors and, while there may be times of stagnation in the turnover in some shares (the property share market, for example, following the 1975 débâcle), the degree of business undertaken when the market is active more than outweighs its erratic nature.

SIZE OF FIRMS.

Of the 280 member firms in the list of 4110 members of The Stock Exchange at 31 December 1976 (on which date as many of the statistics in this book as possible are based) 260 were brokers and 20 were jobbers. Some indication of the size of a firm is given by the number of partners, single-partner firms being forbidden under the rules. Over the past decade, in common with most other professions, the trend has been towards fewer and larger firms.

The term 'partner' normally indicates an individual whose remuneration is taken partly or solely from his share in the profits of the business. In The Stock Exchange, however, it is traditional for some partners to be fully profit-sharing, while others may be remunerated by means of salary and/or commission. In a business where personal contact between the client and the broker is all-important, the client often has more faith in the individual if he sees his name on the firm's writing-paper. For this reason, as well as its being the just reward for services rendered to the firm, non-profit-sharing partners may be included in the partnership list. There is no indication as to which of the partners share the profits and which do not, although all are liable to an unlimited share of any loss which may be incurred if the firm becomes a defaulter.

The total number of employees in member firms currently totals about 12,500 and the size of staffs varies from several hundred in the largest firms to only half-a-dozen in the smallest. The individuals who are permitted to enter the trading floor of The Stock Exchange itself are listed, and the breakdown is in Table 1 below.

TABLE 1

	At 31 December 1976	
	Brokers	*Jobbers*
Partners[1]	2082	224
Associated members[2]	1539	265
Authorised clerks[3]	547	132
Unauthorised clerks[4]	291	96

[1] including 30 corporate and 6 external members
[2] including 135 unattached members
[3] including telephone dealing and accredited clerks
[4] including unaccredited clerks

Authorised clerks are employees of member firms who are permitted to transact the business of buying and selling in the market. Unauthorised clerks, who are distinguished by the fact that the name badge of the firm which they wear is blue instead of silver, are not permitted to transact business, and are only used by their firms for obtaining prices, conveying messages, answering calls, etc.

MEMBERSHIP

All members are subject to the Rules and Regulations of The Stock Exchange (whose 220 General Rules and 57 Appendices are contained in a book of 409 pages) and to all decisions of their elected Council. But over and above these printed rules and regulations, members are constrained to observe the strict etiquette and traditions of their profession.

The Council has wide powers in its control of Members' activities, particularly in ensuring the financial viability of firms (Rule 79a) and in the conduct of a Member's affairs. A Member found to have committed misconduct, which includes 'conduct unbecoming the character of a Member' may be subject to heavy penalty, running from a reprimand, through censure, withdrawal of the right to enter any Trading Floor, suspension from dealing in any manner whatsoever, to the ultimate punishment of expulsion (Rules 17 and 18).

Members must obtain permission from the Council if they wish to accept any other unlimited liability or to take other employment outside The Stock Exchange (Rule 27). In addition a Member must elect whether he wishes to act as Broker or Jobber and may not act as both (Rules 86 and 87).

The Rules and Regulations are constantly under revision and are frequently updated by amendments, new Rules and Permanent Notices. They are currently the subject of scrutiny by the Office of Fair Trading to determine whether any of them constitutes a restrictive practice.

The full requirements for becoming a member are considered in Chapter 9.

CONDUCT OF BUSINESS

The conduct of business between members or between members and their clients is also strictly governed. In the former connection the most important rules are probably:

> The Stock Exchange does not recognise in its dealings any other parties than its own Members: every bargain therefore,

whether for account of the Member effecting it or for account of a Principal, must be fulfilled according to the Rules, Regulations and usages of The Stock Exchange (Rule 73).

A Member or Authorised Clerk may not accept instructions or adopt any procedure which would in any way or for any purpose override his duty to execute each transaction to the best advantage according to his judgement at the time of dealing (Rule 73A).

All disputes between Members not affecting the general interests of The Stock Exchange which arise out of Stock Exchange transactions or are connected with Stock Exchange business and including partnership disputes, shall be referred to the arbitration of a Member or Members of The Stock Exchange: and the Council will not take into consideration such disputes unless arbitrators cannot be found, or the arbitrators are unable to come to a decision (Rule 75 (1)).

In addition members abide by a strict etiquette in transacting business on the market floor. The framework for this behaviour is laid down in 'The Stock Exchange Code of Dealing' and honorary market officials are available on the floor itself to advise on procedure or adjudicate on interpretation.

THE COUNCIL

The drafting and the enforcement of these rules is a matter for the Council, a body of forty-five members, fifteen of whom are elected each year for a three-year term of office. The Government Broker is an additional ex-officio member.

The Council is elected by secret ballot (Rule 2) and from its members elects a chairman and two deputy-chairmen (Rule 4). They also appoint standing committees, which currently cover the following subjects:

Property and Finance
Membership
Quotations
Commissions and Dealing
Settlement Services
Information and Communication Services
Planning

The power of the Council is absolute, as shown in Rule 12A, which states:

> In all matters brought under the consideration of the Council, their decision whether expressed by a Resolution or otherwise shall be final and must be carried out forthwith by every Member concerned, provided that where a Resolution is required by the Rules to be confirmed such Resolution shall not be valid or put into force until confirmed.

As mentioned earlier, it is not the intention to discuss the operation of The Stock Exchange as such in this volume, but to concentrate on the work of the stockbroker. While members are expected to know the principal rules and regulations, the Code of Dealing and to study the notices which emanate from the Council from time to time, in general terms the efficient operation of the Council and its secretariat is best reflected in the fact that the majority of members are only consciously aware of its existence when some major item (such as the TALISMAN settlement system) comes up for discussion, or when they have a personal problem on which advice from a member of the Council is sought.

THE REGIONAL UNITS

It has already been mentioned that there are more stockbroking firms outside London than in the capital itself, although they make only a contribution of about one-quarter of the total equity turnover and a lower proportion in fixed-interest stocks. As a result of unification The Stock Exchange owns freeholds or leaseholds in 15 towns or cities outside London, dealing floors being operated in five of them.

The five regional exchanges—Scottish, Northern (including Belfast), Midlands and Western, Irish and the Provincial Brokers Stock Exchange (co-ordinating the activities of brokers operating in areas without a local exchange)—now act as units of The Stock Exchange, but still elect their own regional committees and chairmen to discuss local problems and provide an invaluable communication link with the national centre.

The eleven regional members of the Council are elected from within their own regional membership, although it is possible that this distinction may cease after 1982.

THE ASSOCIATION OF STOCK AND SHARE DEALERS

Under the provisions of the Prevention of Fraud (Investments) Act, 1958, all those carrying on the business of dealing in securities must operate under the authority of a principal's licence, issued under the regulations of the Department of Trade. Members of recognised stock exchanges and recognised associations of dealers in securities are specifically exempted in the Act, so that none of those mentioned in the previous paragraphs requires a licence.

The largest recognised association of dealers in securities is the Association of Stock and Share Dealers, whose membership at 31 December 1976 numbered some fifteen firms.

TRANSACTIONS OUTSIDE THE STOCK EXCHANGE

So much for the industry and the profession of stockbroking. Before turning to the detailed organisation of a stockbroking firm, one last point must be made clear. The law does not require that every sale and purchase of securities shall be made through the channels of a stockbroker or authorised dealer in securities. Fathers may transfer stocks and shares to their children, willing buyers and sellers may carry out transactions together, or a financial institution may undertake the normal functions of a stockbroker by placing shares with others with whom it has connections.

A recent development in this connection has been the establishment of the ARIEL (Automated Real Time Investment Limited) system, which came into existence on 11 February 1974. ARIEL was formed by a number of the Accepting Houses who found themselves giving very large amounts of commission to stockbrokers, without receiving adequate remuneration in the management of their investment departments. At the same time they had the genuine belief that The Stock Exchange dealing system was obsolete and that new electronic methods would ultimately supersede it. They therefore set up a network, which now covers some 65 subscribers, whereby offers and bids for securities may be shown on all screens and interested parties may be linked anonymously to negotiate a deal between themselves. ARIEL represents about 1 per cent of the total equity turnover on The Stock Exchange.

In addition one of the firms of licensed dealers, M.J.H. Nightingale & Co. Ltd, has developed an over-the-counter market for securities of companies which, for one reason or another, are not yet prepared to obtain an official listing. Ten companies currently use this facility, with dealings in thirteen securities.

THE STOCK EXCHANGE UNLISTED SECURITIES MARKET

For many years the facility has been available for dealings in the shares or stock of either private or public unlisted companies to be carried out through the medium of The Stock Exchange. In 1978, following various submissions to the Wilson Committee, The Stock Exchange published a booklet (*The Stock Exchange Unlisted Securities Market*) explaining this facility and the provisions of Rule 163 (2). Over 800 companies currently make use of this market.

The Stock Exchange makes no charge for giving permission to deal under this Rule, but reserves the right to withdraw the facility if activity becomes so great that the Council decide a full listing is more appropriate. Prices are published in the Daily Official List and in the Saturday edition of the *Financial Times*. The investor is also protected by the Stock Exchange Compensation Fund on the same terms as apply to investors in listed securities.

ORGANISATION OF A STOCKBROKING FIRM

Stockbrokers are becoming more and more expert in the critical appreciation of management in those companies which they investigate. Rapidly increasing costs are making them more aware of the beams in their own eyes. For years the main drive in almost every firm of stockbrokers has been to increase turnover, whether by broadening its connections or by expanding the business done with its existing clientele. Now that the advantages of size have created large organisations, the administrative problems have increased with them.

In the smaller firms, where all the partners may work in the same room, policy decisions can be taken at any time as a matter of course. With a staff of a dozen or twenty, an increase in the salary of one individual does not necessarily throw the whole wage structure out of line. But when the partnership exceeds thirty and the staff numbers several hundred, the administrative organisation approaches that of an industrial concern.

Each firm will have its own management structure and I can only speak with any authority about my own. We felt it important to cover the essential divisions which any concern, in any field of commercial operation, must cover—production, sales and service, finance, administration (including personnel) and research. The organisation chart shown in Figure 1 includes also a management committee, composed of the heads of the principal departments, reporting to the partnership at monthly meetings. The chart includes also the specialist departments dealing with fixed-interest, foreign securities and corporate finance. In my own firm there is an additional refinement whereby all executive decisions are left to the senior partner and managing partner, so that the time spent in committee is reduced to a minimum.

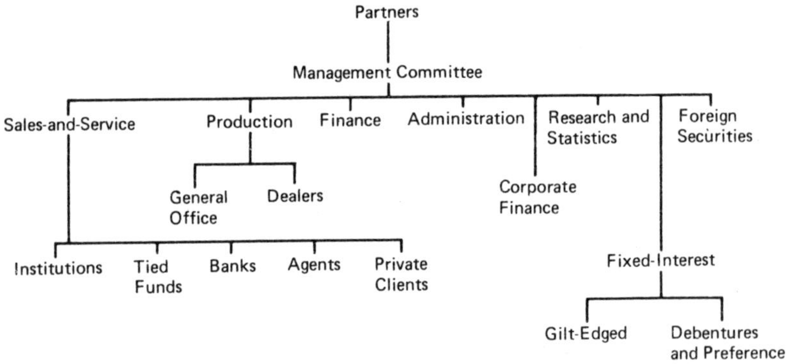

FIG. 1 Organisational Chart

The division of responsibilities between partners in some such organisation as that illustrated may seem unduly obvious, but partnerships which have grown up either out of mergers or out of gradual expansion tend to become haphazard in their administration. Unless some cut-and-dried organisational chart is drawn up, many jobs can be duplicated and others left undone. Some firms, for example, have little sophistication in the costing of bargains for different classes of client. Others have no budget, either for capital or current expenditure, or monthly targets for trade. And priorities in research projects which are requested by the different sales and service departments cannot easily be allocated unless some partner is responsible for the overall programme of the research department.

The organisational chart also simplifies to some extent the problem of the private client who is an acquaintance of a partner or member of the firm. It is almost impossible to refuse to deal personally with a close friend or acquaintance, and yet much time and effort is probably wasted in almost every firm by partners whose talents would be more economically employed on their own specialised side of the business. No gynaecologist is expected by his friends to advise them on matters of general health, but every stockbroker, whatever his specialist activities, is expected to be a general practitioner as well. The chart puts the individual's responsibilities before him in black and white, and he is obviously doing a disservice to his partners if he does not introduce his friends to the partner in charge of the relevant department and leave him to serve them.

The organisational chart also provides a convenient guide for the division of this book into chapters. Since the firm is decentralised into departments, each one can be studied in some detail. Remembering always that the larger firms will probably be more decentralised than the smaller concerns and that a number will have specialist departments not mentioned here—or overseas branch offices, for example—the greatest emphasis is placed on the first department, the sales-and-service to the client.

2 Sales-and-Service

To the majority of stockbrokers the concept of a salesman immediately conjures up the image of knocking on front doors or standing behind a counter. Foreign brokerage houses employ both these techniques, American bond salesmen travelling from house to house and Japanese firms setting up shop on railway stations and in department stores. In Great Britain the accent is applied much more on service, but the partners and senior executives of stockbroking firms are nevertheless the only sales outlet for the services which those firms have to offer. In the smaller firms members will also be involved in the production work of buying and selling securities and perhaps in office routines as well, but in the larger organisations there is a clear division of responsibilities.

The services which are offered depend partly upon the classification of the client and partly upon the wishes of the individual. It is convenient, therefore, to consider the sales-and-service organisation under the heading of the various types of client, and many firms have different departments for dealing with each type.

INSTITUTIONS

This is a fairly loose classification covering the leading financial organisation—about 280 insurance companies, some 220 investment trusts, the largest of the pension funds, over 350 unit trusts and about 50 merchant banks. (For assets and share of the market, see Appendix 1.) The majority of these institutions utilise the services of a large number of stockbrokers and have investment departments fully capable of making their own decisions about the merits of any particular investment. Considering first the ordinary share market, the services which institutions require are as follows:

(*a*) SPECIALISED INFORMATION

Where a firm of stockbrokers makes a particular study of an industry or a company, institutions will rely upon them for up-to-date and reliable information. Those firms with strong connections in a single industry, which produce frequent studies of the prospects of the industry and the component companies, will tend to attract institutional business in this field. The sales force of a stockbroking firm has therefore a double task in handling institutional business in its own specialist companies and industries: it not only has to make out a case for a purchase or a sale, but it also has to provide an after-sales service, keeping the institution informed of the progress of the company for many years to come. A stockbroker may, in fact, receive higher praise from an investment manager for picking a loser and still keeping in touch, than for picking a winner and forgetting about it. On the whole the after-sales service of British stockbrokers is superior to that of their American counterparts, who tend to put greater effort into the sale and less effort into the service.

Each of the institutions mentioned requires a somewhat different approach. The insurance companies, with large funds accruing daily and future liabilities, tend to look towards income growth. They are somewhat more sophisticated than the majority of pension funds in spreading their interests into overseas securities. The pension funds, most of whom are able to reclaim all the income tax levied by the Inland Revenue and are not liable to capital gains tax, often take the view that the tax disadvantages of overseas securities outweigh the benefit of geographical spread of their portfolios. The investment trusts have a more difficult problem of investment, since, except for the relatively infrequent occasions when they raise additional funds by means of new issues, they have little new money available for investment, and a major purchase must be matched by the sale of an existing security. The same applies, but to a lesser extent, to unit trusts. Unit trusts on the whole have been growing in recent years, the new units sold to the public outweighing the old units encashed. The last of the institutions, the merchant banks, operate a variety of funds which may include all those mentioned so far, together with charitable trusts, private trusts, company business and the funds of wealthy individuals.

(*b*) MARKET BIDS AND OFFERS

It is not always easy for the larger institutions to obtain shares in the quantities that they require, and they are thus the most likely buyers when substantial lines are offered on the market. Jobbers who have either bought a line of shares, or agreed to negotiate a purchase, approach one or more stockbrokers who they think are the most likely to find buyers. The offer is normally 'subject', meaning that the shares may not be available at a later time since the offer may be made simultaneously to others. A 'firm' offer, on the other hand, indicates that the shares are offered only to the one party. In most firms of stockbrokers one individual in the Institutional Department has the responsibility of examining each offer to decide whether it is worth approaching the institutions with it or not. If it appears sufficiently attractive, calculations will then be made giving the data that individual institutions require and the other members of the department will begin to ring the various insurance companies, pension funds and so on, offering the shares, either 'subject' or 'firm' as the case may be. An institution which is given a 'subject' offer will realise that acceptance does not ensure that the shares have been bought, but that confirmation must be given after the deal has been completed with the jobber.

The competition between firms of brokers to obtain such offers from the market and to place the shares with their clients is such that speed in obtaining an answer is vitally important, since otherwise a competitor may have carried out the deal.

Those institutions which give rapid answers to offers, or conversely to bids of this nature, even if the reply is in the negative, will usually be among the first to receive this type of service. Those which require meetings of investment committees before an answer can be given are less likely to be approached.

Many institutional investors will give serious consideration only to offers which are 'in the office' of the broker who approaches them. This term indicates that the broker is acting for the seller, and is trying to place the shares with his own connections. On the other side of the coin institutions with lines of stock to sell will take note of firms with exceptional placing power or whose dealers show particular skill in the market.

(*c*) PLACINGS

The attractions to an institution of receiving an offer of shares from a broker who is also acting for the seller are threefold. Firstly, the origin of the shares is known. While the broker will never divulge the identity of his client, he can give a general indication of the reasons for the sale. It may be a deceased estate, a family trust which already has an excessive proportion in these shares, or simply another institution who may be taking a profit. If the shares themselves are suspect, the broker will not be prepared to offer them to his own clients, since he must bear some responsibility for the future success of the investment. Secondly, the offer is unlikely to have been hawked round the market, which usually indicates that many other institutions have examined it and found it unattractive. Finally, as the broker is acting directly with the seller, if the institution feels that the price is too high, a counter-bid a few pence lower can be relayed directly to the seller.

From the stockbrokers' point of view the matching of buyer and seller in his own office is also attractive. Under the rules of The Stock Exchange he is not allowed to sell shares direct to his clients, without first offering them to the jobbers in the market. This protects the seller against receiving less from the stockbroker's own clients than he would if the shares were offered freely elsewhere. Nor, if the jobbers are unable to match either side of his bargain, is he permitted to pass the shares directly between his clients, without obtaining written consent from two firms of jobbers in that particular market. Even if he has carried out these requirements he is then only permitted to charge commission to the originator of the business.

As a result a broker with a large order which he believes he may be able to match will always approach a firm of jobbers *before* starting the matching operation. He discusses with them the terms of a 'put-through'. If the order is for the sale of a large line of shares, he will arrange to sell the entire line to a jobber and buy them back at a fractionally different price for the buyers. The broker then has the right (and the obligation) to charge commissions on both buying and selling transactions. The jobber receives the small 'turn' in the price differential and also has the right to demand that some of the shares be retained by him, or taken off his book.

The larger the quantity in the original selling order compared with the normal number of shares in this company quoted in the market, the greater the discount that the seller may have to accept below the market price. In some cases a discount of as much as 10 per cent may be fixed for a very substantial number of shares in difficult market conditions.

When the broker and jobber have agreed the number of shares wanted by the jobber and a fair price for both buyer and seller, this must be agreed by the originator of the business. The members of the Institutional Department are then free to telephone their connections offering them a participation in the placing.

On occasions the jobber will 'protect' the selling broker at a price a little below the placing price. If the placing operation is unsuccessful, therefore, the broker can still sell the shares in the market, the jobber having taken the risk that, with some of the likely institutions having already been covered, he can dispose of the holding in the normal course of jobbing over a period.

(*d*) MARKET PRICES AND OTHER INFORMATION

Many firms cement the good relations between themselves and their institutional connections by a regular service of prices, reports of dividend increases, budget news, etc. Too many telephone calls of this nature are naturally discouraged by the institutional investment managers, who have better uses for their time, but they require to be kept in touch with market movements and usually delegate this service to one or two firms with whom they enjoy particularly close relations.

In recent years The Stock Exchange has developed MPDS (Market Price Display System) giving prices of some 700 securities on a 22-channel TV-type service. The investment manager has only to switch to the appropriate channel to see the movement in any particular market—gilt-edged, oils, industrials, etc.—and so obtain a 'feel' of the situation. Five channels are available for up-to-date news, index movements etc., so that dividend announcements or other important matters can be covered. The opinion of most investment managers regarding this service seems to be somewhat akin to their views on their wives—they rarely appreciate their value until they break down.

(*e*) COMPANY VISITS, CONFERENCES, ETC.

The importance of seeing a company in operation and of meeting the top management has become more apparent in recent years as the management of British companies has begun to be more broad-minded in its welcome to existing and potential institutional shareholders. Many firms of stockbrokers arrange parties of institutional clients to visit those companies with whom they enjoy particularly close relations or of whom they think particularly highly. Investment conferences, to which leading speakers are invited, and other facilities are also arranged by a number of firms.

(*f*) OTHER SERVICES

The allocation of underwriting or the placing of new issues, the publication of research material and service to institutions in fixed-interest and overseas securities are discussed in the relevant chapters under those headings.

TIED FUNDS

The institutions which have been discussed above are those which employ their own investment managers and which do not rely upon any single firm of stockbrokers to advise them. There are a number of funds, however, which rely entirely or in part upon one or more firms of stockbrokers, with perhaps an investment panel or sub-committee to decide overall policy. Among these are the local authority superannuation funds, the great number of charitable trusts, the universities and colleges, a large proportion of industrial pension funds and a vast number of private trust funds. Reference has been made to these as 'tied funds' because they do not utilise the competing services of a large number of stockbrokers, but rely upon the advice of only one or perhaps two.

The service which these funds require is very different from that of the institutions. Since no one is permanently employed full-time on investment matters, the day-to-day market situation is of little interest. Where a placing below the market would be of advantage to the fund, and the security fits well into its investment policy, the stockbroker will automatically reserve a participation, referring if necessary to one or more members of the investment panel or sub-committee. What these funds most require is either the absolute management of their investments or advice on their management. This is usually given in two ways.

(*a*) PERIODIC VALUATIONS AND REVIEWS

At regular intervals (normally half-yearly or annually) the portfolio of investments is valued and a review is prepared for the trustees. No standard pattern is followed, but it is normal procedure to prepare a summary of the portfolio as well as the valuation and recommendations for action.

A word of warning on the interpretation of such a valuation must be given. Market and cost prices reflect only the history of today and yesterday. Investment is concerned with return on capital, by income or appreciation. Investment decisions must be based on the future of the securities, not past paper losses or gains.

(i) *Summary*
It is important to present an overall picture of the fund, divided into the various classes of investment, and to show the proportions both by cost and by current market values. A typical summary would divide the portfolio between fixed-interest holdings and equities. The fixed-interest might be divided into the following classes: British Government funds, corporation and county stocks, public boards, Government issues, foreign stocks and bonds, debentures and other loan stocks, and convertible loan issues.

In the case of ordinary shares, however, the portfolio is further broken down into industrial classifications. It is common practice to classify these under the same headings as the *Financial Times*-Actuaries Industrial Indices, to give a yardstick for comparison of performance. Some funds break down their total portfolio into industrial groups, lumping together the fixed-interest and the ordinary shares in each industry. A cardinal rule of investment in ordinary shares is to obtain a reasonable spread between different industries in order to ensure that a recession in any one sector of the economy does not prejudice the total portfolio. Fixed-interest securities, however, are not risk capital, and the objective of a balanced portfolio in this class of security must be to ensure that the spread of redemption dates is satisfactory. It would be quite misleading to summarise, for example, 5 per cent of the total portfolio in breweries and 5 per cent in stores, where the brewery section comprised only debentures and the stores section only ordinary shares.

Both values at cost (or book) and market will be shown. From the comparison of the two sets of figures it is possible to note which classes of security have shown appreciation or depreciation, and, of the ordinary shares, which industries have performed better than others. It is also useful to show the percentage of the portfolio (again both by book and market values) in each class of security and each industrial group.

Finally, it is usual to show the income, including a comparison of the average yield on the cost of each group and on the current market prices. The definition of yield is given in the following paragraphs.

(ii) *Valuation*
A valuation may be either a simple list of share holdings with market

prices and values, or a full-scale review. In the latter case, the following may be shown for ordinary share holdings:

Amount or number of shares
Description of stock or share
Current middle market price
Current value
Book value
Capital Gains Value (where appropriate)
Latest dividend
Latest earnings on ordinary capital or dividend cover
Income, based on the latest dividend paid
Gross yield on current market price
Gross yield on book price
Price/earnings ratio

Where comments are required on individual investments, these are normally given in the body of the report accompanying the valuation.

(iii) *Recommendations*
The gilt-edged and other fixed-interest holdings would probably be discussed with the relevant departments for advice in regard to necessary action, and consideration of the factors affecting changes in these holdings or investment criteria for new holdings will be deferred until later chapters. In the case of British ordinary shares, however, the department dealing with tied funds will usually be responsible for recommending the action to be taken. In the case of static funds, trusts and charities with no new money available for investment, the addition of a new holding to the portfolio can only be made at the expense of all or part of an existing holding. Pension and superannuation funds, on the other hand, with regular new money for investment, will require constant recommendations of additions to their portfolios.

Five figures are normally quoted as basic information in the recommendation of an investment or a sale: price, dividend, earnings on ordinary capital, dividend yield and price/earnings, ratio.

(1) *Price*. The price of an ordinary share, by itself, has no real significance in assessing whether or not the share is correctly valued. Moreover, investors should not let themselves be led into the trap of comparing the market price with the nominal value. There is

normally no greater risk in buying a 25p. ordinary share at 475p. than a £1 share at 100p. The price of the share is only significant in relation to the rate of dividend declared and possibly, with some reservations, the previous price record of the share and the asset value.

(2) *Dividend.* Most dividends are now shown in the press in terms of net pence per share.

(3) *Earnings.* The earnings on the ordinary capital is also expressed in pence per share. The press may give the figure for dividend cover, calculated by dividing last published earnings by the last annual dividend paid. In the case of a company earning 25p on its ordinary capital and paying 10 p, the cover would be 2½ times. An indication is therefore given of the extent to which earnings could fall without uncovering the dividend payment, or, taking a more optimistic view, the scope for improvement of the dividend if the directors decided to be somewhat more generous in their distribution.

(4) *Yield.* The net yield on an ordinary share is the percentage ratio of the latest declared annual dividend to the current price, and this is the amount received on £100 invested by someone paying tax at the standard rate. The most useful figure for comparative purposes is the gross yield which can be calculated by multiplying the net yield by the factor: 100 ÷ (100 minus standard rate of tax %). The figure for yield represents one of the basic premises upon which the investing public decides whether a share is too high in price, too low, or correctly valued.

The comparison is often made between the income yield obtainable on a fixed-interest security and that on an ordinary share, and care must be taken not to confuse the two figures. In the case of a fixed-interest security, such as War Loan 3½% standing at a price of 22½, an investment of £100 would provide a return (neglecting the expenses involved in investing) of 3.5 × 100 ÷ 22½ = £15.56p per annum. The yield on War Loan 3½% at this price is therefore referred to as £15.56p, and this sum will be received as interest by the investor for as long as the stock or the investor is in existence.

The income which will be derived from a holding of an ordinary share, on the other hand, cannot be assessed in advance. In the first year of holding the share an investment of £100 will produce a net income to a standard tax payer identical with the yield, provided that the dividend paid is the same as that of the previous year. The reason for buying ordinary shares, however, is in the anticipation of improved profits and with them increased dividends. The comparison between the actual income 'yield' on a fixed-interest security and the 'dividend/price ratio' of an ordinary share should therefore be avoided.

The 'yield' on an ordinary share is best used as a yardstick to estimate the public's opinion of the prospects of the share.

(5) *Price/Earnings Ratio.* The ratio of the price to the earnings (P/E ratio) indicates the value of the share in terms of latest published earnings, irrespective of dividend. A P/E ratio of 10 would indicate that an investor would be paying a price equal to ten times the last year's earnings. This figure may be used to compare different shares in the same industrial group to determine their relative values.

(6) *Remarks.* Many firms of stockbrokers, in preparing lists of recommendations, attach either one of the statistical cards prepared by the Exchange Telegraph Company, or one of their own statistical sheets. In cases where trustees prefer a précis of the company's activities without too much additional paper, a short paragraph may be attached to the list of recommendations.

(*b*) ATTENDANCE AT MEETINGS

One of the partners or senior executives from the Tied Funds Department will usually attend a meeting of the trustees to discuss the report and comment upon the recommendations for action. This maintains the personal contact between the stockbroker and his client and provides the trustees with the opportunity of obtaining additional information and enlargement upon any of the points made in the report.

From the stockbroker's point of view the tied fund has the advantage of continuity provided that he maintains a satisfactory service. Where he is fully responsible for investment advice it is obviously in his interest that the fund should show a better-than-average performance, since the stockbroker's business usually grows on personal recommendation rather than on any form of advertising.

Between meetings the portfolios of the 'tied funds' will be examined, particularly when the investment policy pursued by the firm indicates the sale of an existing security or a switch from one security to another. Records of clients' holdings under the headings both of the clients' names and of the security are normally kept either in a computer or manually. In either system clients should be assured that action can quickly be taken on their individual holdings.

Advice will also be required concerning 'rights' issues of ordinary shares, where action must be taken either to subscribe for the shares allocated or to sell them. Very often funds consider that all 'rights' issues should be accepted in order to avoid reducing the stake in the company concerned. In fact the terms of rights issues will be studied carefully by members of the Tied Funds Department to assess whether a better destination cannot be found for the available money.

Similarly, the terms of takeover bids or other matters affecting the rights of shareholders must be examined and the trustees advised of any recommendations.

BRANCH BANKS

The widespread network of branches throughout the country enables the banks to provide a unique service to investors, and the majority of small business comes to the stockbroker through this source. The relationship of trust and respect that the local branch manager enjoys with many of his customers assists in giving them confidence when dealing with investment matters. In the past the clearing banks have preferred not to take any responsibility for advice regarding investment, but have simply handed on to their client the opinion of a firm of stockbrokers. In recent years, however, one or two have opened new departments concerned with advice and management of investment portfolios. Since 1976 all banks have formally accepted financial responsibility for their customers' stock exchange dealings.

The department dealing with bank business is largely occupied with producing short summary reviews in answer to enquiries from branch banks. The head offices of the banks are usually omitted from this department since, operating either for the bank itself, particularly in the gilt-edged market, or for the employees' superannuation and pension funds, they are normally included under the heading of institutions.

Banks operate on various systems when placing orders with stockbrokers. Some allocate a specific branch to a firm of stockbrokers, so that the branch manager deals direct with his counterpart in the Banks Department of the firm. Others bring all their orders from their branches to one of their City offices and allocate the orders among firms of stockbrokers from the centre. In many cases the amount of business allocated to a firm will depend, not only on the service which the firm offers to the bank, but also on the balances which lie to the credit of the firm's account. The central allocation system makes it simpler to adjust the business allocated on this basis, but may cause some lack of personal contact between branch manager and broker, particularly where the broker is located close to a provincial branch. All accredited banks are entitled to a return of one quarter of the stockbroker's commission for business which they introduce.

AGENTS

The principal agents directing business to stockbrokers are solicitors, accountants and, a small but growing body, investment counsellors. All these agents also accepted liability for their clients' transactions in 1976.

(*a*) SOLICITORS

The majority of work for solicitors concerns either trusts or deceased estates. Following the Trustee Investments Act, 1961, the department dealing with these clients has been required to divide portfolios into Narrower and Wider Ranges, and, where appropriate, allocate securities to the Special Range. The effect of this Act, in its simplest terms, has been to permit trusts, whose investment powers were limited under the 1925 Trustee Act virtually to Government securities and little else, to invest up to one half of their assets in certain ordinary shares, with the balance in a somewhat broader selection of fixed-interest securities. The service to those trusts introduced by firms of solicitors is likely to be similar to that offered to a firm's own tied funds.

In the case of deceased estates the stockbrokers are first required to produce a valuation of the quoted securities for probate purposes. The prices for such valuations are taken as 'a quarter up' on the lower of the two quotations published in the Stock Exchange Daily Official List on the date of death. Normally this price is accepted by the Capital Taxes Office without question. In special circumstances (such as the death of a holder with a very large number of shares in one company for which the jobbers in the market would not have been prepared to bid the normal price), the stockbrokers may be asked to put forward a case to the Capital Taxes Office for reducing the probate price.

The Agents Department may also be asked to advise on securities which should be sold to provide the moneys required for Capital Transfer Tax and to prepare lists of securities for division between a number of beneficiaries, so that the interests of each are safeguarded.

(*b*) ACCOUNTANTS

Firms of accountants are often asked to advise on the portfolios of trusts and on the holdings of their private clients. The service which they require from their stockbrokers varies widely from one firm of accountants to another, but in the main is similar to that offered to the broker's own trusts or private clients.

(*c*) INVESTMENT COUNSELLORS

Some firms of investment counsellors have been in existence for many years, but following the American pattern the numbers have increased considerably. The larger merchant banks have only been prepared to manage an investment portfolio if its value was in excess of £100,000, and the preoccupation of some firms of stockbrokers with institutional business left a void in the direct management of portfolios of around £50,000. Private clients with this size of fortune have felt (often with justice) that the larger firms of stockbrokers have taken too conservative a view of their affairs. Investments of the smaller funds have been limited to unit trusts and the larger funds have been invested in a wide spread of leading securities and the only advice the clients have received is to stay put.

The investment counsellor has thrived on a more dynamic approach. He has been prepared to recommend both switching out of existing securities and taking an interest in the smaller and less well-known concerns. The client has the feeling at least that he is being looked after, whether the investment changes are successful or not. It is often difficult to judge which policy would have been the most advantageous to the client, but there is little doubt that the majority of investment counsellors today are highly experienced in investment work and that they have the advantage of being served by a number of different firms of stockbrokers, obtaining information from each on the subject in which they are most expert.

From the stockbroker's viewpoint, although the investment counsellor appears to be doing the stockbroker's job and charging a fee for it, his work is largely complementary. Some stockbrokers, with clients requiring a particular service which they are either not prepared or not competent to give, have recommended investment counsellors to these individuals. It is normal then for the investment counsellor to place orders for these clients back through the originating broker.

All the agents listed above, besides being entitled to charge a fee to their clients, are also entitled to a fifth share of the broker's commission on transactions carried out, provided that their names are included on The Stock Exchange Register of Agents. This list is renewed annually, agents applying for re-election, sponsored by a member firm of stockbrokers and paying a yearly fee of £100.

PRIVATE CLIENTS

The service given to private clients depends very largely on the requirements of the client and the type of firm which is handling the business. Private clients can be divided into two quite distinct categories—discretionary and non-discretionary: the former give *carte blanche* to their brokers to buy or sell within agreed guidelines; the latter require to confirm a recommendation that is made to them. An intermediate group gives discretion over part of their portfolios to encourage their stockbroker to include them in participations which are arranged too quickly to permit obtaining confirmation.

(*a*) VALUATIONS

The introduction of long-term capital gains tax in the Finance Act, 1965, caused an immense increase in the work of the Valuation Department. Not only must the value of each holding at 6 April 1965 be recorded, but also, where known, the cost of the original purchase with adjustment for intermediate sales and purchases. One of the inevitable problems in this connection concerns 'rights' and 'capitalisation' issues. In general it is assumed that a client will have taken up rights and capitalisation issues offered to him unless the sale has been carried out through the stockbrokers. Many clients, however, instruct their banks to sell such issues or assign them to their children or, in the case of rights, allow them to lapse without informing their stockbrokers. Much time is wasted in the Private Clients Department attempting to agree the list of securities on the firm's records with that of the client's bank, where they are normally held.

Some clients hold the view that, because the amounts they have for investment are relatively small, they are bothering their stockbroker when they require advice or ask for a meeting. The economics of investment for the various categories of client are discussed later, but quite apart from whether or not a client's business is remunerative to the firm, almost all stockbrokers feel they have a duty to the public to give their advice and act for even the smallest clients. In fact the amount of personal trouble and worry that is caused to the stockbroker is almost in inverse proportion to the wealth of the client. The institutional investor, sophisticated in these matters, appreciates that stockbrokers inevitably make mistakes either in the selection of an investment or in the timing of a purchase or sale. With their wide spread of interests they can afford to take some rough with the smooth. To an individual, however, with a small capital and therefore a narrow spread of investment, a substantial fall in the price of only one or two securities can cause considerable worry. The member of the Private Clients Department is likely to spend more sleepless nights worrying over his clients' holdings than any of those engaged in the Institutional Department.

(*b*) STOCKBROKERS' UNIT TRUSTS

In order to cut down the mass of small orders which a large number of private clients brings with it, some stockbrokers operate unit trusts within their own firms. The costs of operation can be reduced compared with unit trusts run by recognised management firms, but a unit trust does not always satisfy the requirements of the client. Many of them like to follow the prices of their shares in the daily press and some like to feel that they are supporting their own investments when they purchase goods or utilise the services of companies whose shares they hold. Investment trusts and unit trusts have the advantage of giving an investor with a relatively small amount of capital a wider spread of interest than he could otherwise obtain, and a compromise is probably the best solution, a fair proportion of a small investor's holdings being held in investment trusts or unit trusts, with direct investment in other securities to suit his particular requirements.

(*c*) REQUIREMENTS OF PRIVATE CLIENTS

Individuals who have not previously transacted business with stockbrokers are inclined to approach the problem of investment in much the same light as shopping for Christmas. They write to say that they have money available and can they please have some recommendations. If advice is to be given on a sound basis, the stockbroker will require to know much more about the background of the client and exactly what it is hoped to achieve from the investment.

In particular the stockbroker will want to know:

(i) *The Income Position*

If the client's tax rate is very high, it would obviously be unwise to recommend an investment that is primarily an income-producer. Alternatively, if the client pays income tax at a lower figure than the standard rate, investments must be considered where a full reclaim of tax may be made from the Revenue.

(ii) *Cash Requirements*

It is important to consider whether the client may require to realise all or part of the investment to pay some known liability (such as the purchase of a car or school fees) in the relatively near future. If such is the case, investments should be selected which are easily marketable and possibly where the capital, in money terms, is relatively secure.

(iii) *Children or Other Beneficiaries*

In the case of elderly clients it may be appropriate to know the ages and income positions of children or other beneficiaries under their wills. An elderly person, with no close next-of-kin and with little income, may be better advised to purchase an annuity than to buy stock exchange securities. A high tax payer, who wishes to provide for his grandchildren, may be well advised to form trusts and part with some capital, despite the imposition of Capital Transfer Tax.

(iv) *The Existing Portfolio*

Finally, the stockbroker will want to know what shares the client holds already. Although, for example, shares in the oil industry may look attractive at the time, it would obviously be inadvisable to recommend them to a client who already holds a high proportion of his portfolio in this industry, or whose sole income from employment is derived from this source.

(v) *The Objective of the Investment*

Having taken into account the client's own financial position, the immediate requirements for liquid funds and the existing investments, the stockbroker is now in a position to discuss with the client the objective of the investment that is to be made. At the same time, he may recommend alterations to the existing portfolio in the light of this knowledge.

In some cases the choice of investment lies largely between the alternatives of a security producing the maximum income and one which it is hoped will produce the maximum capital appreciation. But in many cases the client hopes to achieve something of each. There is a general misunderstanding that, because stockbrokers work in the City and are close to the market, they must have inside information about the affairs of companies and the likely effect of this information upon the price of the shares. If this were true, most stockbrokers would gladly divorce themselves from any concern with their clients' affairs and be content to make substantial fortunes for themselves using their own funds. Unfortunately it is almost inevitable that the only time when stockbrokers have reliable inside information is when they are concerned in some operation on behalf of a company and then, of course, they are unable either to reveal it to their clients or to act upon it.

SOURCES OF INFORMATION

One of the tasks facing the stockbroker, particularly the non-specialist partners handling private client affairs, is the enormous quantity of reading matter which it is necessary to consume in order to keep up to date. He is expected to be an expert on all the 3500 companies quoted on the London market, as well as having a fairly detailed knowledge of at least the U.S.A., Europe and Japan. The sources of information can be divided into five: the ticker-tapes and direct computer services; the press; the statistical services; the jobbers; and the firm's own Research and Statistical Department. The partners and executives operating in the sales-and-service departments are expected, therefore, to have a general knowledge obtained from the first four of these sources, and only to make enquiries of the research side of the business on the more detailed or abstruse points.

(*a*) THE TICKER-TAPES

Two ticker-tape services are currently in operation, one provided by Reuters and the other by the Exchange Telegraph Co. The former tends to specialise more in general and international items of news, and the latter in company news and stock-exchange prices. But both offer a valuable service of immediate information concerning company announcements, Budget summaries, etc., relayed direct to the subscriber's office.

Direct computer services are provided by SCAN (Stockmarket Computer Answering Network), DATAstream and by Centre File. SCAN is inclined primarily towards share valuations and analytical data—price/earnings ratios and yields at various prices, profitability ratios and trends, together with fixed-interest calculations of a wide range of U.K. and foreign securities; DATAstream with more sophisticated economic and analytical data and portfolio valuations; while Centre File was set up primarily as a central accounting organisation for subscribing members to carry out general office production routines, with portfolio valuation and direct access to company information as a secondary facility.

(*b*) THE PRESS

(i) *Daily Newspapers*

The *Financial Times* is obligatory reading for all stockbrokers and maintains an exceptionally high quality of reporting. Its range is considerable, so that it takes the student some time to be able to find his way about in the paper and discover the section which contains the information he requires.

Of the more serious daily papers, *The Times*, the *Daily Telegraph* and the *Guardian* all have substantial City coverage, the first two having special business supplements, although the investment impact of editorial comment in the *Daily Mail* and the *Daily Express* is probably greater, owing to their wider readership. Stockbrokers tend to skip through a number of daily newspapers to ensure that they do not miss some report or comment which might affect the prices of shares in which their clients are particularly interested.

(ii) *Weekly Publications*
Apart from the City comment in the national Sunday papers, such as the *Sunday Times*, with its special business supplement, the *Sunday Telegraph*, the *Observer* and the *Sunday Express*, one weekly periodical is almost entirely devoted to investment matters, namely the *Investors Chronicle*. This publication gives a range of general and specific investment reviews and is widely used for reference purposes. Another periodical widely read for more general economic and political coverage is *The Economist*. The intermittent reports of the Economist Intelligence Unit on specific industries or fields of interest are highly regarded, but more likely to be utilised by the research departments than by the sales-and-service organisations.

(*c*) STATISTICAL SERVICES
The Exchange Telegraph Co. Ltd produces statistical sheets covering industry and company information, and stockbrokers often send their clients copies of these cards with recommendations, since they show a record of the company's progress, together with any up-to-date information that has been published; replacement cards can easily and inexpensively be obtained from the company.

The white Extel card is up-dated annually, while brown cards are issued with interim results and news items. The Exchange Telegraph also produces specialist services dealing with statistics, with Australian and European securities, and with unlisted companies.

One of the problems of having an easily available book of reference to take to meetings when enquiries may be made about shares not listed for discussion has been solved by the *Extel Handbook of Market Leaders*, containing information and statistics covering a range of some seven hundred leading U.K. companies and published semi-annually in January and July.

(*d*) THE JOBBERS
For the small firms, particularly those who are unable to afford their own research or statistical offices, the jobbers form a useful centre of information. Many of the jobbing firms maintain their own research sections and take pains to investigate the companies in whose shares they deal. In addition, where stockbrokers publish reviews of industries or companies, they often send copies to the jobbers dealing in those shares. 'The market' therefore becomes particularly

well informed about a company, and their opinion can be obtained by any broker who cares to ask.

In addition the jobbers indicate the public's reaction to information and the public's forecast of the prospects. If a client asks, 'What dividend does the market expect will be paid?', the jobbers will provide the answer. If that dividend is declared, and results are in line with anticipation, then it is unlikely that the price of the shares will move.

In the past some cynics have given their view that jobbers will give a 'market opinion' which happens to suit their own books. If they want to sell shares, the opinion will be favourable; if they want to buy them, unfavourable. In practice, this rarely occurs. With fierce competition between different jobbing firms, the jobber depends for his livelihood upon the goodwill of the brokers with whom he deals. He must, therefore, be at pains to be as impartial as possible in giving information of this sort, but will adjust his quotation of the shares to suit his own book.

(*e*) RESEARCH AND STATISTICAL DEPARTMENT

The work of this department is considered in detail in Chapter 4.

SPECULATIVE BUSINESS

The great bulk of stock-exchange transactions can be classified as investment business, since the institutions, charities, trusts and private investors who are looking for a relatively long-term home for their funds predominate. It would be idle to deny that speculative business also plays its part, although the amount of speculation is far less than the headlines in the daily press would indicate. The speculator, in fact, can be a useful aid to the market, and the introduction of the new capital gains taxes in the Finance Act, 1965, had a marked effect upon the freedom of trading. The absence of the professional speculator has caused wider price movements with greatly reduced turnover. When some crisis developed in the past, due to bad domestic or international news, and sellers forced down the price of stocks, it was usually the professional speculators who decided that the fall had gone far enough and whose buying steadied the market.

Those stockbroking firms which specialise in private-client business may also accord to the speculator additional services in carrying out closing bargains, arranging contangos, dealing in options or transacting business on margin.

(*a*) CLOSING TRANSACTIONS

Settlement for transactions in the great majority of the securities on the London market is made on a fortnightly accounting basis (see Chapter 3). As a result a security purchased during the account period may be sold later in the same account without the necessity of payment. Similarly a security sold during the account can be bought back at a later date without the necessity of delivering the stock. In either case the client pays or receives the difference between the cost of the purchase and the proceeds of the sale.

Transactions on this basis attract smaller expenses than normal investment transactions. While commission on the 'opening' bargain is charged at the normal rate, the 'closing' bargain attracts no commission and the charge to cover Government transfer stamp duty will be refunded, since the security will never be registered in the name of the client.

Transactions 'for the account' usually indicate that the client has insufficient ready cash to take up the shares he has purchased or may not actually possess the shares he has sold. As a result stockbrokers whose business is primarily concerned with investment rather than speculation may indicate to their clients after one or two closing transactions that this is not the type of business that they like to undertake.

(*b*) CONTANGOS

The account period of a fortnight (or occasionally three weeks where a Bank holiday is involved in the period) is a relatively short time for a stock to move sufficiently to cover the expenses of the 'opening' transaction and produce a worthwhile profit. In order to offer the facility to clients of prolonging the period, some stockbrokers will try and 'carry over' the transaction into the next account by means of a 'contango'. In order to effect this operation, a jobber or another broker must be found who wishes to 'carry over' the stock in the opposite direction. The client who has bought shares (the giver) will give a rate of interest for the privilege of not paying for them until the following settlement, the 'taker' accepting a rate for delaying the delivery of the security. 'Carry over' transactions are executed on the last day of the Account (so that the client can close the bargain if a 'carry over' is not possible). Transactions are matched on Preliminary Day, which is the first day of the new Account.

A client's request to 'carry over' a transaction again indicates that either he does not have the ready money to pay for his stock, or the stock to deliver, and many firms of stockbrokers will not accept 'carry-over' instructions.

(*c*) MARGIN TRADING

Financial facilities are also offered by some firms in the form of 'margin' trading. The broker may accept a fractional payment of the total cost of a purchase (usually not less than 20 per cent) and finance the balance from his own resources. Should the price of the share fall sufficiently to endanger the broker's advance, the client is required to put up further capital or the shares can be sold at the broker's discretion. The amount of trading on margin is extremely small in The Stock Exchange, with the result that no fixed margin limits are laid down by the Council. In Japan, for example, where a substantial proportion of the transactions on the Tokyo market may be on margin account, margin transactions can only be undertaken in specified securities, and the proportion of the cost to be put up either in cash or in collateral is strictly governed.

(*d*) OPTIONS

In every commodity market, whether wool or metal or foreign exchange, opportunity is given to insure against fluctuations in price by 'forward' dealing. By this means a premium can be paid to cover the risk involved in delivering or receiving the commodity at a future date. The stock market is no exception. The insurance premium is termed 'option money' and the option is the right, usually over a period of three months, to buy a given security or to sell it at a fixed price. The individual who gives the option money is called the 'giver', and the other party, usually a firm of brokers rather than jobbers specialising in this field, is the 'taker'. Those who believe a share may rise in price take out 'call' options, which give the right to buy at the fixed or 'striking price' at any time in the three-month period. Those who take the opposite view take out 'put' options, giving the right to sell at the striking price during the period. The option, whether for a put or a call, is usually quoted at the same price, but the striking price will be slightly different. It is also possible to take out a 'double option', or 'put and call', giving the right either to sell or buy during the period. The cost of the double option is approximately twice that of the single option, but the striking price is the same for both.

An option enables the 'giver' to benefit from any substantial fluctuation in the price of a volatile stock, with the outlay of a limited amount of capital and a known loss should the option not be exercised.

The 'striking price' of a call option is the offered price of the share in the market at the time of dealing, plus an allowance to offset the *ad valorem* stamp duty and the cost of contango interest during the period of the option. For a three-month option, at current rates, the striking price would be about 2 per cent above the offered price of the share. For a 'put' option, the striking price would be the bid price in the market at the time of dealing. In the case of double options the striking price is usually the middle market price at the time of dealing.

During the period of the option the 'giver' has two courses open to him if the transaction shows a profit which he wishes to secure. If the option is for the 'call' he can either:

(i) close the transaction with the 'taker' of the option by selling the shares to him; or
(ii) sell the shares in the market in the ordinary way, or carry them over, if necessary, until the option expires, and exercise the option on the next Declaration Day.

For a 'put' option the alternatives are exactly the same, with the exception that the shares will be bought rather than sold.

If the option has not been closed at the end of the period, the giver has to 'declare' it (state whether or not he intends to exercise it) on Declaration Day, the Thursday before the Making-Up Day of the account (see Table 2, pp. 52–53 in which the option expires. If a profit can be taken, or at worst some part of the loss saved, the stockbroker will exercise the option on behalf of his client, otherwise it will be allowed to lapse.

The holder of an option is entitled to all rights, dividends, etc., that accrue during the period of the option. Dividends and rights are settled in cash, but capitalisation issues in shares.

The expenses of taking out an option are not much different from those applied in buying and selling shares in the ordinary way. Commission is charged at the same rate as though the 'giver' had carried out the transaction at the striking price, and contract stamp is charged at half the normal rate. The other half of the contract stamp is payable at the time of exercising the option. No further commission is chargeable, either on exercising the option or on dealing against it.

The somewhat unwieldy and expensive system of dealing in options has resulted in a new form of option instrument, the traded option, first developed in the U.S. by the Chicago Options Board Exchange. A similar Options Exchange in London has recently opened.

(*e*) BULLS AND BEARS

It may be appropriate at this point to define the terms 'bull' and 'bear', which are well known in stock exchange parlance. Anyone who has purchased shares in the anticipation of a rise is termed a 'bull', while anyone who has sold shares in the anticipation of a fall is termed a 'bear'. A 'stale bull' or a 'stale bear' is someone whose initial judgement was at fault and who finds that the price of the stock has gone in the opposite direction, leaving him with a loss. An 'uncovered bear' is a seller of a security who does not possess it but is hopeful of buying it back at a profit, while a 'covered bear' is a seller who can deliver the security if required. The term 'bear covering', which may often be seen in the press to explain a sharp rise in price, indicates that a number of earlier sellers were buying back their stock. Finally, the adjectives 'bullish' or 'bearish' are widely used to indicate optimism or pessimism in regard to future movements of prices.

CONCLUSION

The change which has taken place in stockbroking since the Second World War lies primarily in the emergence of the institutions, particularly the insurance companies, pension funds and unit trusts as a powerful influence in the markets for ordinary shares. The numbers of very rich private clients have simultaneously fallen, owing to the heavy impost of taxation. The combination of these two factors has caused a requirement for a much higher degree of technical skill in stockbroking and a far smaller dependence on private connections. In this day and age, however charming a stockbroker is as an individual, he will not achieve the really important business unless he provides a first-class technical service.

The first leg of this service lies in an efficient system of production from the skill of dealing in the stock market at the best price, through all the accounting and other paperwork which makes up the transfer of securities from seller to buyer.

3 Production

In a service industry such as stockbroking, the production side of the business is almost entirely concerned with paper. In common with most professional partnerships in any walk of life, stockbrokers have neglected their general offices and devoted much more time and effort to improving their sales-and-service facilities and their research departments. In the past the entire work of the general office was left in the care of the office manager or to the least effective partner as one only fitted for administration. This attitude of mind has had two effects: first, it has resulted in an antiquated system of accounting and delivery of securities, since until recently there has been no concerted effort by member firms of The Stock Exchange to improve it; second, there is a marked lack of uniformity between the various firms in the systems operated in their own offices, which makes any major advance difficult to achieve. It is only recently that management has come to be appreciated as a central and vital function in stockbroking.

Economies in production may, in fact, be the key to much of the future growth in the industry. The rise in wages and salaries, the rents on modern offices and the vicious increase in rates, together with the rise in prices of raw materials (printing and stationery in particular) have been unusually marked in the City of London. More and more firms, therefore, are paying increasing attention to new production and organisation methods.

The simplest method of describing the somewhat complex procedures that are carried out in the execution of an order to buy or sell shares is to follow the route taken by such an order from the moment it is received by letter or telephone from the client to the time that he in turn receives either a cheque in payment for the stock sold or his certificate showing his entitlement to the stock purchased.

In order to illustrate the examples chosen, a number of names will be mentioned and it may simplify matters if a code is used which will indicate their application:

All *clients'* names will begin with C.
,, *jobbers'* ,, ,, ,, J.
,, *brokers'* ,, ,, ,, B.
,, *shares'* ,, ,, ,, S.

Four principal departments are involved:

(*a*) the dealers in The Stock Exchange who actually make the 'bargain';
(*b*) the accounting sections who settle the money side of the transaction;
(*c*) the transfer sections who physically handle the deeds transferring the title between buyer and seller; and
(*d*) the settlement departments of The Stock Exchange who carry out certain central functions.

It should be appreciated here that the various sections mentioned may only exist in the larger firms and, in those with smaller staffs, one individual may carry out the work of several different sections.

STOCKS AND SHARES

Under current company law all shares must have a par or nominal value. If a company has an authorised ordinary capital of £1 million divided among 1 million ordinary shares, each share will have a par or nominal value of £1. Had there been 4 million shares, each share would have a nominal value of 25p.

In the distant past all risk capital (preference and ordinary capital) was quoted as shares, and these were individually numbered. The recording of the numbers of each share transferred became unduly burdensome to company registrars and, as a result, many companies altered their ordinary capital to ordinary stock. The quotation then applied to 'stock units' rather than shares. Subsequently the law was altered to permit transfer of unnumbered shares.

Since the term 'share' is more widely understood by members of the public, in the examples which follow this word will be used throughout, to avoid the constant repetition of 'stock or share'.

It should be noted that loan capital, which will be discussed more fully in later chapters, is always quoted as 'stock' since the owner does not possess a share in the concern, only a participation in a loan to it.

Let us suppose that a client, Mr Charles Cuthbertson, wishes to sell 1000 J. Sainsbury ordinary shares and to reinvest the proceeds in the purchase of Shell Transport & Trading Co. Ltd registered ordinary 25p. shares. His instructions may be given verbally on the telephone, or may be addressed either to an individual or to the firm by way of correspondence, cable or telegram. In any event the instructions will be passed, first of all, to the Order Department.

ORDER DEPARTMENT

This department may be located in the stockbroker's office situated outside the confines of The Stock Exchange itself, or in his 'dealing box' adjoining the trading floor (see Figure 2). The name 'box' adequately describes the room, which is usually a small office containing a number of telephones direct to the firm's switchboard and to important clients, and in some cases telex machines or teleprinters for direct contact with provincial units and other centres throughout the world. The box is a convenient centre into which all orders are passed for execution in The Stock Exchange and from which information is passed to the sales-and-service departments operating from the main office or, in some cases, to clients direct.

Firms who do not have boxes normally telephone their instructions direct to their dealing staffs through the private telephones on the trading floor (nos 1–348 round the perimeter of the market in Figure 2). Dealers may be called to the telephone by a paging system, or may be connected directly to their office by means of a portable radio link.

Stockbroking firms resident outside London who wish to deal with a London jobber may do so either through a London broking firm or by telephoning directly to the jobber's pitch.

DEALING STAFF

Three categories of individual make up the dealing staff: members of The Stock Exchange, who enjoy all the normal rights and privileges of membership, but who may or may not be partners of the firm; authorised clerks, who are employees of the firm, authorised to deal in securities, but who do not share any financial responsibility; and unauthorised clerks (or 'Blue Buttons'), who are permitted on to the floor but are not authorised to buy or sell

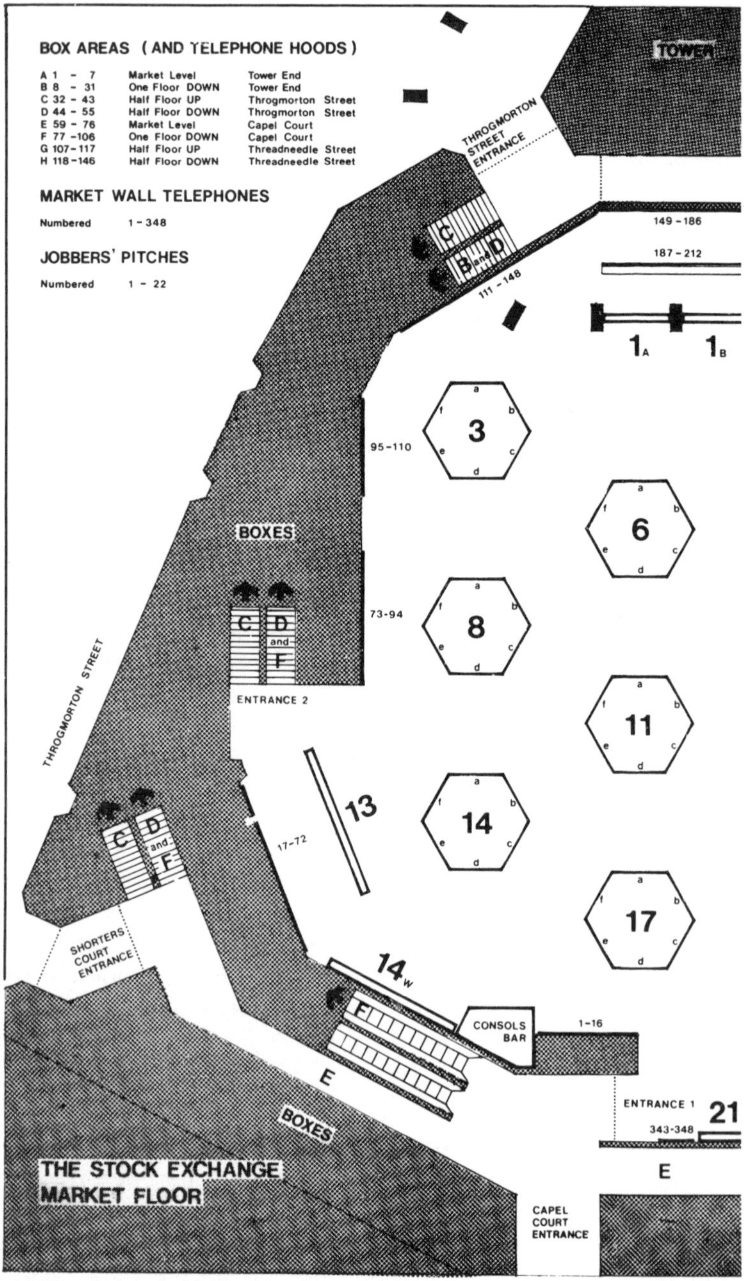

FIG. 2 Plan of The Stock Exchange

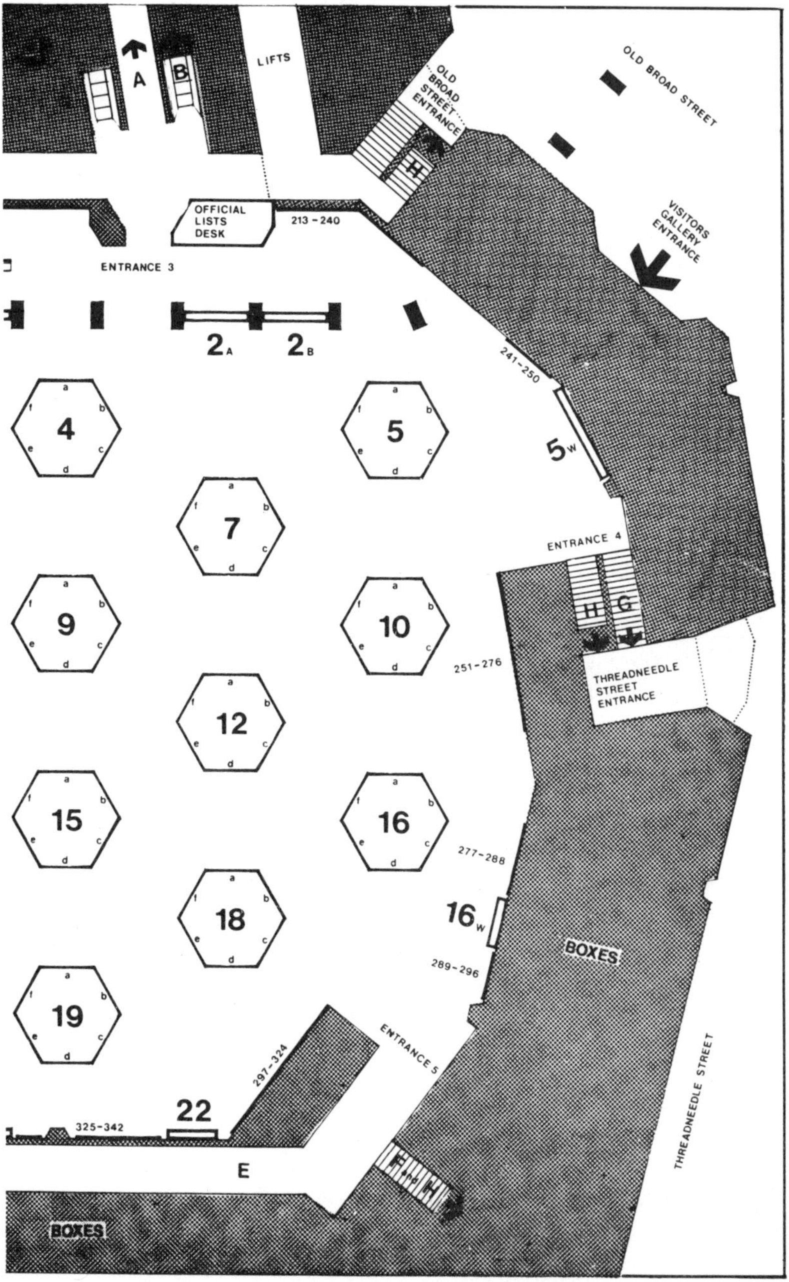

LIFTS
A
B
OLD BROAD STREET ENTRANCE
OLD BROAD STREET
H
OFFICIAL LISTS DESK
213-240
VISITORS GALLERY ENTRANCE
ENTRANCE 3
2A
2B
241-250
4
5
5W
7
ENTRANCE 4
9
10
H
G
251-276
THREADNEEDLE STREET ENTRANCE
12
15
16
277-288
16W
18
BOXES
289-296
19
ENTRANCE 5
297-324
22
325-342
E
F
H
BOXES
THREADNEEDLE STREET

securities. Members and authorised clerks are difficult to distinguish from each other at a distance, each wearing a silver badge in the buttonhole or along the top of the breast pocket, inscribed with the name of the firm. On closer examination it will be seen that the badges of authorised clerks are also surrounded with a black line. In the case of the unauthorised clerks the badge is coloured blue, indicating to the jobbers that the individual may not actually deal in securities.

One of the dealers will receive from the order room the details of Mr Cuthbertson's order, and will immediately enter the market to carry it out. Speed is important, particularly in times of great activity, since prices can change materially in a matter of minutes.

At the time of writing the London market place is the most modern in the world. 'The House', as it is called, is hexagonal in shape and the layout is depicted in Figure 2. The main entrance lies at the top of the diagram (A) with escalators (B) to the strongrooms in the basement and to the visitors' gallery on the floor above. The visitors' gallery contains not only a glass-walled viewing platform, but also a cinema, where the Stock Exchange film 'My Word is My Bond' is shown at regular intervals, and an exhibition room. Entrance to the gallery is free and half-a-dozen attractive guides are available to give detailed explanations of the workings of the market. Below the gallery are three large projection screens on which facsimiles of company announcements can be projected. Standing in the gallery above entrance 3 it is possible to look down on almost the entire market floor, which contains a number of 'pitches' around the walls (1a and 1b, 2a and 2b, 5w, 16w, 21, 22, 14w and 13 in clockwise order) and in the shape of hexagonal stands spaced across the floor (4–12 and 14–19). There is no systematic pattern in the layout of the market, but Government and quasi-Government securities are concentrated at the far side of the market (15d and c, 17c, 18f, 19a, b and c, 21 and 22) with corporate debentures round the further fringe (13, 17c and f, 19d and c, and 18c). Dealers in foreign shares stand in the top right-hand area of the plan (1b, 4a and b, 2a and 5) or immediately in front of the viewer (6a and b, 9a and 7f). The remainder of the floor is devoted to leading U.K. ordinary shares, with option dealers sitting to the right of the plan (5e, 5w, 10c, 16w and 18a). The new Traded options market takes place around stand No. 3.

Almost all jobbers have on display a board showing the principal stocks or shares in which they deal and on which they mark price movements, normally upward movements in blue or black and downward in red. In leading stocks and shares there will be competition between several firms of jobbers, and even in the least popular securities there is almost always more than one firm interested. This competition between jobbers tends to keep their margins down and provide the smallest differential between the prices at which shares can be bought or sold.

The dealer who has been given Mr Cuthbertson's order to execute will approach the jobbers in the most direct order, irrespective of whether he is endeavouring to deal in the sale of Sainsbury or the purchase of Shell, but for simplicity in explanation let us suppose that he carries out the sale first.

He will approach the nearest jobber in the industrial market (whom we shall call Jones & Co.) and enquire: 'What are Sainsbury?' The jobber will reply: '164 to 167.' This indicates that the jobber will *buy* shares at 164p or sell shares at 167. He may in fact simply reply, 'Four–seven', assuming that the dealer will be aware that the 'big figure' is 160p.

The dealer notes that he can sell his shares to Jones & Co. at 164p, and moves on to another jobber, Johnson, in the same market. Here his enquiry might receive the reply: '165 to 168.' He has therefore improved his selling price to 165p and reduced the margin between the selling and buying prices from 3p to 2p.

A third jobber, Jakes, might also call them '164 to 167', so that the best bid has been made by Johnson. The dealer returns to sell the shares to him.

Both dealer and jobber note this transaction in their own dealing books and the dealer moves on to check the price in Shell among two or three jobbers and to reinvest the sum of about £1600 raised by the sale of Sainsbury. At length he finds the cheapest offer of Shell is made by Joseph & Co., buys about 300 shares at 480p and enters this bargain also in his dealing book.

This example answers one or two questions which are always asked about transactions on The Stock Exchange. Firstly, the jobber is not in a position to raise his price when a buyer approaches him or to lower it when a seller makes enquiries, because he never knows until the moment of concluding the deal whether the broker is a buyer or seller of the shares. Secondly, it illustrates the relatively narrow margin on which jobbers operate in the popular shares. To be quoted a 3p price in Sainsbury from the start (a difference of less than 2 per cent) is normal. When the dealer came to reinvest in

Shell, a higher-priced but more marketable share, he would also have found a 3p difference between buying and selling prices in the initial quotation (equivalent to 0.625 per cent on a price of 480p). It must also be remembered that jobbers are taking considerable risks when they deal in large numbers of shares in volatile markets. One of the largest firms of jobbers in the industrial market has averaged a profit of $\frac{3}{8}$p per share in recent years.

It will be noted that prices move in multiples of 1p, but in shares of very low value prices are quoted in $\frac{1}{2}$p or $\frac{1}{4}$p. In gilt-edged and other loan capital, where prices are quoted per £100 nominal, the variation is in fractions of £—$\frac{1}{2}$, $\frac{1}{4}$, $\frac{1}{8}$, $\frac{1}{16}$, $\frac{1}{32}$ and $\frac{1}{64}$. The quotation of a Government stock standing at 80 might therefore be $79\frac{7}{8}$–$80\frac{1}{8}$.

Thirdly, it illustrates the motto of The Stock Exchange—'Dictum Meum Pactum' ('My word is my bond')—for neither the broker nor the jobber signs any contract on the deal, their respective words being sufficient evidence that a bargain has been transacted.

And finally, it times the change of ownership of the shares. From the moment that the dealer said to the jobber, 'I sell you one thousand Sainsbury' as far as The Stock Exchange is concerned Mr Cuthbertson ceased to be the owner of the Sainsbury shares. And from the time he said to Jones & Co., 'I buy Shell', Mr Cuthbertson became the owner of these shares. If, one minute later, a take-over bid had been announced for J. Sainsbury that caused the shares to rise suddenly by 50p, the firm of stockbrokers would still be responsible for delivering one thousand shares for the payment of only 165p a share. (Incidentally, the share selected for this example in the first edition—Smith's Crisps—was taken over shortly after the book was published!) When stockbrokers act for a client they are entirely responsible for completing his transactions, to the extent of all the financial resources of all the individual partners. As a result they are understandably cautious in checking the credit-worthiness of new clients.

Having concluded the transaction, the dealer will report back to the order room so that, where instructed, the client can be informed on the telephone of the prices at which the sale and purchase were effected. The details of the two bargains will also be transmitted to the general office for the preparation of the relevant documents.

LIMIT ORDERS

In the simple example quoted, the client merely instructed his broker to sell one security and purchase another. On many occasions, however, the client will fix a price at which he wishes the transaction to be carried out, and reference is made to such an order as a 'limit'. Such limits are given to one of the jobbers dealing in the shares but every firm of brokers also maintains a Limit Book in which such orders are entered, and it is often the duty of one dealer to keep a constant check throughout the day on all the limits which are nearing completion. Where no specific time-limit is set, clients are circularised at regular intervals to enquire whether their limit instructions still hold good.

Some reinvestment orders may also be fixed at limit prices, so that the purchase may only be carried out if the sale can be effected, or vice versa. Such orders are referred to as 'contingent'.

MARKING

The dealing staff has an additional duty to perform concerning each transaction carried out during the day, which is known as 'marking the bargain'. Slips are provided in the House with columns for the name of the stock or share, the price, the date, the name of the firm of brokers and any special remarks. The marks are reproduced daily in the Stock Exchange Daily Official List. They provide figures against which a client can check that his own transaction has not been carried out at an unduly high or low price.

The total number of marks is also used as an indicator of the activity in markets, although it is only an approximate guide. The marking slip does not contain the number of shares transacted, so that a single mark can represent one share or 100,000 shares. Marking, although normal, is only compulsory in the following special cases, but appeals against marking may be made to the Honorary Market Officials on the floor of the House. These senior retired or semi-retired members will also advise on dealing disputes and the interpretation of the Code of Dealing or the Rules.

(i) *Bargains between Non-Members*

It has already been explained that brokers in the U.K. are not permitted under the rules to match buying and selling orders in their own offices, without first offering the business to the jobbers in the market. If the jobber can carry out one side of the transaction, either bidding or offering, then the broker must deal with him and disregard the matching order. Where the jobbers are unable to compete on either side of the transaction, the broker may carry out the deal, charging commission only to the client initiating the business, and the marking slip must be signed by two firms of jobbers agreeing to the business as 'between non-members'. A special symbol is attached to the mark in the list the next day.

(ii) *Bargains at Special Prices*
A broker may have an order in a very large line of shares, often valued at some hundreds of thousands of pounds, and a jobber may either supply these shares or buy them, as the case may be, at a price outside the normal quotation. Alternatively the broker may carry out a 'put-through', as described in the previous chapter, again at a price outside the normal quotation. In either case the mark will bear a symbol denoting a bargain at a special price in the lists.

'Put-through' business is a source of some contention both inside and outside The Stock Exchange. The fractional difference in price mentioned earlier as the jobber's profit is normally one-half of the standard stockbroker's commission rate, although it may be a smaller figure when the size of the transaction is very large. The broker who carries out the business, because he has in effect made two transactions, selling for his original client and buying for his other clients, is entitled to charge commissions on both sides of the transaction and welcomes this opportunity. This situation has resulted in a number of large transactions being made outside The Stock Exchange altogether. A merchant bank or a firm of overseas brokers, for example, with a large line of shares to place and with friendly relations among the likely buyers in the shape of insurance companies, pension funds and other investment institutions, is able to offer a line of shares at a price exclusive of either the broker's commissions or the jobber's turn.

Some brokers feel that, while the jobber should obviously receive some reward because it is on his quotation of price that the 'put-through' is based, a rate of half the commission is too high and that this is one reason why business by-passes The Stock Exchange. The leading jobbers, on the other hand, who would be prepared to risk taking a substantial line of shares in the hopes of gradually selling them over a period with the possibility of a higher profit because of the enhanced risk, find that these opportunities become increasingly scarce.

It should also be remembered that the jobber carries a residual risk if the broker becomes a defaulter. Failures of broking firms in the past have made this point unpleasantly clear.

A bargain may be carried out at a special price for an entirely different reason. Where the number of shares that a broker has to sell (not to buy) is so small that the work of taking delivery of the shares makes the transaction unremunerative to the jobber, he may bid a price a few pence lower to compensate for this. This mark will bear the same symbol in the lists as a 'put-through' at a special price.

(iii) *Previous Day's Bargains*
The marking board closes at 2.15 p.m. each day, while The Stock Exchange itself remains open until 3.30 p.m. and dealing between jobbers and brokers continues on the telephone until 5.30 p.m. or later. As a result the bargains for account settlement carried out after 2.15 p.m. are omitted from the lists published the following morning and will be shown with a symbol denoting 'previous day's business' one day later.

MARKET BOOK
In most firms the entries from the dealers' own books are transcribed into a consolidated list termed the Market Book. This gives a record of all bargains transacted and will be used later in the day to check against the contract notes in order to ensure that none has been completed incorrectly or omitted.

ACCOUNTING PERIODS

Before explaining the preparation of a contract note, however, a word should be said about Stock Exchange accounting periods.

In the U.S., Canada, Japan and a number of other overseas stock exchanges, shares sold or purchased on one day must be delivered or paid for four or five business days later. The delays inherent in our transfer system (although greatly reduced by the Transfer Act of 1963), the requirements of the jobbing system and certain concessions in the rules on commissions have caused The Stock Exchange to divide the year into twenty-five accounting periods. The majority of these are fortnightly periods, with three-weekly accounts covering some national holidays. Taking one of the normal fortnightly accounts, any shares purchased in the two business weeks from, say, Monday 1st to Friday 12th must be paid for by Tuesday 23rd (see Table 2 below). Similarly, a client who sells shares in this period, provided that he has delivered his securities and signed the necessary transfer forms, will be paid on the 23rd. It follows that anyone who buys shares and sells them again within the period of the account does not require to pay for them at all, and is not liable for the 2 per cent *ad valorem* stamp duty levied on the purchases, and anyone who sells shares early in the account and buys them back again later does not require to deliver them. The fortnightly accounting system therefore encourages some degree of short-term speculation, although this has been considerably reduced by capital gains tax.

TABLE 2 Accounting dates

Day of the week	*Description*	*Date in Example*	*Details*
1st Week			
		October	
Monday	First day of end-October account	1	First day for dealing in normal way for transactions to be settled on 23 October. Securities usually declared 'ex-dividend'.
Tuesday		2	
Wednesday		3	
Thursday		4	
Friday		5	
2nd Week			
Monday		8	
Tuesday		9	
Wednesday		10	
Thursday		11	First day on which forward dealings for next account may be made ('new time' bargains).
Friday	Last day of end-October account	12	Last day of dealing in normal way for settlement on October 23rd.
3rd Week			
Monday	Contango Day	15	
Tuesday	Making-Up Day	16	
Wednesday	Ticket Day	17	
Thursday	First intermediate day	18	
Friday	Second intermediate day	19	

Day of the week	*Description*	*Date in Example*	*Details*
4th Week			
Monday	Third intermediate day	22	
Tuesday	Account Day	23	Date of settlement of all transactions in end-October account.

CASH TRANSACTIONS

While the majority of dealings in the stocks and shares of companies are settled at the end of each account, there are two exceptions—gilt-edged securities and almost all new issues.

The gilt-edged market covers securities issued by the central Government, Dominion and colonial Governments, local authorities and certain public boards. Transactions in these securities are normally settled on a cash basis, delivery and payment being made the following day.

New issues, both of companies coming to the market for the first time and capitalisation or rights issues of established companies, are normally transferred on allotment letters or renounceable certificates. In either case the seller signs the reverse of the document of title, renouncing his right to the stock or shares, and delivery without the payment of stamp duty can be effected by the purchaser for a limited period. In effect, therefore, new issues transferred in this way have many of the attributes of bearer documents and are considered in more detail in a later paragraph (see p. 81).

GENERAL PROCEDURE FOR THE DELIVERY OF SECURITIES

At the end of each accounting period, when hundreds of thousands of shares have changed hands through the medium of the jobbing system, there is a mammoth job of matching buyers against sellers. In addition to this a broker who may have bought many thousands of the same shares for different clients has the task of identifying which shares belong to whom as they are delivered.

The advent of the computer has provided a method whereby this operation can be carried out centrally by the Bargain Accounting office of The Stock Exchange (The Centre).

Checking

First, it is important to ensure that the original data are correct. Every broker submits daily to The Centre details of the transactions carried out during the day. These are matched overnight with the corresponding input from the firms of jobbers and lists of both matched and unmatched bargains are circulated early on the following morning. The prime entries are thus entered into the computer for the processes that make up the settlement procedures.

At the end of the account The Centre produces a slip of paper for each purchase, entitled a ticket. This bears the details of the purchase, together with a reference number from which the broker can identify the buyer of the shares. In London there is no penalty for 'odd lots' as there is in New York. In other words, a seller can get the same price for 233 shares that he could obtain for 200, whereas in New York, since certificates are made out in round numbers of hundreds and tens, the small odd number of shares will not command such a high price. The Centre may match a buyer of 1000 shares against sellers of 500, 220, 150 and the last 130 out of another seller of, say, 357. The ticket for the 1000 shares therefore has to be split into the requisite amounts to make up the total, and these split tickets are despatched by The Centre to the brokers who acted for the four different sellers.

This system would work perfectly if, during an account, the total number of shares sold in a given company exactly matched the total number purchased. In practice, of course, this situation rarely occurs. The function of the jobber is to make a market and, as a result, at the end of an account he almost always finds himself either 'long' of shares (having bought more than he has sold) or 'short' (having sold more than he owns). Where he is long of shares the remedy is simple, for he receives the shares himself and pays for them. Jobbers have a special reduction of the normal 2 per cent *ad valorem* stamp duty on shares which are held in their names for less than two months in order to assist them to keep a free market.

Where the jobber has sold short of shares, however, the situation is obviously more complicated. The normal remedy is simply to postpone delivery of the shares until the following account, but, when delays are likely to be protracted, facilities are available for borrowing securities through the services of 'money brokers'. Where certain rights are attached to shares purchased but not delivered (i.e. dividends, capitalisation issues, etc.), the jobber is responsible for making these good at the time of delivery.

Where the jobber has exactly matched sellers and buyers, he is no longer concerned in the delivery of the shares. The Centre has passed to each of his sellers a ticket showing the buying broker and the price the buying broker paid, and it is up to them to settle direct.

Under the simplest of systems, the selling broker would only have to pin the ticket to the documents of transfer and, on Account Day, deliver them to the buying broker and receive payment.

If the selling broker and the buying broker settled the payment between themselves, how then does the jobber receive his remuneration? The answer is also simple. The Centre not only acts as a clearing house for the delivery of securities, but also maintains accounts for the differences owed by brokers and jobbers.

BARGAIN ACCOUNTING

At the time The Centre issues the tickets for an account, it also produces two lists: the one showing the 'shapes' into which each broker's purchases have been split and the broker to whom the relevant tickets have been sent; the other showing the tickets he will receive in respect of his sales and to whom the stock should be delivered.

CENTRAL STOCK PAYMENT

Under the simple system described, each selling broker would receive a cheque from each buying broker (or jobber) for each piece of stock delivered, and would pay cheques to each buying broker (or jobber) for all stock received. The Central Stock Payment Office of The Stock Exchange co-ordinates all these payments so that each member firm receives only one cheque for all stock delivered and pays only one cheque for all stock received.

The physical delivery of tickets and the securities themselves (with the exception of gilt-edged and some bearer securities) is also centralised, so that messengers are not constantly walking round the City between member firms.

CONTRACT DEPARTMENT

Returning to the example of Mr Cuthbertson's sale and purchase, the details of the two transactions were transmitted from the 'box' to the Contract Department. Different firms of brokers use different forms of transmission, some collecting written slips at intervals from the House, some using telephone reporting or direct transmission on teleprinter or facsimile machines. The destination of these reports, however, is the Contract Department, and all of them will bear the same essential information—the name of the client, the number of shares bought or sold, the description of the share, the price, and the name of the firm of jobbers with whom the transaction was carried out. The report will also contain other relevant instructions—in the example quoted, that the Shell shares purchased are a reinvestment of the proceeds of the sale of J. Sainsbury shares.

SOLD	BY ORDER OF	008	Our Ref. IES087	Bgn Date VAT Point 12 APR 77
C.Cuthbertson, Esq.				CUTHB11C 00
J. Sainsbury Limited Ordinary Shares of 25p Each				
AMOUNT	PRICE			CONSIDERATION
1000	£1.65			1650.00 N
0-76764-0			Transfer Stamp	0 N
			CONTRACT STAMP	0.60 N
			Commission	24.75 T
	1.5% on £1650.00			
			VAT 8.00%	1.98
	FOR SETTLEMENT 3 MAY 77		TOTAL = £	1622.67
VAT SUB TOTALS	TAXABLE ITEMS EXCLUDING VAT 24.75	EXEMPT ITEMS 0		

Fig. 3 Sold Contract Note Details

BOUGHT	BY ORDER OF	008	Our Ref. IEB072	Bgn Date VAT Point 12 APR 77

C.Cuthbertson, Esq.

CUTHB11C 00

Shell Transport & Trading Company Limited Ordinary Shares of 25p Each (Registered)

AMOUNT	PRICE		CONSIDERATION
325	£4.80		1560.00 N
0-80340-3		Transfer Stamp	32.00 N
		CONTRACT STAMP	0.60 N
	1.5% on £1560.00	Commission	23.40 T
		VAT 8.00%	1.87
	FOR SETTLEMENT 3 MAY 77	TOTAL = £	1617.87

VAT SUB TOTALS	TAXABLE ITEMS EXCLUDING VAT	23.40	EXEMPT ITEMS	0

FIG. 4 Bought Contract Note Details

The Contract Department prepares the invoices for the business carried out. These invoices, termed contract notes, may be calculated manually, on accounting machines or by computer. They are signed by the firm of brokers and in law are binding upon them. Extracts from the sale and purchase contract notes to illustrate our example are shown in Figures 3 and 4 and contain the following information:

Dates. The date of the bargain and the settlement date by which payment must be made for shares purchased or on which payment should be received for shares sold.

Description. The full description of the share.

Amount. The number of shares.

Price. The price at which the transaction was executed.

Consideration. Number of shares × price.

The following three figures in the case of a sale and four in the case of a purchase represent the expenses of the transaction, i.e.:

Transfer Stamp Duty. An *ad valorem* duty of 2 per cent is payable on the purchase of U.K. registered securities with the following exceptions:

(*a*) The majority of gilt-edged securities;
(*b*) Debenture and unsecured loan stocks;
(*c*) New shares in renounceable form;
(*d*) Shares transferable as bearer documents;

all of which are exempt.

Registered charities and overseas residents are subject to half the normal rating, which is shown in Table 3 below.

TABLE 3 U.K. Transfer Stamp Duty

			£ p
Any registered stocks and shares (subject to stamp duty) where the amount or value of the consideration for the sale does not exceed £5			10
Exceeds:			
£5	but does not exceed	£10	20
£10	,, ,,	£20	40
£20	,, ,,	£30	60
£30	,, ,,	£40	80
£40	,, ,,	£50	1 00
£50	,, ,,	£60	1 20
£60	,, ,,	£70	1 40
£70	,, ,,	£80	1 60
£80	,, ,,	£90	1 80
£90	,, ,,	£100	2 00
£100	,, ,,	£120	2 40
£120	,, ,,	£140	2 80
£140	,, ,,	£140	3 20
£160	,, ,,	£180	3 60
£180	,, ,,	£200	4 00
£200	,, ,,	£220	4 40
£220	,, ,,	£240	4 80
£240	,, ,,	£260	5 20
£260	,, ,,	£280	5 60
£280	,, ,,	£300	6 00
£300—for every £50 and also for any fractional part of £50			1 00

The duties on transfers not on sale and not by way of voluntary disposition are liable to the fixed duty of 50p.

Contract Stamp. A stamp is affixed to both sale and purchase contract notes based on the value of the consideration, as shown in Table 4 below:

TABLE 4

Up to	£100		nil
Over	£100 but does not exceed	£500	10p
,,	£500 ,, ,,	£1500	30p
,,	£1500		60p

Commission. The full details of commission rates are shown in Appendix 2. The minimum rate is almost invariably applied by all firms of stockbrokers, but, where commission is 'at discretion' brokers will set their own scales, depending upon the types of business they wish to encourage. The paperwork involved in a typical transaction, which is described later in this chapter, illustrates the uneconomical nature of small business.

Concessions. A number of concessions are available, the most important being for the larger bargains (see Appendix 2) and for closing transactions.

Closing. A transaction opened during one account period and closed for the same client during the account need attract commission only on the original purchase or sale. In the case of bargains for cash settlement, the closing bargain may be carried out free of commission within a period of twenty-eight days for gilt-edged securities and fourteen days for new issues passing in scrip form or as letters of renunciation.

Agent's Commission. Orders executed on the instructions of a recognised bank, other than for principals of the bank, attract a refund of commission of one-quarter. Firms and individuals on the list of authorised agents (solicitors, accountants and others specialising in investment) may obtain a refund of one-fifth of the commission on orders for their clients, provided the commission is in excess of £10.

Employees of the firm of stockbrokers are also entitled to a share of the commission on business which they have introduced, at the discretion of the firm, normally up to a maximum of a half-share for individuals who are members of The Stock Exchange. Other employees, providing they are on the Register of Attachés and Clerks, may receive up to one-third of the commission. Where a return of commission is given to banks or other agents outside the firm, a note to this effect must be shown on the contract note.

Value Added Tax. VAT is charged on brokers commission for business on behalf of U.K. residents, currently at the rate of 8 per cent.

Total. In the case of the sold contract note the expenses are deducted from the consideration and the total proceeds to which the client is entitled entered at the bottom of the page. In the case of a purchase the expenses are added to the consideration to produce a total cost.

In the example it will be noted that it was impossible to reinvest exactly the proceeds of the sale, so that Mr Cuthbertson will have a small credit balance of £4.80 at the settlement date.

The contract notes are checked. The contract stamps are affixed and they are then signed by one of the partners of the firm. Since the contracts are binding, care is taken to see that no mistakes occur at this stage, and the contract notes are despatched to the client.

Before proceeding further, a word of warning should perhaps be given to the reader. The object of the remainder of this chapter is to show the logical steps which are taken in both the accounting procedures and the delivery of the documents of title. The exact steps taken are a mystery even to some members of The Stock Exchange themselves, but unfortunately they make fairly dry and unpalatable reading. The reader who prefers the more entertaining work of the Research Department and other specialist sections is advised to skip lightly on to Chapter 4.

BOUGHT AND SOLD CONTRACT JOURNALS

Separate books of account are kept for purchase and sale transactions. The first of these are the Contract Journals. Each journal is, in effect, a list of all the contract notes, columnised so that totals may be obtained of all the separate entries.

These journals form the first entry in the accounting system, and we shall follow through each posting to the various ledgers as the accounting system is described. The journals also give an immediate indication of the business carried out. It is common practice for one of the partners to examine these journals each morning to keep a check on the firm's business. From this he can assess whether the total commissions appear to be satisfactory, whether any particular client (or occasionally even a member of the staff) is engaged in speculative transactions, whether each department is keeping up to its target and so on.

In the case of my own firm the accounting procedures are carried out by computer. While the illustrations will be in the form of print-outs, the procedures are little different from manual or machine posting. The daily postings to the various ledgers should agree with the sub-totals of the bought and sold contract journals.

CHECKING THE BARGAIN

While The Centre produces a list of matched and unmatched bargains every morning, the jobber often does not know exactly the number of shares bought or sold at the time of dealing. In our example the dealer would have bought 'about 300 Shell' after calculating in his head the approximate proceeds of the sale of J. Sainsburys. The computer at The Centre is therefore programmed to accept matches within certain limits of divergence acceptable to the jobbers.

Mismatches in excess of the limit are agreed verbally between broker and jobber and an adjusting figure passed to The Centre. At this point the daily totals in monetary value are agreed, forming the basis of The Centre's accounting system.

The question is often asked what happens if either the jobber or the broker repudiates the bargain. With the many thousands of bargains each day there are occasionally cases where one or other side has no record of a bargain (after checking with all the other likely firms who might have dealt, on the assumption that the dealer booked the bargain to the wrong firm); where both sides appear to have either sold the shares or bought them; or where the number of shares or price does not agree. Normally, if the error is not obviously the fault of one party, any resulting loss is divided between the jobber and the broker. On very rare occasions, where the dispute cannot be resolved amicably between the member firms, it is referred to the arbitration of one or more members.

ACCOUNTING PROCEDURES

In the settlement of any transaction at least five people are involved — the selling client, the selling client's broker, the jobber, the buying client and the buying client's broker. Each broker accepts responsibility for the liabilities of his clients, so that in the example the number can be reduced to four, since it is only Mr Cuthbertson with Broker & Co. who are concerned and not the individuals who supplied him with Shell or bought his Sainsbury shares. The procedure is further simplified by The Centre acting as an intermediary in inter-firm accounting. Instead of payments to and receipts from each firm of jobbers and each firm of brokers, The Centre lists all transactions and accepts or delivers balancing cheques. The principal ledger accounts would, in the simplest case of an exactly matching bargain be reduced to two—the Client's Account and the Jobbers' Account. In practice, however, since deliveries making up a total purchase may come from several brokers in split amounts, or sales have to be split similarly, it is necessary to ensure that each individual transaction is complete and that no errors in the financial settlement have occurred. An additional account is therefore added, a Ticket Account for each bought and sold bargain.

CLIENTS' ACCOUNTS

A specimen sheet from a computer system for Clients' Ledgers is illustrated in Figure 5, showing the two bargains taken in our example. In the case of the purchase bargain all the items shown in the columns of the contract note (Figure 4) are debits to the client's account. While these items are going to be credited individually to other accounts in order to provide the balancing entries required, it is obviously unnecessary to list them individually in the client's account. The total amount is therefore posted in the *debit* column.

A similar procedure is adopted for the sale bargain, but in this case net proceeds are posted to the *credit* of the client, while the relevant expenses involved are credited to the Contract Stamp and Commission Accounts, and to the VAT Account. Again, by posting the net proceeds to the client's *credit*, the same effect is achieved as posting the consideration to his credit and the individual expenses to his debit. The client's account now shows a small balance in favour of Mr Cuthbertson, being the difference between the proceeds of the sale and the amount reinvested.

Unless other instructions are given by the client, a cheque for £4.80 would normally be posted to him on Settlement Day, provided the sale documents have been received in good order.

JOBBERS' ACCOUNTS

At the end of each account The Centre provides for each firm of

PRIVATE CLIENT'S LEDGER

25 April 77

C. CUTHBERTSON ESQ.

Client Ref. CUTHBIIC 00

For settlement 3 May 77

DATE	AMOUNT	STOCK	PRICE	REF.	DEBIT	CREDIT	BALANCE
1977		To balance brought forward					0
12 April	S 1000	J. Sainsbury Ord 25P	£1.65	SBJ IES087		1622.67	1622.67CR
12 April	B 325	Shell Transport and Trading Ord 25P	£4.80	BBJ IEB072	1617.87		4.80CR
3 May		CHQ		02 10507	4.80		0

FIG. 5 Clients Ledger Extract

JOBBER'S ACCOUNT LEDGER

A. BROKER & CO.

ACCOUNT 1 SETTLEMENT DATE 3 MAY 77.

DATE	DR - AMOUNT	- CR	NARRATIVE	PRICE	LEDGER	FOLIO	DEBIT	CREDIT	BALANCE
	SAINSBURY (J) ORD 25p		0-76764-0	NON-CLEARING					
12 APR 77	1000		SD BGN	1-65	SBJ	1EB087	1650-00		
27 APR 77		500	SD TKT	1-67	TKT	1EB087/001		835-00	
27 APR 77		300	SD TKT	1-64	TKT	1EB087/002		492-00	
27 APR 77		200	SD TKT	1-63	TKT	1EB087/003		326-00	3-00 CR
		(0)	BALANCE ON STOCK						(3-00 CR)
	SHELL TRANSPORT & TRADING CO. ORD. 25p (REGD) 0-80340-3 NON-CLEARING								
12 APR 77		325	BT BGN	4.80	BBJ	1EB072		1560-00	
27 APR 77	300		BT TKT	4.80	TKT	1EB072	1440-00		
27 APR 77	25		BT TKT	4.80	TKT	1EB072	120-00		0.00 CR
12 APR 77		125	BT BGN	4.80	BBJ	1EB094		600-00	
27 APR 77	125		TFR JOBBER 990 BGN ILS034 CLOSED/CLOSING BARGAIN		JAC	1T 00610	608-75		8.75 DR
21 APR 77	125		SD BGN	4.87	SBJ	1LS034	608-75		
27 APR 77		125	TFR JOBBER 990 BGN 1EB094 CLOSED/CLOSING BARGAIN		JAC	1T00610		608.75	0.00 CR
		0	BALANCE ON STOCK						(8.75) DR

FIG. 6 Extract of Centre Account

brokers a Jobbers' Account of all transactions carried out (Figure 6). The sale of 1000 Sainsbury at 165p has been matched by three purchases—500 at 167p; 300 at 164p; and 200 at 163p. The difference in the balance column, therefore, is due to these small variations in price. The Centre will send to A. Broker & Co. three split tickets for delivery of the shares.

The sale of Sainsbury shares produced a *credit* on the client's account and this is matched by The Centre opening a *debit* on the Jobbers' Account. Similarly The Centre opens *credits* for the three split tickets.

In the case of the purchase of Shell, the reverse applies. Two tickets will be despatched by The Centre on behalf of A. Broker & Co., who will receive 300 from one seller and 25 from another. In this case there is no difference in the balance column since the tickets will bear the buying price of £4.80. The remaining entries show a purchase and a sale of the same stock within the account, where the bargain was closed at a small profit.

As the purchase of Shell produced a *debit* on the client's account, this is matched with a *credit* on the Jobbers' Account at The Centre. The Centre also opens *debits* for the three split tickets.

SOLD TICKET ACCOUNT

The considerations on the three sold tickets (Nos IES087/001, 002 and 003), posted as a *credit* to the Jobbers' Account at The Centre, must be matched by a similar *debit* entry elsewhere. These three entries open the Sold Ticket Account (Figure 7). Although transfer stamp is charged on a purchase, the selling broker is responsible for affixing the correct stamps on the deeds, and these amounts are listed, with the buying brokers name and reference, as *debits* to the ticket account.

When the securities are delivered and a credit posted to A. Broker's account at The Centre, representing payments from the three buying brokers, Blakehouse, Bryant and Benjamin, the amounts should equal exactly the total of consideration plus stamp on each split ticket. These figures are posted to the *credit* of the Ticket Account, which should now balance exactly.

BOUGHT TICKET ACCOUNT

Two selling brokers are involved in the delivery of the Shell

1ES087 C. CUTHBERTSON

DATE	DR-	AMOUNT	CR	NARRATIVE	LEDGER	FOLIO	DEBIT	CREDIT	BALANCE
12 APR 77				SAINSBURY (J) ORD 25p 1000 at £1.65 JOBBER 998 JOHNSON 0 CLOSING					
27 APR 77	500			CONSIDERATION AT £1.67 STAMP (BLAKEHOUSE I367)	STK	1ES087/001	835-00 17-00		835-00 852-00
27 APR 77	300			CONSIDERATION AT £1.64 STAMP (BRYANT 298)	STK	1ES087/002	492-00 10-00		1344-00 1354-00
27 APR 77	200			CONSIDERATION AT £1-63 STAMP (BENJAMIN Z196)	STK	1ES5087/003	326-00 7-00		1680-00 1687-00
3 MAY 77		500		Z123 TFRZZS998 BLAKEHOUSE I367	TKT	IT 01204		852-00	835-00
3 MAY 77		300		Z123 TFRZZ5998 BRYANT 298	TKT	IT01210		502-00	333-00
3 MAY 77		200		Z123 TFRZZ5998 BENJAMIN Z196	TKT	IT01212		333-00	0
		0		TICKET ACCOUNT CLOSED					

FIG. 7 Sold Ticket Account

purchase, one for 300 and one for 25. Each has received a split ticket from The Centre bearing the identifying number and the amount due. In addition they will have affixed the stamps in payment of Transfer Stamp Duty to the transfer forms and will require payment to cover this outlay.

The *debit* entries of £1440 and £120 in the Jobbers' Account therefore must be matched by *credit* entries for the same amounts and these open up the Bought Ticket Account (Figure 8). The *credit* of the stamp duty matches the *debit* for this duty contained in the overall debit entry in the Clients' Account.

As the selling brokers, Bull and Bear, deliver their shares, payment is made via The Centre and a *debit* for the amount due is entered in the Ticket Account. The total of credits should now exactly balance the debits and the bought ticket account is closed (Figure 8).

Loss of Stamp over Splits

It will be recalled that, on consideration over £300, the Transfer Stamp Duty moves in steps of £1 for every £50 or part of £50 of the consideration. In the example quoted, where the ticket for 325 Shell has been split into one for 300 and one for 25, the considerations on the transfers at the purchase price of 480p amounted to £1440 and £120 respectively. The stamp duty shown on the bought ticket account amounted to £29 and £2.40, making a total of £31.40, whereas Mr Cuthbertson was charged £32.00 on his contract note. In most cases a higher charge results from splitting.

The money value of all transactions is agreed daily with The Centre, debits and credits being posted to the accounts of both brokers and jobbers, and The Centre allocates the cost of stamps on splitting between the firms of jobbers concerned.

TRANSFER OF SECURITIES

The settlement side of the production departments is complemented by the work of the transfer departments, who must ensure that the documents of title are received or delivered in good order.

1 EB 072 C. CUTHBERTSON

DATE	DR	AMOUNT	CR	NARRATIVE	LEDGER	FOLIO	DEBIT	CREDIT	BALANCE
				SHELL TRANSPORT+ TRADING ORD 25P 325 AT £4.80					
				JOBBER 999 JOSEPH 0 CLOSING					
27 APR 77			300	CONSIDERATION AT	BTK	1EB072/001		1440.00	1440.00
				£4.80 STAMP (BEAR 1234)				29.00	1469.00
27 APR 77			25	CONSIDERATION AT £4.80	BTK	1EB072/002		120.00	1589.00
				STAMP (BULL 128)				2.40	1591.40
3 MAY 77	300			Z002 TFRZZ8998 BULL	TKT	IT02138	1469-00		122.40
3 MAY 77	25			Z002 TFRZZ8998 BEAR	TKT	1T02139	122-40		0
			0	TICKET ACCOUNT CLOSED					

FIG. 8 Bought Ticket Account

ACCOUNT LIST BOOK

S.E. LIST NUMBER 0-76764-0 SAINSBURY (J) ORD. 25p XD=15 NOV 76 BCD= 1 DEC 76 ACCOUNT I

12 APR 77	1ES 087	£1.65		JOHNSON 1000	C. CUTHBERTSON	CUTH 811C000
				500 at 1-67 300 at 1-64 200 at 1-63		

S.E. LIST NUMBER 0-80340-3 SHELL TRANSPORT + TRDG ORD 25p REG XD=25 APR 77 BCD = 5 MAY 77 ACCOUNT I

12 APR 77	1EB072	£4.80	325	JOSEPH	C. CUTHBERTSON	CUTH 811C000
12 APR 77	1EB094	£4.80	125	JOSEPH	MRS. A.CLEGG	CLEGG 05A000
13 APR 77	1FB121	£4.82	500	JONES	MR. G. CRABB	CRABB 059000
21 APR 77	1LS 034	£4.87		JOSEPH CLOSING 125	MRS. A. CLEGG	CLEGG 05A000

FIG. 9 List Book Extracts

LIST BOOK

It is necessary to keep a record of the transactions not only under the names of the clients, which can be found from the Clients' Ledger, but also under the heading of the share. A List Book of all transactions is used for checking names, claims for dividends and rights, and capitalisation issues.

The List Book provides a record in alphabetical and chronological order of transactions carried out in each stock. Figure 9 illustrates the sale bargain in our example, listed under Sainsbury, and the purchase bargain, listed under Shell. In the latter case one or two other transactions have been included in the extract. It will be noted that, where the number of shares appears before the jobber's name, the bargain is a purchase and where it appears after the name it is a sale. Mrs Clegg bought 125 Shell on 12 April and closed the transaction within the account by selling again on 21 April.

NAMES DEPARTMENT

It has already been stated that, at the end of each account, The Centre produces tickets for every purchase transaction, split into the optimum shapes. These are sent to the deliverers (selling brokers) and each ticket bears details of the firm delivering the security; the transfer consideration, stamp and bargain value; the number of

Deliverer	Settlement Date	Deliverer's Client Ref	Deliverer's Bargain Ref	Ticket Number	
250 A BROKER & CO	3 MAY 77	-	IES 087	1367	001

Transfer Consideration	Security Code	Bargain Conditions	Stamp	Bargain Value
835.00	0-676-400	-	17.00	835.00

Quantity	Security	Bargain Price	Settlement Total
500	SAINSBURY (J)	1.67	852.00

Centre Control Number	Bought Bargain Date	Issue Date	Jobber	Taker's Client Ref.	Taker	
70611 028069	13 APR 77	27 APR 77	998	-	BLAKEHOUSE	990

Issued by the SETTLEMENT CENTRE, ST. ALPHAGE HOUSE, FORE ST LONDON EC2Y 5DA

FIG. 10 Bought Bargain Ticket

shares, title of the security and its code number; the bargain price and the sum of money (settlement total) due from the taker to the deliverer.

One of the three tickets covering the sale by Mr Cuthbertson of his 1000 J. Sainsbury is illustrated in Figure 10. It is entitled a 'bought' ticket, since it refers specifically to Blakehouse & Co.'s purchase of 500 shares and will end up attached to the documents delivered by A. Broker & Co. to Blakehouse & Co. In addition to the information covering the transaction itself, the code numbers of the member firms are important – 990 for Blakehouse & Co.; 250 for A. Broker & Co.; and 998 for the jobber with whom Blakehouse & Co. dealt on the purchase transaction. A Broker & Co.'s number (250) also appears on the form of transfer of the J. Sainsbury shares at the top left hand corner (Figure 11). The coding system provides a simple method of identifying member firms in the central delivery system.

SOLD TRANSFER DEPARTMENT

When the letter enclosing the sale contract is sent to the client, a sale transfer form will be included for Mr Cuthbertson to sign and return with the certificate for the shares sold. The transfer form is completed only in respect of the columns showing the number of shares in both words and figures and his name and address (Figure 11).

Most clients, if they are wise, keep their share certificates in a bank. To save them trouble a delivery order may be enclosed, instructing the bank to deliver the relevant certificates to the broker. This will be signed by Mr Cuthbertson and sent on to the bank.

On receipt of the share certificate, the Sold Transfer Department will mark it with the sold ticket number for identification, before filing it in a suitable place to await delivery in due course.

When Mr Cuthbertson returns his sold transfer, duly signed, it is married up with his certificate, coming from his bank. The Ledger Department is informed that the securities sold have been received with all the documents in order and the client may be paid on Account Day.

The transfer and certificate are then filed to await the receipt of the tickets from the buying brokers. In the example taken, three tickets will be received from Messrs Blakehouse, Bryant & Bryant, and Benjamin. It is therefore necessary to split the transfer deed,

STOCK TRANSFER FORM

FNS 3 (Above this line for Registrars only)

Consideration Money £..

Certificate lodged with the Registrar

(For completion by the Registrar/Stock Exchange)

IES087.

Full name of Undertaking. J. Sainsbury Limited.,

Full description of Security. Ordinary Shares of 25p Each.

Number or amount of Shares, Stock or other Security and, in figures column only, number and denomination of units, if any.

Words: One Thousand

Figures: 1000. (units of)

Name(s) of registered holder(s) should be given in full; the address should be given where there is only one holder.

If the transfer is not made by the registered holder(s) insert also the name(s) and capacity (e.g., Executor(s)) of the person(s) making the transfer.

In the name(s) of

Charles Cuthbertson Esq.,
76, Snowy Lane,
Bashford,

I/We hereby transfer the above security out of the name(s) aforesaid to the person(s) named below *or to the several persons named in Parts 2 of Brokers Transfer Forms relating to the above security:*

Delete words in italics except for stock exchange transactions.

Stamp of Selling Broker(s) or, for transactions which are not stock exchange transactions, of Agent(s), if any, acting for the Transferor(s)

PLEASE SIGN HERE

Signature(s) of transferor(s)

1. Charles Cuthbertson.
2. ....
3. ....
4. ....

Bodies corporate should execute under their common seal.

Date..........

Full name(s) and full postal address(es) (including County or, if applicable, Postal District number) of the person(s) to whom the security is transferred.

Please state title, if any, or whether Mr., Mrs. or Miss.

Please complete in typewriting or in Block Capitals.

I/we request that such entries be made in the register as are necessary to give effect to this transfer.

Stamp of Buying Broker(s) (if any)

Stamp or name and address of person lodging this form (of other than the Buying Broker(s))

FIG. 11 Form of Transfer

which is carried out by preparing three 'broker's transfer forms', one for 500 at 167p per share for Blakehouse, one for 300 at 164p per share for Bryant & Bryant, and one for 200 at 163p per share for Benjamin. At the same time the reverse of the original transfer form is completed, showing the breakdown of sales. If Mr Cuthbertson only sold a part of his total holding of J. Sainsbury and his certificate was for 3000 shares, a balance of 2000 will be due to him in due course.

STAMPING

The three 'broker's transfers' must now be stamped with the *ad valorem* duty in each case. The amount is marked in pencil on the left-hand side of each transfer and they are sent to the Inland Revenue Stamp Office for the requisite stamps to be affixed to the transfers. For this purpose the Stamp Office issues special forms not unlike the paying-in books issued by banks, a duplicate copy of which will be kept in the office for posting the individual stamps to the *credit* of the Stamp Account.

CERTIFICATION

The certificate representing the underlying shares sold must also be 'split', and this operation can be carried out either at the office of the company's registrars or the Certification Office of The Stock Exchange. Since the Certification Office is within easy reach of all brokers' offices, most of the certification work is carried out there.

The three broker's transfer forms, properly stamped, and the original form, duly signed by the client, are sent to the Certification Office, together with the certificate. If the documents are in order the office will certify the three broker's transfers accordingly, return these to the broker, and despatch the original transfer and certificate to the company's registrar.

In the selling broker's office, the Sold Transfer Department pins the bought tickets to the transfer forms, which are now ready for delivery and the sold Delivery Record sheet is completed (Figure 12).

In addition, selling brokers will keep a record of all deliveries in bargain order for reference purposes.

PAYMENT OF THE CLIENT

A client who is in credit will be sent a statement of account on

21 APR 77

	C. CUTHBERTSON		CONSIDERATION	CHARGES	COMMISSION	PROCEEDS
1ES087	JOHNSON 0-76764-0	J. SAINSBURY Ord. 25p		1.98		
	CUTHBT 1C000					
	1000 J SAINSBURY Ord.	£1.65	1650-00	0-60	24.75	1622-67

VAT: 8.00%

BUYERS' TICKET No.	NUMBER OF SHARES	TICKET PRICE	WHO PAYS	CERT. No. OR CERTD.	DATE DELIVERED
L367	500	£1·67	BLAKEHOUSE		3 MAY 77
298	300	£1·64	BRYANT	CERT'D	3 MAY 77
2196	200	£1·63	BENJAMIN		3 MAY 77

FIG. 12 Sold Delivery Record Sheet

Account Day. In the case of Mr Cuthbertson a cheque for the small balance of £4.80 will be enclosed. Clients in debit will be sent a statement a week before Account Day to enable them to pay their accounts by that date.

BALANCE CERTIFICATE

Mr Cuthbertson is still due the balance of 2000 shares out of the total certificate for 3000 J. Sainsbury. On receipt from the registrar of the company the balance certificate is sent, according to the instructions on the client's record card, to his bank for safe keeping.

BOUGHT TRANSFER DEPARTMENT

During the period of the account in which the Shell purchase occurred, the Bought Transfer Department, who will handle the securities as they are delivered, has been given details of the purchase. A record sheet is prepared (Figure 13) to follow the various stages which the stock will undergo until it finally reaches the client in the form of a certificate.

First of all the clerks in the department will refer to the Clients' Register and mark on the record sheet the requisite particulars. Mr Cuthbertson's full name and the address at which he wishes his shares registered must be inserted. This name and address may be different from the client's usual postal address. He may prefer the address of his bank, for example, if he is likely to be away from home from time to time. He may not wish his identity disclosed to someone who looks through the records of shareholders, which can be examined at Companies House, and may prefer the shares to be placed in the name of a nominee company. All these details should be available from the Clients' Register. Details of the address to which the certificate should be sent and any particular instructions regarding the payment of dividends are also entered. In the example quoted the client prefers that dividends should be paid directly into his bank account. A form of request must therefore be sent to the client for signature, instructing the registrar of the company where to pay all dividends.

As the stock is delivered, the boxes at the bottom of the form are completed. On 3rd May, 300 shares were delivered by Bear & Co. and the seller (or transferor) was Dr C. Cantor. A certificate accompanied the transfer form. On the same date the balance of 25

CLIENT
CUTHBIIC000

DIVIDENDS MANDATED TO
Lloyds Bank Ltd
Little Wren
Cambridge

CERTIFICATES TO
Lloyds Bank Ltd
Little Wren
Cambridge

TICKET HELD BY

PAID	RATE	BARGAIN DATE
17 May 77	6.778	12 April 1977
EX DIVIDEND	**BOOKS CLOSED**	
25 Apr 77	5 May 77	

IEB072/001

Shell Transport and Trading Ord 25P @£4.80

325

	1560.00 32.00
PAY	1592.00

REGISTRATION DETAILS
Charles Cuthbertson
76 Snowy Lane
Bashford

GIVEN TO	DATE		
Johnson & Co.	27 April 1977	A. Broker & Co.	990

DATE	NO. OF SHARES	DELIVERED BY	TRANSFEROR(S)	CERTIFIED OR CERT NO.	REGISTERED	CERTIFICATE COLLECTED	DESPATCHED
C. Cuthbertson							
3.5.77	300	Bear & Co.	Dr C. Cantor	Cert No 7284			
3.5.77	25	Bull & Co.	Sir C. Colinworth	Certd	6.5.77	6281=325	18.5.77
	325						

FIG. 13 Bought Delivery Record

shares was delivered by Bull & Co., the seller being Sir C. Colinworth, and the transfer was certified.

The delivery of the 325 shares is now complete. The two transfers are therefore completed with the full name and address of Mr Cuthbertson from the details on the delivery record. These two documents, together with the certificate for the 300 shares, are attached to the delivery record and passed to the Registration Department.

REGISTRATION DEPARTMENT

It is now the job of this department to turn the transfers received into a certificate and to ensure that this is received by the client safely. The documents are recorded and then despatched to the registrar of the company concerned (in this case Shell), the date of despatch being marked at 6 May 1977. In due course the registrar will acknowledge the transfers and give a date when the certificate will be available. This date is entered into a diary so that the certificate may be collected on the correct day. On this date the Registration Department clerk turns up the delivery record for instructions as to the despatch of the certificate. Mr Cuthbertson likes them sent to his bank. The number of the certificate and the date of despatch is completed in the delivery record and the transaction is now complete.

DIVIDEND DEPARTMENT

The examples selected have dealt only with a straightforward sale and purchase of securities. The stockbroker has an additional duty to ensure that his client is protected in regard to all dividends and other rights which may be attached to the securities bought or sold. On the first day of each account, Contango Day for the previous account, stocks and shares whose dividend announcements have been declared recently are quoted 'ex dividend' (xd). A buyer of these stocks or shares after this date is not entitled to the dividend or interest payment, although this may not be made for some weeks to come, unless the transaction is made under special provisions.

A list of 'ex dividend' securities is published in *The Stock Exchange Weekly Official Intelligence*, which also contains information regarding the amount of the dividend, the date of the closing of the company's transfer books and the date of payment of the dividend. The transfer books are closed to enable the registrar of the company to pay the dividend to shareholders on record at the closing date. The 'ex dividend' date is normally selected so that it is virtually impossible for someone to buy shares which are not entitled to the dividend and register the transfer with the company before the books are closed. Any delay in delivery or of registration may, however, mean that a purchaser of shares is not registered in time to receive the dividend, although he is entitled to it.

Little difficulty would arise if all securities were delivered on Account Day, for the buying broker would know that all deliveries on a given date in a particular stock were entitled to the dividend, while a fortnight later all deliveries of this stock must have been purchased 'ex dividend'. The inevitable delays in delivery—a large number of trustees, all of whom are required to sign the sale transfer form; the seller on holiday abroad; or the jobber having sold short—make it imperative to scrutinise each delivery in order to protect the buyer's interests.

Where the transfer books of the company concerned have closed and the buyer is entitled to the dividend, the Dividend Department will make an immediate claim on the selling broker, in duplicate through The Centre. Settlement of this claim must then be made within fourteen days.

In many cases, although the transfer books have not actually closed by the date of delivery, insufficient time is available to register the shares in the new holder's name before that date. A claim is therefore made to the selling broker, which must be settled within twenty-eight days. In the event of delays in settlement, recourse may be made to The Centre.

The number of dividend claims, although greatly improved recently, is still quite considerable. Nothing is more infuriating to a client who has filed his return of income for the previous year than to receive a claim for a dividend paid many weeks previously. It is always difficult to persuade the client that the selling broker has no control over the registration of the stock in the name of the new buyer. This action lies entirely in the hands of the buying broker and, while in the opinion of The Stock Exchange six months is a maximum reasonable delay in claiming a dividend between members, in law a client may claim back dividends over a period of seven years.

BOUGHT BARGAINS

Before the delivery of the security, the Dividend Department will examine the list of securities due to be received and open accounts in the Dividend Ledger for those where the books will be closed before the stock is due. On the assumption that the Shell purchased in our earlier example fell into this category, the entry in the Dividend Ledger would be as shown in Figure 14.

BOOKS CLOSE	PAID	XD	RATE	TAX
5 MAY 77	17 MAY 77	25.4.77	6.778p.	NET

SHELL TRANSPORT & TRADING ORDINARY

Amount	Claimed by	Date	Other Reference	Ticket Number	DEBIT	Amount	Claimed From	Date	Other Reference	Ticket Number	CREDIT
325	C. CUTHBERTSON	12 APR 77		1EB072	£22.03	300	BEAR & CO		1233	1EB072	£20.33
300		,,				25	BULL & CO		1234	do	£ 1.70

FIG. 14 Dividend Account Extract

At the head of the page of the title of the stock is given with details taken from *The Stock Exchange Weekly Official Intelligence*. In the *debit* columns on the left-hand side the number of shares, the client, the date of the bargain and the identifying ticket number are recorded, together with the amount of dividend due. At the same time the matching *credits* are posted to the accounts of the clients concerned.

When securities are delivered, the Dividend and Transfer Departments are usually responsible for checking that they are 'good delivery'. They must confirm that either the correct certificate is attached, or that the transfer form is certified; that the stamp duty is correct; that the stock is correctly described on the transfer form; and that either the original form is signed by the seller or a broker's form contains the broker's stamp. If the date on the ticket, which is pinned to the transfer form, indicates that the security was purchased in the previous account, *The Stock Exchange Weekly Official Intelligence* is examined to ensure that no dividend claims are involved. If the date indicates an earlier purchase, the daily Official List must be studied.

Referring to the example, *The Stock Exchange Weekly Official Intelligence* will indicate that the transfer books have closed, so that the seller, although not entitled to the dividend, will receive it from the company. The Dividend Department therefore calculates the amount of the dividend due, and prepares the dividend claim which is sent to the selling broker in duplicate through The Centre. The *debit* entries in the Dividend Ledger will then be completed as shown in Figure 14, and the first three columns of the *credit* entry may be made, leaving only the amount in the last column to be completed when the selling broker pays the claim.

SOLD BARGAINS

Much the same procedures are carried out for ensuring that prompt claims are made on clients who have sold securities for dividends to which they are not entitled.

Buying brokers' dividend claims are checked to ensure that the seller has in fact received the dividend. The claim is entered as a *debit* of the Dividend Account, and opens the matching *credit* of the buying broker's account. The balancing entry to the *credit* of the Dividend Account and the *debit* of the client's account follow, and the transaction is completed with the receipt of the client's cheque and the despatch of the firm's cheque to the buying broker.

DIVIDENDS ON AMERICAN AND OTHER FOREIGN SECURITIES

This somewhat specialised function of the Dividend Department is considered in Chapter 8.

RIGHTS DEPARTMENT

In just the same way that the Dividend Department ensures that clients do not miss dividends to which they are entitled or do not retain them if others are entitled to them, so the Rights Department plays the same role in regard to rights and capitalisation issues.

Whenever a company announces a rights or capitalisation issue, the relevant dates are published in *The Stock Exchange Weekly Official Intelligence*, issued each Monday. The Rights Department prepares a list of companies, recording the date when the share will be quoted 'ex rights' or 'ex cap.', the dates when the company's books close, the last date of renunciation and, in the case of rights issues, the dates of payment of the calls. Unlike the procedure in the payment of dividends, shares are not quoted 'ex rights' and 'ex cap.' on the first day of a new account, but on the day after the allotment letter or other document of title is posted to shareholders. In many cases an additional check will be made by a member of the Rights Department visiting the Quotations Department of The Stock Exchange daily to note those shares which are being quoted 'ex' on that day.

The Rights Department then examines the List Books to locate the bargains carried out in these securities over a number of past accounts. The 'open positions' are examined, a record made of shares which have been bought and which are not yet delivered by the selling brokers, or deliveries which cannot be registered before the books of the company close. Claims for the rights are then made on the selling brokers or clients.

The books kept in the department are very similar to those kept by the Dividend Department.

When the documents have been received, either from selling brokers due to clients or from clients due to other buying brokers, they are held in the Rights Department until the total for each bargain is complete. Split tickets will mean a number of pieces to make up the whole, and the sale of part of a holding by a client may mean that only part of his allotment of new shares is required by the buyer. When the total of the new shares is completed for each bargain, they are handed over to the Bearer Department.

BEARER DEPARTMENT

All securities which are transferable by bearer or semi-bearer document pass through this department. Three types of share fall into this classification.

(*a*) ALLOTMENT LETTERS AND RENOUNCEABLE CERTIFICATES OF STOCKS AND SHARES IN U.K. COMPANIES

The majority of new issues, both original quotations and issues by companies already quoted, are carried out by means of allotment letters or renounceable certificates. In both cases the company pays stamp duty at the time of the issue, and for a period of several weeks (or months in some cases) transfer is free of stamp duty. The original allottee is only required to sign the appropriate part of the document, renouncing his right to the underlying security, and it is then delivered from hand to hand like a piece of currency.

Allotment letters differ from renounceable certificates in one major respect. The former must be exchanged for a definitive certificate at a stated date, while the latter also acts as the certificate itself. In the following paragraphs, to avoid repetition, both documents will be referred to as allotment letters.

All purchases and sales of new shares on allotment letters are made for cash settlement. A bargain carried out on one day, therefore, may be settled by delivery and payment the next. The settlement for this type of security is carried out in a similar fashion to registered stock through The Centre.

Allotment letters are delivered on a three-part 'tag' set (two white copies, one pink), showing the name and number of the delivering broker, the date of the bargain, the stock and the amount of money due. The selling broker keeps the bottom copy, pins the top two to the allotment letter and sends the securities to The Centre. They in turn keep one copy and send on the other, together with the stock, to the jobber.

The jobber, in turn, pins on a new 'tag' set for each allotment letter due for delivery to buying brokers and returns the security through The Centre.

The Centre sorts the debits and credits on the tag sets and prepares a statement of balances owed by or due to all the jobbers and brokers concerned. Each stockbroker's balance should agree with the total of the white tags (stock sold) and the pink tags (stock bought) in the Bearer Department.

The Bearer Department will hold the allotment letters for purchases until the full delivery is complete and will also hold up registration of new shares until the last possible date. A client may decide to sell the new security at the last moment and, should the allotment letters have been sent to the company for registration, the broker will have to deliver the security on a form of transfer, losing the *ad valorem* stamp duty of 2 per cent.

One other important function of the Bearer Department is the paying of calls on rights or other new issues. Where payment is due on a fixed date, the Bearer Department will again wait until the last moment before paying, if the value of the rights appears to be in doubt. There is no point in paying a call on a security which may fall below the value of the call immediately afterwards.

The Bearer Department is also responsible, in some offices, for acquiring application forms for new issues and seeing that these are completed for clients and despatched to the issuing bankers, with cheques, before the closing date.

(*b*) BEARER BONDS

The shares of a number of international companies and many foreign loans are transferable in bearer form. These documents contain a series of coupons attached, which entitle the owner to dividend or other distributions. On delivery they must be carefully checked to ensure that the bond has not been damaged, that it has been stamped, and that the coupons are intact. A record is made of all the bonds received and the number of each one. Under Exchange Control Regulations, bearer securities must be held in safe keeping by an authorised depositary, such as a bank, and not by an individual. The Bearer Department will therefore despatch the completed delivery to the client's bank.

Bearer bonds are not good delivery unless they bear *ad valorem* stamp duty at the appropriate rate. This may have been paid twenty years ago, when the rate was considerably lower than today, but bonds not already stamped bear the following duty:

Bearer with coupons attached – 2 per cent of market value per bond.

Inland bearer (British securities such as Shell and British-American Tobacco) – 3 per cent of market value per bond.

Note that under the provisions of the Finance Act, 1967, bearer instruments relating to stock expressed in the currency of a territory outside the Scheduled Territories need not be stamped, if delivery takes place after 1 August 1967.

(*c*) AMERICAN AND CANADIAN SECURITIES

American and Canadian securities are often loosely called bearer stocks, although in fact each one carries the name of a stockholder registered in the company's books. They are very similar to the renounceable certificates mentioned earlier in discussing new issues by British companies. Certificates for American and Canadian securities are prepared in round amounts of hundreds, tens and units, and are renounceable by signing the reverse of the document.

Dealings in both bearer and semi-bearer securities are normally for account settlement. The Bearer Department will keep a book of 'Stock In and Stock Out', entering the exact details of the security, the name in which it is registered and the firm who has delivered it or to whom it must be delivered for record purposes.

Deliveries of stock in overseas markets are considered at the end of Chapter 8.

GILT-EDGED TRANSFER DEPARTMENT

The last department to be reviewed in the general office concerns the transfer of Government securities. In gilt-edged transactions the jobbing system operates at its best. Because the Government is the largest individual owner of gilt-edged and because of the excellent management of the Government debt by the Bank of England, a free market is maintained in almost all Government issues. Jobbers can therefore deal in substantial quantities without the fear of being unable either to supply or get rid of the stock. The banks will lend a high proportion of the capital required when stock is taken on jobbers' books, and the Government Broker is always ready to assist in maintaining an orderly market.

As a result the jobber in the gilt-edged market acts not as a post office between brokers in the delivery of securities, but as a principal. Virtually all gilt-edged stock is delivered out of jobbers' nominees or is put into them. Transfers are exempt from stamp duty, so that little cost is attached.

Gilt-edged transactions are for cash settlement. The day after a purchase transaction, therefore, the Gilt-Edged Department passes the name of the buyer direct to the jobber. On the same day the stock is delivered and paid for. The lack of delay in such transactions means that claims for interest payments are rare and the paperwork involved reduced to a minimum.

In many offices the Gilt-Edged Transfer Department acts as a miniature of the entire Transfer Office. Names are passed, transfers prepared, deliveries checked, dividend mandates prepared, stock sent for registration and certificates despatched to clients, all by only one or two individuals.

One of the problems faced by Gilt-Edged Transfer Departments is the size of individual bargains, running sometimes into several million pounds. Since payment is made against delivery, there must be no delay in obtaining payment from the client. Where institutions are concerned, payment is usually made by a bank against the delivery of the security. In the case of tied trusts, however, with substantial funds, a switch may be made on occasion from securities settled on Account Day into gilt-edged due for payment the following day. A careful check must be kept to ensure that the firm is not out of money overnight or for longer periods.

CONCLUSION

The operation of the production side of a stockbroker's office is the least understood division of the business. Even the system described in this chapter is likely to be superseded in a few years on the introduction of TALISMAN, to which reference is made in Chapter 10.

4 Research and Statistics

The greater emphasis placed on technical investigation for investment has resulted in the rapid growth of research and statistical departments during the last decade. The terms 'research' and 'statistics' are fairly loosely applied and as easily confused as 'research' and 'development' in industrial concerns. In some firms the Statistical Department's materials consist of nothing more than the published statistical services, and operations are largely confined to producing brief reports on companies and reviewing the lists of private clients. In others a highly qualified staff of actuaries, economists, accountants and statisticians may be employed, possibly using their own computer, together with industry specialists, qualified in their appropriate disciplines.

The objectives of the department, however it is composed, must be threefold: to provide evidence on which the firm's investment policy may be based; to investigate securities, either individually or by some other classification, providing a service both to the members of the firm and to clients on the investment merits of these securities; and to develop new methods of investigation, so that additional techniques are available for assessing these investment merits.

EVIDENCE FOR INVESTMENT POLICY

As firms of stockbrokers grow larger and the links in the chain of communication between partners become more extended, there is an inevitable tendency towards individuals stating their own personal investment ideas. It is important that the firm should have a defined investment policy and that all clients should receive broadly similar advice. The Research Department must provide the evidence to support, and even on which to formulate, policy from time to time. Research will be required into both the global and national economic outlook. The work of the department may vary from a simple study of published statistics, with an attempt to identify the trend-indicators, to a full-scale construction of a complicated model of the national economy.

From time to time suggestions are made that the mass of effort which is poured into research and statistical studies could well be pooled in some common research organisation. On the face of it this proposal seems sound enough. Work in any one broker's office is almost certainly being duplicated elsewhere, but the broker maintains his connections, in particular his institutional connections, by the service he is able to offer, and must therefore compete on knowledge. The most important service is the presentation of his investment recommendations in a form which shows that he is either better informed, or has been able to reach more effective conclusions, than his competitors. The operation of the Research Department is vitally important as a source of information and evidence to the sales-and-service departments.

The primary purpose of the Research Department is to comment on the economic outlook, both domestic and international, since investment strategy is generally more important than day-to-day tactics. As a result major firms of stockbrokers have developed substantial reputations in the economic arena, some as monetarists, others as Keynesians, but all producing reasoned arguments for future investment policy.

On the more immediate problems of portfolio management, only the activities of the Research Department in connection with ordinary shares are considered here, the investigation of fixed-interest or overseas securities being considered under the headings of the relevant departments.

The science of investment analysis can be divided into two separate but overlapping functions:

1. The selection of investments.
2. The timing of a purchase or sale.

The problems of selecting an investment and timing the action on it are interrelated in that, however good the management or prospects of a company, its shares are almost certain to fall in price in sympathy with a general market recession. Conversely the shares of a small company in which dealings are relatively rare may hold up against a general downward trend either because the market is never tested or because the restricted marketability makes it almost impossible to deal. A study of the high and low points printed on the penultimate pages of the *Financial Times* shows that, in any given year, the low price of many leading shares will be as much as a third below their highs, although the *FT*-Actuaries Share Index may only have varied by 10 per cent. In the short term, therefore, timing can be said to be even more important than selection.

For pension and superannuation funds, with very long-term liabilities and with new money available for investment for many years to come, it is comforting to think that a fluctuation of even as much as 30 per cent is of relatively little account compared with the doubling or trebling of the value of the investment which may be anticipated over the very long term.

THE SELECTION OF INVESTMENTS

Much of the work of the department consists of plodding through the published information available, selecting relevant passages in reports, analysing statistics, comparing information available from data banks, and gradually building up a survey of an industry or a case for an investment. The one vital factor which cannot be accurately established from a study of facts and figures or even company reports, however, is the future quality of management. Their success or failure in the past can be judged by an examination of the record of the concern, suitably discounted by comparison with like companies; but this gives no indication of their performance in the future. As a result, the second source of information lies in direct contact with industry, and visits to companies, combined with meetings with management at all levels, have become a much more common occurrence. The stockbroker is able to form his own judgement of the competence of the executives from personal acquaintance. The third source of information available to the Research Department lies in the work of outside experts—economists, market research consultants and others—who are commissioned to undertake certain specific tasks.

PUBLISHED INFORMATION

Apart from the statistical services mentioned earlier, a mass of published information is available to the investment analyst, and one of the problems is to ensure that the highly qualified staff are not bogged down in reading material which they may never use again. The essence of an efficient Research Department, therefore, is to be able to refer readily and easily to information when it is required.

Most of the larger firms maintain their own reference libraries, where up-to-date files are kept on industries, companies and general subjects. A useful bibliography for research departments has been produced by Professor Richard Brealey of the London Business School, *Bibliography of Finance and Investment* (Elek Books, 1974).

Even the largest firms would find it uneconomical to subscribe to all the trade papers and other sources of information listed, and many analysts find that the City Business Library, Basinghall Street, London, E.C.2, and the Library of the London Chamber of Commerce, 92 Cannon Street, London, E.C.4, provide all the reference works they require. A larger collection of trade papers, particularly technical journals and those published in the U.S.A., are included in the Patent Office Library in Holborn (25 Southampton Buildings, London, W.C.2).

For those who want a more comprehensive source of production and trade statistics, including those of overseas areas, the Statistics and Market Intelligence Library of the Department of Trade at Export House, 50 Ludgate Hill, London, E.C.4, may well provide the answers.

Two further sources of published information should be mentioned—the Registrar of Companies at Crown Way, Maindy, Cardiff, with a branch office at Companies House, 55 City Road, London, E.C.2, and the Registrar of Companies for Scotland, 102 George Street, Edinburgh 2. A study of a company's file may prove most rewarding. For those concerns with a varied product group, different subsidiaries, manufacturing different articles or operating in different industries, the detailed figures from each company file may give a very fair breakdown of the group's profits in the various industries with which it is concerned.

COMPANY ACCOUNTS

It is not within the compass of this book to deal in any detail with the study of company accounts, nor to discuss the relevance of the various figures. Every shareholder, however, receives a copy of the company's accounts annually and some mention of one or two of the items seems appropriate here, even if their significance is fairly elementary in terms of the work of a Research Department.

(*a*) *Balance Sheet Figures*

The balance sheet gives the financial position of the company or group on one day in the year. The following items are worth noting:

(i) *Capital*. The capital of a public company provides some measure of its size (e.g. the provisions of the Trustee Investments Act, 1961, limits investment to those companies with issued share capital of £1 million or more). In addition, the relative amounts of various classes of capital (debentures, loans, preference and ordinary) indicate the gearing of the equity. Where the service of the prior charges takes a high proportion of available profit, the equity is said to be 'highly geared', and a small fluctuation in such available profit will have a marked effect on the earning for the equity.

(ii) *Reserves*. Reserves comprise both capital reserves and revenue reserves, and indicate the surplus worth of a company over and above its issued capital. It is common practice for companies to capitalise reserves, giving 'scrip' issues to shareholders, so that reserves large in relation to issued capital indicate the prospect and extent of future capitalisation issues.

(iii) *Fixed Assets*. Fixed assets include properties, plant and machinery. Where freehold property is a significant item, it is important to note the last date of revaluation. Where new values are written into the balance-sheet after a revaluation, a balancing adjustment will be made to the reserves.

(iv) *Current Assets*. Current assets include such items as cash, investments, debtors and stocks. The figure may reveal whether the company has a surplus of cash resources or whether it is carrying too large an amount of stock. Examined in conjunction with current liabilities (q.v.), an indication may be given as to whether there is sufficient working capital, and therefore whether additional funds are required.

(v) *Current Liabilities*. Included under this heading are such items as creditors, tax payments due, dividend payments and bank overdrafts. Where large overdrafts are shown they may well indicate the need to raise fresh capital, particularly if they have increased sharply since the previous year.

(vi) *Net Asset Value*. The net asset value per share is calculated by ascertaining the total of net assets available for the ordinary and dividing it by the number of ordinary shares in issue. In general terms the net assets available for the ordinary are represented by the balance-sheet totals of ordinary capital, plus reserves, less fixed-interest capital, but it is usual to deduct also any figure for goodwill. Great care should be taken in comparing asset values of companies in dissimilar industries. Shipping companies, for example, may have asset values well in excess of the market values of their shares; companies carrying out services or marketing may have very low asset values relative to the market prices of their shares.

(*b*) *Profit and Loss Account*

(i) *Profit Record.* The record of net profits before tax over a period of years may prove misleading as a guide to progress, since new acquisitions during the period could have affected these figures. The profit record therefore will probably be shown in terms of earnings on the ordinary capital, adjusted for capitalisation issues and the 'bonus element' in rights issues. The adjusted record will now give a clear picture of the earnings available for ordinary shareholders over the period and will indicate the measure of growth that has taken place.

(ii) *Dividend Record.* Dividend records are adjusted in the same way. It may be that a company has never increased its dividend through the years, but that frequent capitalisation issues or rights issues have been made. In cases such as this, the effective increase in dividend can look quite startling. On the other hand, when compared with the earnings record, it may simply show that there has been virtually no growth in the company's earnings, but that the directors have been successively more generous to shareholders by distributing a greater proportion of profits.

The imposition of dividend limitation in the U.K. in 1972 has distorted the recent trend and, on occasions, rights issues have been made as much to take advantage of Treasury dispensation on dividend increases as to raise new capital.

(*c*) *Profitability*

Two measures of profitability are in common use—the ratios 'earned on total sales' and 'earned on capital employed'.

(i) *Earned on Total Sales.* The trend in the ratio of net profit from trading, before interest charges and before tax, to total sales gives an indication of whether the company is improving, maintaining or reducing its sales margins.

(ii) *Earned on Capital Employed.* The trend in the ratio of net profit before tax to the total capital employed in the business gives an indication of whether the company is improving, maintaining or reducing the return on its assets. This figure can be very valuable since it often indicates a turn-round in the fortunes of the company. The earnings on the ordinary capital may continue to show an improvement while those on the capital employed may show a fall. One of the difficulties faced by the analyst is to arrive at a true figure for the capital employed. This is usually taken as the balance-sheet assets total, less current liabilities, including bank overdrafts and intangibles such as goodwill, patent rights and 'excess of cost' of subsidiaries over book value. Some analysts take the figure at the commencement of the year, some at the year-end and some as the average of the two, so that there is no standard practice in this connection. Only the trend of the amount earned on capital employed over the years is of real value, and any comparisons between these ratios for companies even in the same industry may be misleading. One company may have recently revalued its assets, for example, or some exceptional capital expenditure may have been undertaken which cannot produce full profitability in its first few months of operation.

(*d*) *Cash Flow*

Cash flow is used to describe the amount of money the company has available for spending each year, generated from its own trading operations.

No precise definition of the term has been generally accepted, but the 'gross cash flow' is usually taken to be the net profit after tax plus the amount set aside for depreciation. The 'net cash flow' is the net profit after tax, less the dividends payable, plus depreciation. In these calculations profits from the sale of investments and tax provisions no longer required are excluded (as being non-recurring) when arriving at the net profit figure.

The figure for 'cash flow' is of interest in two respects. If the company's annual programme of capital expenditure is obviously much greater than the net cash flow, additional permanent finance may be required. Those companies which are engaged in heavy expenditure on plant and machinery, with high depreciation levels, may show an apparently misleadingly low earnings record on their ordinary capital. These are the very companies, however, which, when the new plant is fully productive, may be expected to show above-average improvement in their profits.

(*e*) *Inflation Accounting*

At the date of going to press no definitive standards have been established for inflation accounting. When these are finally agreed, there is little doubt that the skills of the investment analyst will be even more in demand in the interpretation of the new figures.

COMPANY VISITS

A decade ago chairmen and directors of companies viewed requests for visits by stockbrokers with extreme suspicion. They took the view that no individual should be given *any* information about the company that was not available to the body of shareholders in general meeting or through the company's publications. While this is an understandable attitude of mind, it has now been proved to be somewhat dated. Stockbrokers and other investment analysts who visit companies respect and even encourage the principles of chairmen and directors. They do not request confidential details, such as the current level of profits or a forecast of the dividend. They are concerned to obtain a more balanced view of the company's activities than can be achieved by reading the chairman's reports, and to get an impression of the management by meeting the individuals face to face.

It should be emphasised here that considerable experience is required to obtain any value out of company visits, and, if used as a single tool in the investment investigation, they can prove to be extremely misleading. Unless the analyst has visited works before and knows the points to observe, he may obtain an entirely unrealistic view. Managements are inevitably shy of exhibiting the least efficient of their processes and tend to show only the divisions which are working smoothly and well. Stores of finished stock, for example, may be considerably larger than needed technically or are usually held in the industry. This may be all too easily concealed from the untrained eye. Over a period the analyst develops a nose for the well-run workshop and can detect the smell of the inefficient firm. In the same way that some highly-placed executives can be excellent talkers and indifferent, or even disastrous, managers, so the evidence of all company visits must be viewed in a highly critical light.

Managements are easily put off by too many and too pointed questions and will often talk more readily about their competitors in the same field than about their own concerns. A company visit may often produce more valuable information about another company in the same industry than about the organisation to which the visit has been paid, but any judgement of a competitor is usually a fair guide to the ability of the judge.

One of the problems facing the analyst is to remember the salient points which have been discussed and to record them. In the middle of an informal talk with the managing director, when he is just getting warmed up to the company's new developments, the production of a large pad of paper and a pencil spells death to the conversation. Every interview and visit has to be conducted with a different approach. It is usual to submit the resulting memorandum to the management for amendment or for the erasure of any information held to be confidential.

The preparatory work which must be done before a visit to a company is very considerable. The reports and accounts for at least the past five years must be studied and the chairman's remarks examined so that intelligent enquiries can be made about the company's products or services. Some firms have a standard *pro forma*, the main headings of which are committed to memory by the visiting analyst so that the ground is adequately covered and no important facts omitted. The completion of a report in this form also assists the publication of a memorandum on the company if this is to be sent to clients at a later date.

Each firm of stockbrokers will have its own method of preparing such a *pro forma*, but one specimen example might include the following details:

General	Name of company
	Visited by
	Date of visit
	Introduction to company
	Issuing house to company
Details of Visit	Works, factories, offices, etc., visited
	Names, functions and ages of directors and executives met
Management	Impression of existing management
	Method of selection:
	(*a*) Internal
	(*b*) External
	Does management selection ensure
	(*a*) sufficient outside knowledge and experience?
	(*b*) sufficient technical experience?
	What management training provisions are there?
	What is outlook for management in future?
	(*a*) Approx. ages of existing management

(*b*) Are suitable replacements available?
Management tree or chain of command of the company
General comments

The Industry Names of leading competitors
Company's views on competitors
Company's share of the market
Is it increasing/decreasing?
Is the market increasing/decreasing?
Industry's exports

Marketing and Sales Products sold
Are they up to date?
Sales outlets:
(*a*) Wholesalers
(*b*) Retailers
(*c*) Direct
Does sale pattern change?
What market research has been done?
Any special advantages or difficulties?
Experience in other countries, particularly America
Export sales
Advertising
General comments

Production Production grouping—continuous, batch, on-off, etc.
Shift work
Layout of production flow
Age and type of machines used
Handling of products down the line
Size of average batch and time on the shop floor
Stock record and stock control
General comments

Labour Labour relations
Unions and their attitudes
Total number of employees (divided in groups if possible)
Payment, piecework, etc.
Incentive schemes
Pensions schemes

	Training
	Special labour problems
Raw Materials	Main raw materials
	Where are supplies drawn from?
	Do stock losses/profits materially affect P. & L. account?
	Method of stock valuation (last in—first out, etc.)
Finance	Methods of financial control
	Is company largely self-financing?
	Major capital expenditure programmes planned
	Taxation situation
Future	Company's five-year plan
	Areas of future problems and future expansion
Properties	Last date of revaluation
	Approx. area of factories
	Estimate as to whether properties are fully utilised
Current Trading	Is the industry generally running at higher level in current year?
	Are profit margins being maintained?
	Is company's trade affected by any exceptional circumstances?

It is, of course, not always possible to obtain answers to all these questions, and in particular circumstances there may be other and more important points which should be made. On current trading, in particular, considerable tact must be used to avoid asking direct questions which may lead to the disclosure of confidential information.

Company visits are one of the most pleasant and interesting of the investment analyst's tasks. Generally more is learned about an industry and its prospects in half-an-hour's conversation with a leading member of management than in several days sitting in the back room of a stockbroker's office. In particular the emergence from the somewhat rarefied atmosphere of the City to the more realistic and down-to-earth environment of the industrial North or the Midlands provides a breath of fresh air which stimulates the analyst's perception.

Conversely, members of management can derive considerable value from City visitors, being all too prone to accept left-wing political criticism of the role played by capital markets in the past.

ORGANISED MEETINGS AND VISITS

Meetings addressed by leading industrialists and visits to companies are arranged by the Society of Investment Analysts. This body was formed in 1955, with a founder membership of seven, and a total of ninety within a few days. At the end of 1976 it comprised a membership of some 1500, drawn not only from firms of stockbrokers but from all institutions and other investment organisations.

It is a rule of the Society that remarks made by speakers at their meetings must not be quoted in circulars or other investment material, with the result that replies to questions and the facts disclosed in these addresses tend to be more uninhibited than in more formal gatherings.

EXTERNAL WORK

Many firms employ the services of leading economists to prepare for them periodic reviews on the economic outlook and to act in a consultative capacity when specific questions require to be answered. This does not imply that the economists within the firm are incapable of a reasonable assessment of the situation, but the advantage of an outside mind, not hemmed in by current City thought, and constantly mixing with other economists in discussions of theory and practice, can be considerable.

From time to time market research consultants are employed by stockbrokers to investigate trends in the sales of consumer goods and to report on the development of new methods of merchandising. A major investigation of this type is fairly costly and is therefore not undertaken as a matter of routine.

Industrial experts are less easy to find for outside consultation. If their opinion is of real value they are most likely already fully employed in their own company and less well informed about others in the same field.

Outside financial journalists are employed by a number of firms to convert the work of the Research Department into a readable article, when a company or industry review is planned. Some journalists also work under contract to produce regular investment reviews for circulation, normally to private clients.

TIMING

It has been mentioned earlier that the investing public's yardstick for equity share prices is still the yield (or to put it more accurately the percentage dividend/price ratio), allied to the price/earnings ratio. The yield will vary with both the price and the dividend. The share price may fluctuate for a number of reasons: in sympathy with either the market in general or the section of the market in which it lies; or the investment rating of the share itself may have altered, due to changed profits, an announcement of special importance, or a hundred and one different eventualities; or some technical factor may have forced the price of the share temporarily out of line. The object of the analyst in studying timing is firstly to estimate whether the market in general is likely to move upwards or downwards, and secondly to select shares which are either dear or cheap in relation to other comparable shares. At any given time investment trusts and unit trusts will switch from one share which looks relatively dear to another which looks relatively cheap, since by this means they will improve upon the average performance of the market. Funds with long-term liabilities and new money accruing regularly will select those shares which are cheap in relation to the whole market, since regular purchases of such stocks over a period will also give above-average performance. Some method of indicating which shares are standing out of line from their normal course must therefore be of advantage.

CHARTS

A number of research departments utilise charts of share prices or price indices in attempting to forecast the movement both of the market in general and of particular securities. At its simplest a chart illustrates the movements of the past in a clear and obvious manner, but the majority of chartists expect to derive considerably more information than just a historical record. Their experience suggests that prices move in certain identifiable patterns, and that these patterns will be repeated in the future.

OTHER METHODS

There are almost as many aids to investment timing—point and figure methods, volume and price correlations, and a range of new ratios calculated on computers—as there are investment analysts. It is not within the compass of this book to name more than the most widely used. But when it is possible to increase the capital invested by 50 per cent in a single year on a leading share (as shown by the differential between high and low mentioned earlier), it can be realised that successful timing is of even greater importance than successful selection.

RESEARCH INTO NEW METHODS AND TECHNIQUES

The work of the Research Department outlined so far deals only with the day-to-day problems of investment. Its long-term role, however, must be to find new and improved methods of selecting investments and techniques for improving timing.

The use of the computer in this connection is still only in its early stages. In America a number of firms have developed methods of examining the mass of statistics available to select and compare the performance of individual companies. Naturally the work which is currently under examination in the research departments of stockbrokers is a highly guarded secret, but it is evident that new and more sophisticated computer techniques will be developed in the future. It is only by having an additional precision tool and acquiring the skill to use it that a firm of stockbrokers can obtain an advantage over its competitors.

5 Finance

The previous chapters have been devoted to the work of individual operating departments. The financial control of a partnership may be devolved upon one individual or become the responsibility of an executive committee, depending upon the way in which the firm is managed.

Money is one of the basic raw materials of the stockbroker, and it is natural that the financial aspects of the business should be handled with particular care. These may be broken down under three main headings: the financial standing of the client; the financial stability of the firm, including the provision and best uses of the partnership funds; and budgetary control, including the costing of bargains, the annual budgets of current and capital expenditure, and trading forecasts.

THE FINANCIAL STANDING OF THE CLIENT

Except in special circumstances (arbitrage dealing, for example), the stockbroker acts as an agent for his client, rather than as a principal, but he is nevertheless responsible for the settlement with other members of The Stock Exchange of any transactions which his firm has undertaken.

A partner in a firm of stockbrokers is liable, to the extent of all his worldly goods, for the transactions of his firm. As a result clients are carefully scrutinised before they are accepted. It is normal to request a banker's reference, indicating the credit-worthiness of the individual, and the Stock Exchange Council requires that an application for each new client is made to the Stock Exchange Mutual Reference Society, which keeps a file of complaints and which will also direct an enquirer to the press-cutting files of the Records Office.

One of the problems facing stockbrokers on the introduction of a new client is the extent of his resources. The first transaction may be for a relatively small number of shares, a sale order possibly being accompanied by a relevant certificate, so that obviously little risk is attached to the transaction. If the newly-accepted client then gives instructions to buy a large number of shares in a highly speculative concern, does the stockbroker accept the instructions or refuse to deal?

Most firms have their own internal regulations regarding this sort of dilemma, just as they take the necessary precautions against mystery voices which give telephone instructions to buy or sell securities in times of hectic trading, or individuals who identify themselves, on the telephone for example, as one of the directors in a company for whom it is known that the firm of stockbrokers acts. But some clients tend to look askance at stockbrokers, whom they accept implicitly as being of good financial standing, if the firm makes detailed investigations as to the client's credit-worthiness.

THE FINANCIAL STANDING OF THE STOCKBROKER

The financial viability of stockbroking firms is more closely monitored than that of any other service industry or profession. Financial statements are required to be submitted to the Council offices and to The Stock Exchange accountants monthly, with audited accounts half-yearly on a strict time-schedule. Member firms of stockbrokers must at all times maintain a 'minimum liquidity margin' (the amount by which 'approved assets' exceed 'ranking liabilities'). The size of this liquidity margin should, if possible, be related both to the volume of business transacted by the firm and to the nature of the business. Its calculation has been a matter of debate in The Stock Exchange for many years and at present is computed largely as a rule of thumb. The minimum margin must be equal to the sum of £5000 multiplied by either the number of partners or the aggregate of associated members and attachés, whichever is the greater (Rule 79c). The margin of liquidity should not be confused with the capital of the firm. A compensation fund is available to pay the losses to clients in the event of a failure by a member firm. Although this fund has been built up out of members' subscriptions over a number of years, it is not available to pay the losses which accrue to other firms in the event of failure.

Finally, partners in Stock Exchange firms are not permitted to engage in other activities which may incur a liability on their finances. Rule 30 states (*inter alia*) that a member who wishes to be a principal or an employee in any business other than that of The Stock Exchange must obtain prior consent of the Council.

The Law Society imposes restrictions on firms of solicitors, insisting that clients' funds must be held in a separate bank account from partnership funds. The situation of stockbrokers is very different, since they act to a far smaller degree as custodians of securities and relatively rarely are given powers of attorney for their clients. Stockbrokers nevertheless have to accept delivery of securities on Settlement Day and pay for them punctually, whether they have been put in funds by their clients or not. It is true to say, therefore, that clients who are slow in paying for their purchases may be financed over the short term either by the funds of the partnership, or by those of more punctilious clients, or by a combination of both. Many institutional investors, in order only to part with securities against the receipt of a cheque in the case of a sale, or to pay against the physical delivery of the stock in the case of a purchase, arrange to have the securities delivered to or by their banks against payment.

DAY-TO-DAY FINANCE

Several problems face the stockbroker in the administration of day-to-day finance. The first is that the banks tend to place their business with those firms who maintain reasonably large current accounts. As a result the funds at the disposal of the firm may be spread between thirty or forty accounts with different banks. In order to avoid paying high rates of interest on overdrafts in some banks, while obtaining no interest on credits with others, the cashier has to maintain a careful balance between banking clients.

The second is concerned with the delays in preparing stocks for delivery. The Stock Transfer Act, 1963, reduced many of the delays of delivery and greatly reduced the volume of dividend claims, etc., but about 50 per cent of stock is now delivered on Settlement Day itself, whereas in the past the inefficiency of the system extended delivery throughout the following week or longer. The physical difficulty of preparing some thousands of transfer forms, having them impressed with the correct stamp duty, obtaining certification where required and attaching the necessary documents, together with the requirement during the same short period of checking and listing some thousands of deliveries, requires considerable effort in management and organisation. Priority must obviously be given to those deliveries where the money passing is large, and particularly institutional transactions where payment is made on receipt of securities sold and must be recouped from the buying brokers. Firms with substantial sums at their disposal may find it worth while to arrange the acceptance of institutional or other large sale deliveries earlier than Settlement Day, in order to prepare the documents in advance and spread out the work of the settlement, even if this means some delay between paying the seller and recouping the money from the buyer. This extra advantage of having large partnership funds occurs at a time when the financing of partnerships is becoming increasingly difficult.

FINANCE FOR PARTNERSHIPS

Before the Second World War finance for stockbrokers was not normally difficult to obtain. Candidates for partnership often qualified because of their connections and as a result were likely to be endowed with sufficient wealth to pay for their participation. The emphasis since the war, on skill rather than connections, allied to the high rates of taxation and swingeing estate duties, has brought in a new membership of technocrats, often with little capital behind them. Partnerships have therefore been faced with two problems: increasing the total funds to cope with expanding business, while the remuneration of the partners suffers the penal rates of tax; and finding methods of buying out the elder retiring partners in order to make room for the younger men.

The plight of the firms of jobbers in this respect is much worse, but a detailed discussion is not within the scope of this book. They act as principals, not as agents, and their capital is truly on risk. While the banks will provide temporary finance against the security of the stocks in the hands of the jobbers, the freedom of dealing in large amounts is obviously curtailed when the jobbers appreciate that a sudden move in the market could virtually wipe out the greater part of their capital. The opportunity of making large capital sums has gone, while the chance of losing them is ever-present.

LIMITED PARTNERS

In order to alleviate the problem of obtaining additional funds, the Council introduced in June 1966 regulations permitting external members and limited partnerships. Risk capital may now be obtained from persons and corporations not actively engaged in Stock Exchange business, entitling them to a participation in profits (and losses) of the firm but limiting their liability to the capital introduced.

These provisions are of particular assistance in allowing retired members to retain a share in profits without unlimited liability and giving similar opportunities to widows, family trusts and other connections of members. Members of Lloyd's, provided they have the approval of that institution, may also participate.

In granting permission to corporations to become limited partners, the Council is careful to exclude investment organisations who, by sharing in the profits of the broking firm, could effectively reduce commission charges on business directed to it. Consortium campanies may be formed to assist in the finance of jobbing firms, but no individual institution may hold more than 35 per cent of the capital of the consortium company.

Limited partners may also not hold more than 50 per cent of the capital owned by the general partners, thus effectively limiting them to one-third of the capital of the firm. Under the Limited Partnership Act, a limited partner may not take part in the management of the firm.

The introduction of these regulations offered several advantages over previous practice. Time can be given to members of a partnership to pay out a retiring partner or beneficiaries of a deceased estate, causing less strain on surviving partners. Corporations not active in Stock Exchange investment may be interested to invest in forward-looking firms to finance expansion, and this may, in turn, give existing partners an opportunity of realising some of the goodwill which they have built up over the years.

Member firms who have formed corporate memberships are not prohibited from having limited partners.

CORPORATE MEMBERSHIPS

No provision for reserves can be made out of partnership profits, which must be distributed each year between the partners, and which suffer tax in the hands of each individual at his personal rate. The full earned-income allowance may, however, be claimed.

In order to provide reserves at a less penal rate of taxation, a number of firms elected in the past to form themselves into unlimited companies (corporate members) or limited companies, where the directors assumed unlimited liability. One of the advantages of this move has been to obtain adequate pension provisions for directors and member shareholders. The other taxation advantages and disadvantages vary so radically with successive Finance Acts that further discussion can become out of date before the printing ink is dry.

SERVICE COMPANIES

A halfway house between a partnership and a corporate membership has been offered by the formation of a service company. This is also an unlimited private company owned, jointly or severally, by the partners. The physical operation of the business can be carried out by the service company on a fee basis, and the service company can justly be expected to make a reasonable profit, reducing the profits of the partnership accordingly. The amount of profit which can be put to reserve in the service company is naturally less than in the case of a corporate membership, since the service company's fee will be unlikely to absorb all the partnership profits. Some capital reserves can, however, be built up, while the taxation advantages of a partnership are retained.

PARTNERSHIP TAXATION

In the following context the term 'year' refers to the fiscal year ended 5 April.

Partnerships pay income tax on their business profits on a preceding-year basis. That is to say, the assessment for a given year is based on the profits of an accounting year ended in the preceding fiscal year. When a business is set up, or when it is permanently discontinued, special rules apply. Further, in the 'commencement' period an option is available to the taxpayer (but not to the Revenue) if it is to his advantage to elect for it and in the 'cessation' period the Revenue (but not the taxpayer) will, in relevant circumstances, increase the assessments for the penultimate and pre-penultimate years of assessment. A detailed exposé of the rules regulating the assessments of the 'commencement' and 'cessation' periods is quite outside the scope of this book, but their general effect is that in the 'commencement' period some profits will be assessed twice whilst in the 'cessation' period some profits will fall out of assessment altogether. *Any* change in the partners will be an event which will give rise to the application of these special rules. In fact, the rules will apply as though the business carried on by the old group of partners were a different business from that carried on by the new. The application of these special rules may substantially increase the taxation liability of the firm and, consequentially, of its partners (in relation to that which it would have been had the change not taken place) and, in mitigation, an election is available which has the effect of securing that the assessments are made as though no change had taken place. This election must be made, in writing, and within a specified period by *all* the partners engaged in the business both before and after the change. Whether or not to make this election is a matter of some complexity and it is essential, in all cases, that the firm's professional advisers be consulted. In addition, it should be borne in mind that the application of the special rules can have sufficiently material effects to be a determining factor when deciding on the date when a partner should retire or a new one be admitted.

The great advantage of the 'commencement and cessation' provisions is that it may be possible, if the figures fit, to cause a 'bad' year to be the basis of more than one assessment, to the exclusion, effectively, of a 'good' year.

GOODWILL

Stockbroking is such a personal profession and so much depends upon the confidence of the client in the reliability of the stockbroker's advice that, in general, most firms specially exclude any goodwill element from the cost of becoming a partner. It seems hard, however, that a stockbroker who has built up a successful business should be unable to capitalise on it at his retirement, unless a limited partner can be interested in acquiring a share. In the longer term it seems likely that more and more of the larger firms will adopt corporate status in order to introduce outside capital.

FINANCIAL CONTROL

COSTING

The unit of transaction in stockbroking is the 'bargain', irrespective of whether the amount of money passing is £10 or £10,000. In the various processes of production that have already been mentioned, the amount of work involved, ledger entries, paper circulated, etc., between bargains varies relatively little. The bargain therefore is the most convenient unit to cost, and it should be made clear here that each bargain refers to an individual transaction with a jobber. To buy 10,000 shares may require either one bargain with one jobber, or perhaps three bargains with three different jobbers. Here the purchase by three separate deals would be considered to be three separate bargains.

Occasionally the 'cost of a bargain' appears in the press and figures of between £10 and £15 have been quoted. It is not clear exactly how these costs have been calculated, but it is safe to assume that they refer to purchases and sales of ordinary shares (gilt-edged and fixed-interest securities represent a small proportion of the number of transactions of the majority of firms). It seems likely that the cost figure has been calculated simply by dividing the total number of bargains executed in a given period by the overall expenses of the firm, probably before allowing any remuneration to the profit-sharing partners. On this evidence the conclusion might easily be reached that, if the commission does not amount to something over about £25, a bargain is being executed at a loss.

The immediate counter to this argument which has often been put forward is that of marginal costing: i.e. if the economic business is sufficient to warrant a given size of Production Department, any additional business, however small, adds grist to the mill. The cost figures of a smaller firm in the provinces, however, bear little comparison to those of a large firm in London. London firms who discourage the small private investor are likely to drive more business towards their competitors in the country districts.

The fallacy in drawing any conclusion from such rudimentary costing lies in the fact that a high proportion of effort and expense is incurred outside the Production Department, and this is more closely related to the class of client than to the number of bargains. A private client with only £500 to invest may involve far greater expense in the sales-and-service department than simply executing a deal in ten times that amount. Various systems of costing have been applied in my own office and standards have now been evolved by examination and adjustment over a period of years.

Examples of per-bargain cost during the twelve months to April 1976 (compared with totals taken from a review for the six-months July–October 1964) are shown in Table 5 below.

TRADING PROJECTIONS

In every industrial concern the new financial year is heralded by a general review of trading and a budget of sales for the next twelve months. In stockbroking this exercise is still rarely attempted. The excuse is made that so many variables affect the mood of the

TABLE 5 Firm's costs

Department	*Category*	*Cost per equity bargain* £ p	*Total cost (1964 in brackets)* £ p
Pension and charitable funds	Direct costs[1]	28 86	
	Indirect costs[2]	9 78	
	Production[3]	12 48	
	Administration[4]	1 87	52 99 (6 43)
Institutional Equity	Direct costs	31 64	
	Indirect costs	26 30	
	Production	17 48	
	Administration	1 78	77 20 (9 46)
Private clients (Banks, etc.)	Direct costs	3 89	
	Indirect costs	2 40	
	Production	6 23	
	Administration	0 43	12 95 (4 18)

[1] *Direct Costs* include all those which can definitely be allocated to the relevant department, of which the principal are staff salaries and associated costs, rent and rates, Stock Exchange subscriptions and General Charge, and publications.
[2] *Indirect Costs* include allocations of central or other departmental expenses, of which the principal are research, secretarial, valuations, telephone, messenger and postal charges.
[3] *Production Costs* cover dealing, General Office and settlement.
[4] *Administration* covers financial controls and management expenses.
All costs are calculated after allowing for a basic salary for each profit-sharing partner, but without making allowance for any staff participation in profits. In the year in question the two items almost exactly balanced, leaving the costs per bargain after making these adjustments virtually unchanged.

investor—international affairs, Government decrees, even the weather plays its part—that no useful prediction can be made. Many of these factors, however, make the task of the industrialist equally arduous—particularly in those industries which are traditionally Aunt Sallies for Government tax adjustments or are very vulnerable to the English climate. The motor-car manufacturers and the soft-drink companies still produce their production and sales targets, however often they require to be adjusted. Theoretically the stockbroker is in a much stronger position to fulfil his trading targets, whatever the economic climate, since the majority of his private clients will act if he so advises them. It is this knowledge, that he is in a position of trust, coupled with the natural feeling that it is very often easier and safer to do nothing than to stick one's neck out, that keeps the stockbroker from trading just for the sake of trading, or turning his clients' holdings over just for the sake of the commission involved. This very conflict of interest between himself and his client tends to make him lean over backwards not to take any undue risk, with the result that he is often accused of being too conservative or too uninterested in the client he is endeavouring to protect.

In my own view some sort of trading forecast is essential in almost any business, even if it simply retraces the graph of last year's history, with suitable corrections for known variations and some factor applied for growth. A budget of trading, broken down between the different classifications of clients, gives a series of monthly target figures for the various departments. If these targets are not being achieved, then some remedial action may be taken with a flexible organisation. Without a series of trading targets it becomes too easy simply to complain that business is slack without taking any action to improve the position, with resultant deterioration in the morale of the staff.

BUDGETS OF CURRENT AND CAPITAL EXPENDITURE

The preparation of the trading forecast for the following year also gives rise to an examination of the salaries of personnel and of the staffing needs throughout each department. In examining the costing of bargains and the profitability of each class of client a decision must be made whether the firm intends to give an even more comprehensive coverage to institutions, both of sales-and-service and of research, in the hopes of increasing this very competitive but profitable business, or to streamline the private-client business on the chain-store principle of providing a very efficient service in a limited range of products to a large clientele. At the preparation of the annual budgets of current and capital expenditure, therefore, some indication can be given of the expected overall increase in expenses during the year ahead, and departments will be making out their cases for expenditure in the following year.

The prospective moves for more of the detailed production work to be undertaken centrally by The Stock Exchange, giving less discretion to individual firms, has made this type of annual budget of much greater importance. When the new TALISMAN system is complete, Stock Exchange firms will be able to expand their business to a considerable extent without marked increase in production costs, and the figures on which costing and trading forecasts are based will be much more easily and accurately obtainable.

6 Fixed-Interest

So far the only classification of investment which has been considered in any detail is the ordinary share, the risk-bearing capital of the company. The other broad class of securities is the fixed-interest group, covering gilt-edged securities, company loan capital and preference shares.

The volume of business transacted on The Stock Exchange in fixed-interest sections of the market is very large. For the calendar years 1961, 1971 and 1976, the comparative figures are given below in Table 6.

TABLE 6 Turnover on the Stock Exchange (calculated as an aggregate of all purchases and sales)

	1966		*1971*		*1976**	
	No. of Bargains	*Value (£m)*	*No. of Bargains*	*Value (£m)*	*No. of Bargains*	*Value (£m)*
British Government and British Government-guaranteed, short-dated (having five years or less to run)	117,656	10,581	143,981	22,062	299,874	46,624
Others	254,547	6,025	386,070	25,335	468,276	35,298
Irish government	–	–	–	–	37,981	4,460
U.K. local authority	97,887	694	93,046	1,521	82,403	4,264
Overseas government, provincial and municipal	50,574	138	37,606	218	18,051	198
Fixed-interest stock, preference and preferred ordinary shares	503,989	585	704,301	1,679	392,854	1,424
Ordinary shares	3,118,894	3,565	5,258,345	13,377	3,566,727	14,163

* 1976 figures include all provincial turnover.
Source: The Stock Exchange.

While every firm of stockbrokers carried out some business in fixed-interest securities, probably 80 per cent of the turnover in gilt-edged is handled by twenty firms with specialist departments in this field, and the greater part of the debenture and preference-share business (other than dealings immediately following a new issue) lies in even fewer hands.

It will be seen from the turnover figures just quoted that the business in fixed-interest securities, other than gilt-edged, is relatively small. Some firms divide the two into completely separate departments, but in the management tree I have illustrated they are considered as independent sections working under one control.

Before looking at the operation of the department in more detail, some explanation of the quotations and terminology of the market in fixed-interest securities should be made. The majority of gilt-edged stocks are redeemable, so that the borrower must repay them (or offer an alternative issue of equal value) at the end of the period. Most stocks give the borrower a choice of repayment date, so that Treasury 6¾ per cent 1995–98 must be repaid at £100 for each nominal £100 of stock at earliest on 1 May 1995 and at latest on 1 May 1998. These two dates are termed the 'earliest redemption date' and the 'final redemption date'. During the life of the stock, for every £100 nominal the investor will receive £6.75p per annum before tax. The rate of interest paid on the nominal value is termed the 'coupon', in this case a '6¾ per cent coupon'. On all gilt-edged securities, with the exception of Consolidated 2½ per cent, Annuities 2½ per cent and Annuities 2¾ per cent interest payments are made twice yearly on fixed dates.

The prices of both gilt-edged and company loan stocks are quoted per cent. On 22 April 1977, Treasury 6¾ per cent 1995–98 stood at 57. The value of £100 nominal of this stock, therefore, amounted to £57. The annual return on an investment of £100 in this security (income yield) can also be calculated by dividing the coupon by the price and multiplying by 100. In this case the income yield amounts to £11.84 per cent.

But if the stock is held to redemption the return is obviously greater, since over the period of 18 years to the earliest date or 21 years to the final date, a capital appreciation of £43 per cent must occur. In order to compare the merits of such fixed-interest stocks, a 'redemption yield' is calculated, apportioning the capital appreciation in annual instalments over the period. In the case of stocks standing *below* par it is normal to take the period to the *final* redemption date, and for those standing *above* par to the *earliest* date, thus giving the most conservative picture in either case. If held to maturity, the 'gross redemption yield' gives the effective annual return to an investor who is not subject to tax and, in the example quoted, amounts to £12.60 per cent. In cases where interest has accrued since the last payment or repayment is due at a premium over 100, the calculations must take these factors into account.

For the investor who is subject to tax, the capital appreciation may be more important than the income, and the 'net redemption yield' is calculated with both income tax and capital-gains tax at the appropriate rates.

The prices of gilt-edged and loan capital, with the exception of those British Government stocks with less than five years to final redemption, are quoted to include the accrued interest which has built up since the previous 'ex dividend' date. In order that the comparison shall be accurate, the 'clean' price of the security is taken for calculating these yields, the accrued interest having been deducted.

GILT-EDGED

The gilt-edged market covers securities issued by the British Government, the Dominions and colonies, the local authorities and most of the public boards. The section entitled 'British Funds' on the last page but two of the *Financial Times* divides the list of British Government securities into four sections—short-dated (due to be redeemed within five years), medium-dated (with redemption between five and fifteen years), long-dated (over fifteen years) and undated (where either there is no final date of redemption or the date is unspecified and at the option of the Government).

SHORT-DATED

Securities which have less than five years to redemption are termed 'money stocks', since they provide an alternative to money on deposit or other forms of short-term security. The rate of commission on purchase and sale is extremely low, the rate being left to the discretion of the broker and, in large amounts, being as low as $\frac{1}{64}$ per cent (1.56p per £100) on the nominal value of the stock or even half that figure in very large amounts.

The principal investors in the short-dated market are the banks and discount houses, who require investments which are easily liquidated and which can be bought or sold in large quantities. Stockbrokers who specialise in this field spend much of their time walking round the City between The Stock Exchange, the clearing banks, the merchant banks and the discount market. Their expertise lies in judging the future trend of short-term interest rates, selecting the stocks which appear to be the most attractive on the list and enjoying the confidence of the jobbers in the gilt-edged market, which enables them to deal in very large quantities of stock.

OTHER GILT-EDGED SECURITIES

The largest holders of medium-dated, long-dated and undated gilt-edged securities are institutional. The short end of the medium-dated market is within the reach of the banks, who generally dislike moving beyond a redemption date of about seven years for their funds, other than superannuation funds. Insurance companies with liabilities accruing at given dates may adopt a policy of matching some at least of their assets against these liabilities, obtaining a spread of dated securities in the medium range.

The long-dated stocks are particularly favoured by the life offices and the pension funds, whose liabilities are long-term and whose investment policy is designed to obtain the highest rate for the longest period.

Undated securities are generally regarded with disfavour by the majority of institutions, although they may be purchased in times of high long-term interest rates as a policy move in the management of a gilt-edged portfolio.

MANAGEMENT OF A PORTFOLIO

The service which a Gilt-Edged Department offers to its clients lies primarily in two directions:

(*a*) advice on future trends in interest rates, the money supply etc.;

(*b*) advice on the attractions of one stock as compared with another.

Judgement on both these matters is required, not only in selecting investments for new money, but also in switching an existing holding into a more attractive security.

SWITCHING

The basic principle of 'switching' is to take advantage of price movements to exchange from one gilt-edged stock to another and later switch back again to the original stock, taking a profit on the completed transaction. In effect, at the end of the operation, the fund has the same gilt-edged holdings as at the start, with a profit as well.

While at first sight this savours of speculation, switching is a normal part of the day-to-day investment of all well-known insurance companies and most of the larger pension funds.

(*a*) *Policy Switches*

A policy switch results from taking a view on the trend of interest rates and the resulting prices of gilt-edged stocks. If it is considered that long-term interest rates will rise, longer-dated stocks are sold and shorter-dated stocks purchased. In due course, when it is anticipated that the long-term trend in interest rates is downward, the exchange is reversed by selling the shorter-dated stocks and repurchasing the longer-dated ones. If the interpretation of the movement in interest rates is right, a substantial profit may result, although there is normally a fairly lengthy period before such switches are completed.

In many cases the reversal of the policy switch does not put back into the portfolio the original stock that was sold, since some other stock of approximately the same life may look more attractive at the time of the reversal.

Evidence for a policy switch is largely a matter for the economist. Part of his stock-in-trade is to look forward at the likely pressures on the economy, from which some assessment of trends in long- and short-term interest rates may be made.

Policy switches from medium-dated to long-dated gilt-edged securities may be carried out with no intention of a reversal, being based purely on the fact that longer-dated stocks tend to yield more than medium-dated under normal market conditions.

(*b*) *Jobbing or Anomaly Switches*

A jobbing switch consists of taking advantage of an anomaly in the relative prices of two gilt-edged stocks. For a number of reasons the supply and demand of different stocks varies, so that from time to time one stock will move abnormally compared with another. This can apply even to stocks of similar date. The stock which is relatively high is therefore sold and the other, which is relatively low, bought. If the switch can be reversed within twenty-eight days, commission is only payable on the initial transaction, with the result that most short-term switches are started in the hopes of reversal within a month.

Comparisons between different stocks are kept either in chart form, or, more recently, in terms of figures produced daily on a computer.

TAP STOCKS

When the Government makes a new issue of one of its loans, the full amount of the issue is not generally subscribed by the public, and a large proportion of the stock may be taken up by Government departments or departments under the control of the Government, notably the Department of Health and Social Security, and to a lesser degree the Foreign and Commonwealth Office and the Ministry of Agriculture, Fisheries and Food. The management of the Government debt is carried out through the Bank of England and the Government Broker, so that interest rates and liquidity can be influenced, or the market supported, in various sectors of the market by increasing or decreasing the departments' holdings of certain stocks. The stock that is currently being released by the departments is called a 'tap stock' and is generally offered at a slightly more advantageous price than others of a similar redemption date. From time to time the Government Broker may be instructed to raise or lower the selling price at which the stock is released to the market—the 'tap price'—until the Bank of England considers that sufficient stock has been released to achieve its object and 'the tap is off'.

The release of stock on tap usually presents opportunities to switch from other securities into the tap stock and may provide an attractive home for new money destined for the gilt-edged market.

GILT-EDGED LISTS

As an aid to selecting gilt-edged securities, most firms with specialist departments circularise their institutional clients with lists of securities, giving the relevant details of price, redemption dates, dates of interest payments, together with interest yield and redemption yields both gross and after tax. Computer data banks, such as DATAstream, also supply on-line services to subscribers.

For the firms who do not publish their own lists, the leading jobbers in the gilt-edged market provide a similar service, noting in addition offers of the somewhat rarer issues among the Dominion and colonial stocks, the public boards and the local authorities.

The only stocks which are subject to *ad valorem* stamp duty are those contained in the list of securities guaranteed by the Government and those of certain Public Boards.

NON-INSTITUTIONAL GILT-EDGED HOLDERS

While the majority of the really substantial gilt-edged *business* emanates from the banks and other institutions, the trusts and private individuals still hold by far the larger proportion of the stocks issued. Some indication of this is given in Table 7 below.

TABLE 7 Estimated institutional share of gilt-edged market holdings at 31 March 1976

	Under 5 years stocks (£million)		*Over 5 year stocks (£million)*	
	Nominal	%	*Nominal*	%
Insurance companies	808	6	6054	28
Building societies	1930	14	447	2
National Savings Bank investment account	62	–	325	1
Trustee Savings Banks special investment depts.	187	1	530	2
Pension funds:				
Local authoriy	79	1	653	3
Other public sector	56	–	695	3
Private sector	251	2	1289	6
Investment trusts	51	–	174	1
Unit trusts	6	–	21	–
Other	76	1	23	–
Total Institutions	3506	25	10211	47
Other non-official holdings	7383	54	8048	37
Official holdings	2864	21	3568	16
Total	13753	100	21827	100

Source: The Bank of England.

A number of the issues are exempt from all British taxation, past, present or future, to residents abroad.

Gilt-edged securities held by U.K. residents for more than one year are free of Capital Gains Tax on disposal. All firms of stockbrokers therefore have clients who are interested in the gilt-edged market to some extent, and must keep themselves informed of the trends in this market.

THE DEBENTURE MARKET

The debenture market is a loose term which covers the market in the principal issues of company loan capital:

(*a*) Mortgage debentures, which are loans secured upon a specific part of the assets of the company, normally its land and buildings, and sometimes in addition by a floating charge on other assets.

(*b*) Debenture stocks, which are loans normally secured by a floating charge on all the assets of the company remaining after meeting any prior claim.

(*c*) Unsecured loan stocks or notes, which are loans without any specific security, other than the recognised financial strength of the company concerned.

(*d*) Convertible stocks, which cover all the above types of loan, with the additional right conferred upon the holder that he may elect to exchange the stock for ordinary shares at certain specified dates and in certain conditions.

Issues of loan capital have the advantage over gilt-edged securities with similar redemption dates that they normally offer a somewhat higher yield to redemption. Following continual pressure from The Stock Exchange on the Chancellor of the Exchequer, corporate loan stocks became exempted from *ad valorem* stamp duty in the Finance Act 1976, but commission charges are higher than on gilt-edged and the marketability is much more restricted. The greatest volume of dealing in a debenture or other issue of loan capital is likely to occur in the days immediately after its issue, since in many cases it is partly paid (i.e. only a down-payment of say £25 per £100 stock requires to be paid, the balance of the issue price being payable at a later date or dates), with the result that commission charges are lower.

The section of the Fixed-Interest Department dealing with debentures will examine each offer of or bid for stock from the market, or each new issue, for a number of factors, in particular:

(i) *Size of the Issue* If the issue is very small the marketability becomes practically non-existent. Very small issues must thus be placed in the hands of institutions, who are likely to hold them until redemption, and who may require a higher return for the lack of ability to sell.

(ii) *Security*. The security of the loan is normally quoted as 'asset cover'. If the assets available, at balance-sheet valuation, including the proceeds of the loan issue, amount to three times the principal of the loan, the asset cover will be described as 'three times'. Members of the department will be concerned to investigate just what assets are available as security. An investment-trust debenture, secured upon the assets of the underlying portfolio, obviously has assets which may be readily disposable. A chain-store debenture may be secured by freehold shops in first-class areas, and thus have assets far more easily viable than those of a textile company, whose loan is secured by a mill and machinery which may be of little use to any other concern in the event of a textile slump. Ever since the famous St. Martin Preserving or Tickler case in 1958, where a sale of the undertaking was agreed by the board, without infringing the trust deed of the debenture, investors in debentures have been careful to check in detail the particulars of the issue.

(iii) *Security of Income*. The security of income is indicated by the amount of earnings available to cover the interest payment on the loan. This figure may refer either to the year immediately past, or, if this may have been exceptional, to the average of the past three or five years. Interest cover may be given either as a factor, i.e. 'five times', or as a priority percentage, i.e. '15–20 per cent'. The former method may be misleading, for it does not always indicate that there may be a prior charge, standing before the loan stock in question. The latter method clearly indicates that the prior charge takes the first 15 per cent of earnings, leaving the second stock to take the next 5 per cent.

(iv) *Terms*. In particular the department will examine the terms of the offer: the price; the rate of interest; the dates and terms of repayment of the principal; where the loan stock ranks in relation to other loans made to the company; the powers relating to future borrowings; the provisions in the event of a default; and the provisions for a sinking fund, if any.

From this information the essential yields can be calculated—interest yield, gross redemption yield and net redemption yield after applying taxes at the rates applicable to any particular class of client. These yields will probably be compared with those of the nearest British Government security to establish whether sufficient extra yield is obtainable to make the stock attractive.

The operation of a sinking fund is important, particularly to long-term funds. If the security offers a high return for a relatively long period, sinking-fund drawings may be unattractive, since part of the holding could be redeemed in the future when interest rates may be lower and it would be impossible to secure such a good return for the balance of the term.

On the other hand, for those funds which pursue a flexible policy regarding their debenture portfolios, the restricted market in some issues standing below par provides them with an opportunity of selling at an artificially high level to the sinking fund towards the date when otherwise drawings must be made.

Under British law companies are empowered to buy in their loan stock issues for cancellation and, where existing issues restrict future growth of a business, purchases may be made or schemes of arrangement proposed to circumvent the problem.

Interest paid on debentures and other loan stocks may be deducted from profits before the application of corporation tax. They thus provide a less expensive method of corporate financing than by the issue of fixed-interest share capital.

PREFERENCE SHARES

There are two basic forms of capital under British company law. Loan capital represents borrowings, repayable before any distribution of surplus assets to shareholders. Share capital represents the member's participation in the enterprise, whether or not on terms which afford a preference as to return of capital or to dividend.

Preference capital is classified in the share capital of a company, and thus bears more of the risks of the enterprise than the loan capital. It consists principally of two types:

(*a*) *Preference shares*, the holders of which have certain preferential rights, defined in the Articles of Association, as to the rate of and entitlement to dividend, the distribution of surplus assets, and to voting. The dividend is payable at a fixed rate and may be cumulative (i.e. a dividend unpaid one year will be payable out of the profits of the company in succeeding years), or non-cumulative; the shares may be redeemable, although issues of redeemable preference are now uncommon; and in some cases they may be convertible into shares of another class.

(*b*) *Participating preference shares*, which confer, in addition to the normal rights of preference shares, a further participation in profits, often related to the dividend payable on the ordinary capital.

For many years preference shares have been the unwanted child of the stock market. They have neither the security of gilt-edged or debentures nor the possibility of increased income in good times given by equities. Since the majority have no final date of redemption, their yields can be compared with those obtainable from undated debentures or undated gilt-edged issues, such as War Loan. Preference shares have always been looked on as the highest-yielding class of fixed-interest security.

'FRANKED' INCOME

Preference shares have one advantage over debentures for those funds (particularly investment-trust companies) paying corporation tax. Dividends from preference shares of U.K.-registered companies will have been paid after deduction of corporation tax on the profits of those companies. Provided that a sufficient proportion of these dividends are passed on to shareholders, they will not be brought into the computations for corporation tax on the investment company's profits. Income which has already borne corporation tax is known as 'franked' income.

PREFERENCE YIELDS AND ADVANCE CORPORATION TAX (ACT)

Prior to the introduction of ACT, gross yield calculations for preference shares were made by a similar method to those for loan capital (i.e. by dividing the coupon by the price). Net yields to tax-paying funds were calculated by applying a factor incorporating the rate of tax of the particular fund. Changes in the rate of income tax from year to year resulted in an increase or decrease of the effective yield to such funds, while tax-approved funds were unaffected.

Following the introduction of ACT, however, and a subsequent tax ruling, the situation was reversed. Preference shareholders paying tax at the standard rate will always receive a return based on the ratio of coupon to price; approved funds have lower levels of reclaim with reduced tax rates and suffer in comparison.

VOTING RIGHTS

Preference shares which enjoy a substantial proportion of the voting rights of a company have also commanded a higher price than the return on the investment warranted. In several cases a purchase of the voting preference shares has helped to secure control of a company with much less outlay of capital than would have been necessary to acquire the same number of votes through purchases of the ordinary. Companies faced with possible danger from this direction have reorganised their capital, offering the preference holders a stake in the ordinary or other inducement to agree to the change in exchange for their votes.

RIGHTS IN A LIQUIDATION

Many preference shares are entitled only to repayment at par in a liquidation, although they may have been standing at much higher prices immediately prior to the liquidation date. Following the famous Union Cold Storage case in 1933, where the company sought to repay the three preference issues with only a modest premium over par value by way of compensation, and the decisions in the Wilsons and Clyde Coal Company and Chatterley-Whitfield cases in 1949, where the courts upheld the companies in their decision to extinguish the preference shares at par, many investors have fought shy of high-coupon preference issues. Issues of preference capital now would include the provision that repayment will be at par or the average price over a period before the liquidation takes place, whichever is the higher. There might also be the provision that the consent of preference shareholders must be obtained, at a separate meeting, to any liquidation. Some preference issues also give holders the right to veto further issues of shares ranking above or equal to the issue, and to restrict the company's borrowing above certain limits.

SERVICE BY THE DEPARTMENT

Apart from providing internal advice on economic matters, such as movements of interest rates, the fixed interest department is likely to act directly with institutional clients in respect of corporate securities in two ways:

(i) OFFERS AND BIDS FOR QUOTED SECURITIES

The department will examine the 'marks' each day to ascertain if dealing in any issues has taken place at prices which made them obviously attractive either to buy or sell. It will then keep informed those institutions who normally operate in this field. In particular it will operate for the sinking funds of those debentures issued by companies for whom the firm acts, or bid holders for stock where a sinking fund is operating in the market.

(ii) NEW ISSUES

As mentioned earlier, the greatest activity in debenture and preference issues takes place during the early days after listing has been granted. When a placing of new fixed-interest capital is made in the market, certain amounts must be offered to the jobbers for passing on to brokers other than the firm involved in the issue. The department's role therefore is to examine the details of new issues as they occur, to obtain as much stock as they can in attractive placings and to ration participations equitably between clients. Where their own firm is acting as sponsor to an issue of fixed-interest capital, the department will be required to advise on the terms of the issue and the institutions who are likely to take a participation either of underwriting or a placing of stock. The mechanics of such an issue are described in the next chapter.

7 Corporate Finance

One of the most fascinating sides of a stockbroking business is the Corporate Finance Department, since its duties cover not only the midwifery of bringing new companies to the market, but the cut and thrust of the battle to take over other companies or to defend them against takeover bids. The partners in charge must spend much of their time visiting companies up and down the country—and often overseas—assessing the management, estimating the price which shares in a relatively unknown concern can command at some date in the future, and advising the management on how best they can solve the particular financial problem that faces them. In some cases it may require several years of careful nurturing before a company is ready to obtain a quotation on the London market, and in almost every case it requires an after-sales service to keep clients who have invested in the company abreast of the latest developments.

The new money raised on The Stock Exchange during the year to 31 December 1976 is shown in Appendix 3.

All issues by the British Government are handled by the Government Broker. Other gilt-edged issues, whether for Commonwealth Governments or for the local authorities, are spread among a wider range of firms who specialise in acting for these particular clients. One firm also has a reputation as an issuing broker to water undertakings, most of which are offered by tender.

Issues of capital by companies are more widely spread throughout stockbroking firms. They can be divided into two classes—companies seeking a quotation for the first time and companies whose capital is already quoted. When this book was first written the advantages of a public listing easily outweighed the disadvantages. In recent years, however, Government taxation policy (Capital Gains Tax, Capital Transfer Tax, Investment Income Surcharge and the threat of a Wealth Tax) has both tipped the balance against listing and also sapped investor confidence to the detriment of market levels. In 1976, for example, only 24 new companies were listed, compared with 85 in 1971. This situation is likely to be only a transitory phase, however, and, as confidence is reborn, boards will once again face the decision of 'going public'.

COMPANIES SEEKING A QUOTATION FOR THE FIRST TIME

There are a number of reasons why companies seek listing for their shares, but in the majority of cases they fall into three categories:

(i) To obtain additional capital, whether by the issue of shares or the borrowing of money, as part of the financial development of the enterprise.

(ii) To enable members of the family, for fiscal, financial or other reasons, to make part of their holdings available to the public.

(iii) To improve the marketability of the company's capital and hence the standing of the concern and its products.

(i) PRESENT OR FUTURE FINANCIAL REQUIREMENTS

When a company is unable to generate sufficient capital for its future expansion, either internally from retained profits or by subscription from its present members, or externally from its banking facilities, a number of courses are open to it. A mortgage may be raised privately on the fixed assets with one of the insurance companies or other funds; a link may be established with one of the City 'nurseries' which are prepared to take minority interests in private companies; or the decision may be taken to create additional capital which may be offered to the public by obtaining a quotation on The Stock Exchange. In any event it is likely that the company's bankers or auditors will be consulted, and it is possible that they may pass on the enquiry to a firm of stockbrokers who are known to specialise in this field. The Corporate Finance Department of the firm will then be consulted as to which of the alternatives appears to be the most attractive and, with their connections among the City institutions, will be able to give the necessary introductions if one of the first two alternatives is adopted. In many cases, however, the recommendations may include the issue of share or loan capital, by combining a listing on The Stock Exchange with the raising of new permanent finance from the public.

Once a listing has been obtained, the company will find that it can raise new capital more easily and cheaply. Institutional investors are unwilling to invest a large proportion of their funds in unquoted securities, in particular the insurance funds, following the Insurance Companies (Valuation of Assets) Regulations 1976, which laid down a statutory basis for assets valuation. The investigation which they must carry out before deciding whether shares or debentures of a private company should be included in their portfolios and the difficulty of keeping an eye on the investment over the years, together with the inability to sell easily should they decide to dispose of their holding, does not encourage investment in private companies. As a result, institutions expect a considerably higher return on their money from unlisted securities, and this can be expensive to the borrower or the seller of shares.

(ii) FAMILY INVESTMENT AND FISCAL CONSIDERATIONS

Where a business has been carried on by one family for a number of years, almost all the assets of members of the family may be tied up in the one company. They have, therefore, no spread of interest in their investments. Their advisers may suggest that, however good the prospects for the family concern, they should endeavour to obtain a wider spread among their assets.

As well as the broader aspect of investment, the family may be faced with fiscal problems. Where one member is elderly and his heirs may be faced in due course with a substantial payment of Capital Transfer Tax, the need for a listing becomes doubly important. Money may be raised at a time when public interest in this type of share is active, thus providing a cash reserve from which part at least of the tax can be paid. At the same time a listing on The Stock Exchange (with the condition that dealings take place at least once a year) provides a price which the Capital Taxes Office will accept in the probate valuation without undue delay.

Where an estate contains shares in a private or unlisted public company of which the control is in a limited number of hands, the value for tax purposes may be based on asset valuation. Broadly speaking this arises under the Finance Act, 1940, as amended, where the deceased, within five years of death, had control of the company or received more than 50 per cent of dividends paid by the company or owned more than half the share and debenture capital. A listing may not be of benefit to an estate in reducing the probate value (except in times of pronounced market weakness), but it does furnish an upper limit which is acceptable to the Capital Taxes

Office, and, perhaps more important, it provides a means by which the actual tax may be realised in due course.

Prior to the Finance Act, 1965, a number of applications were made for listing in order to establish a price for long-term capital-gains tax. Since that date one or two companies have come to the market because of the penalties attached to being a 'close' company.

Occasionally listings are obtained for the shares of companies which have previously been under the control of not more than five persons, in order to avoid the risk of higher income tax rate direction if, in the opinion of the Special Commissioners, a reasonable part of the company's profit has not been distributed. When the public holds shares carrying not less than 35 per cent of the voting power of the company, which have been the subject of dealings on The Stock Exchange in the United Kingdom, the company is outside the scope of such directions.

On average, listed companies tended in the past to distribute approximately half their available earnings as dividend on ordinary share capital. With the introduction of dividend controls on public companies in 1972, as a counter-inflation measure, the proportion of profit distributed as dividend has decreased. Nevertheless a dividend policy which will attract public subscription might result in the controlling shareholders paying unnecessarily large sums in taxation instead of ploughing back more into the company. There are, however, technical methods of avoiding this difficulty, which are considered later.

It should be emphasised that there is a fundamental difference between the issue of shares discussed here and that in section (i) above. In the earlier section the company received additional capital, subscribed either directly or indirectly by the public. In the latter case the vendors of the shares are the existing owners, so that the company does not benefit financially. In a large number of cases, however, issues are arranged to give advantage to both parties.

(iii) MARKETABILITY AND PUBLICITY

Marketability has obvious advantages for family concerns, since it provides the owners with the opportunity of liquidating part of their holdings whenever they require to raise money. It also assists growing companies in the acquisition of other businesses by putting a price tag on their shares, which can then be offered in exchange for those of the company they intend to acquire.

In addition to the advantage of easier marketability, the publicity value of a listing is not so immediately obvious. This is probably appreciated more in America than in Britain, owing to the wider spread of share ownership in the United States. A principal reason for the listing in London of shares of overseas companies is to keep the name of the concern before a growing investing public, as well as to attract funds from new sources. For British companies also, regular mention in the financial press, noticed by the majority of executives in the U.K., can provide an efficient and inexpensive form of advertising. Where a public company or its products enjoy a well-known name, its shareholders may become loyal and active customers.

In some industries where the business is very largely carried out by small local concerns, the fact that a company is large enough and respectable enough to be listed can have a marked effect on the relations with its customers and on the engagement of executive staff. The dissemination of information in accordance with Stock Exchange requirements gives confidence both to customers and to employees.

The coin of publicity has a reverse side to it, and this is the principal disadvantage. From being a private company with a small family of shareholders, most of whom are probably known personally to the board, a listed company emerges into the public eye. Its accounts, which may only have been available to investigators at Companies House, are now publicised through statistical services and the press. If the company is progressive and business expands, the directors will have to remember that they must be more reticent about facts and figures to their friends and acquaintances in order to ensure that all members are treated equally. They will almost certainly receive requests from financial journalists and stockbrokers to visit their factories and meet their top-level management. And they will be spurred on by the fact that the public will come to expect a steady trend of rising profits from a well-managed concern. So long as the public has the image of a progressive company, press and investment publicity can only be of value. When things go badly, this additional publicity may become a nuisance, but both investment analysts and financial journalists are sufficiently realistic to appreciate that few companies can maintain an unblemished record without the occasional lapse in the rate of growth.

SIZE OF THE COMPANY

The boards of many companies turn down the suggestion of a quotation out of hand because they consider that the size of their company is small compared with other quoted companies with which they are familiar. The limit laid down by The Stock Exchanges is that the aggregate market value of the company's capital shall not be less than £500,000, with any one class security having a minimum market value of £200,000.

One consideration which must be borne in mind is the cost of obtaining a listing. There are a number of fixed charges which cannot be reduced, so that, for a small company, these can become very costly in proportion to the cash proceeds of an issue.

As a rule of thumb it might be unduly expensive to arrange for the quotation on The Stock Exchange of a debenture for a company with net assets of less than about £1½ million, and for the shares of a company having net profits before taxation of less than around £250,000.

Size alone does not rule out the possibility of eventual listing, since the City 'nurseries' mentioned earlier often arrange for the merger of smaller concerns working in the same field with a view to listing in due course.

INITIATING THE ISSUE

The directors of most private companies of standing have at one time or another thought about obtaining a listing. Often this has been shelved until the pressure of day-to-day work is less severe, or until the expansion of profits has brought the concern into line with others of the smaller quoted companies with which the board is familiar. Very often the matter is raised later as a matter of some urgency.

If management had authorised an investigation into the possibilities of obtaining a listing at an earlier date, there is little doubt that in most cases a more satisfactory result could have been obtained, since the timing of the issue could have been chosen to coincide with a rising trend in the company's profits and with market conditions which were favourable to share issues. Too often the timing of an issue is left to the last moment and becomes a matter of urgency.

New issues are introduced to stockbrokers usually from one of the company's various professional advisers—accountants, solicitors or bank managers—by some personal connection in the company or close to it, or by one of the issuing houses who have been approached to sponsor the issue.

The operation may be sponsored by the stockbrokers acting either on their own (assisted by the New Issues Department of one of the clearing banks) or in conjunction with an issuing house. From the stockbroker's point of view it is both more remunerative and more satisfying to act as sponsor, but for a number of reasons the company in question may prefer to be associated with an issuing house. Where a company is not yet ready for listing, the issuing house may be able to provide temporary finance within its own organisation, either through its private company nursery, or through the medium of funds managed by it. Where a considerable capital reconstruction is required or the issue is very complicated, a leading issuing house probably has more experience than any single firm of stockbrokers, and stockbroking firms who do not have specialist Corporate Finance Departments may not be equipped with the staff who are qualified to carry out the detailed investigation that is necessary before an issue is accepted. The name of a well-known issuing house on the prospectus of a new issue also automatically indicates to the investor (particularly the institutional investor) that a further team of experts have investigated the company.

The disadvantage lies almost entirely in the increased costs which are charged by issuing houses, against those charged by stockbrokers, as sponsors.

NEW ISSUE PROCEDURES

In order to examine the work of the department, the following procedures will probably be adopted during an issue sponsored by the stockbrokers alone.

PRELIMINARY INVESTIGATION

After the initial approach has been made, representatives of the company will probably want to attend an introductory meeting with the partner in charge of the Corporate Finance Department, so that each can assess the quality of the people with whom they are likely to be dealing. The company's problem can then be discussed informally. Either at this meeting or subsequently in a memorandum prepared by the company, the partner in charge of the Corporate Finance Department will want to know certain salient facts about the business—a general outline of the company's products and services, the management structure, premises, labour force and competitors, copies of the accounts for the last five years, together with an estimate of prospects for the current year, which will also require verification by the auditors and sponsors for inclusion in the prospectus. He will also want to know the company's exact requirements and, if a public issue is likely to be the most satisfactory solution, the distribution of major shareholdings.

From the accounts and the memorandum the stockbrokers can tell immediately if a listing is quite out of the question. If, on the other hand, this seems feasible, the next step is probably a visit to the company itself to study it at closer quarters and to meet members of the management at the lower levels. At the same time a thorough investigation is undertaken by an independent firm of accountants, nominated by the stockbrokers.

Following a satisfactory report, the Corporate Finance Department then has to prepare a proposal for the company, which is usually divided into four parts:

(*a*) The capital reorganisation required to fit the company for quotation.
(*b*) The form of capital to be issued.
(*c*) The method of quotation.
(*d*) The terms of the issue.

(*a*) *Capital Reorganisation*

Most companies seeking listing are private companies, so that the transition to a public company and the quotation of its shares are achieved at the same time. Some form of capital reorganisation is almost always required, but each case necessitates individual treatment. It may be necessary to form a holding company or to acquire subsidiaries by the parent company to build up a sufficiently substantial concern for listing. Outstanding loans may have to be repaid. The properties and other assets may need to be revalued. This action in turn may increase the reserves of the parent company from which a capitalisation issue may be made.

A public issue gives an opportunity of simplifying the capital structure and tidying up the classes of capital which are no longer appropriate, e.g. founders' shares, deferred shares and shares with restricted or multiple voting rights.

The essence of any capital reorganisation is to produce the simplest and most straightforward structure which will achieve the required object. All these points will be considered by the Corporate Finance Department and put forward in a written proposal to the company.

(*b*) *The Form of Capital to be Issued*

As explained earlier, the two basic forms of capital under British law are *share capital*, representing the member's participation in the enterprise, and *loan capital*, representing borrowings, repayable before any distribution of surplus assets to the shareholders. In the great majority of companies whose share or loan capital has not yet achieved listing, the issue will take the form of ordinary share capital, since only this form of issue satisfies the various conditions of improved marketability, Capital Transfer Tax requirements and the spread of family portfolios, mentioned at the beginning of this chapter. Issues of loan capital are normally only undertaken by companies with existing listings for their ordinary capital, and as such are discussed later in this chapter.

Application for listing will thus be most likely in the ordinary shares of the company.

(*c*) *Method of Issue*

The department must next decide upon the best method of making the company's capital available to the public. Listing on The Stock Exchange is obtainable by any one of three methods, depending largely upon the size of the issue involved, the public interest in it and the spread of existing shareholdings.

(i) *Issue by Public Subscription/Offer for Sale*. The Companies Act, 1948, stipulates in considerable detail the main headings of information which must be given to potential investors on the issue of share or loan capital, and the requirements of The Stock Exchange are even more stringent. Even when the Companies Act does not require a full prospectus, a Stock Exchange advertisement may have to be published, containing virtually the same information, so that the document setting out the particulars of the issue and fulfilling either the requirements of the Act or The Stock Exchange is commonly called a 'prospectus'. For the technical-minded a summary of the information to be published, in the order in which it is likely to appear, is given in Appendix 5.

All offers to the general public (which includes both institutions and private investors), as opposed to existing shareholders, must comply with these requirements unless specific exemption is granted by the Council of The Stock Exchange, to whom application for listing is made. In the case of substantial issues by well-known concerns, new shares are occasionally offered direct to the public by means of a full prospectus. This is normally called an issue by *public subscription*. In the case of smaller or less well-known companies, or where existing shares are being sold, the firm of stockbrokers sponsoring the issue may offer to purchase the entire issue on a given date, subject to the listing being granted, and that capital is subsequently resold to the public by the stockbrokers. This is called an *offer for sale*. The detailed procedure by which these two methods are carried out is almost identical, the only difference being that in the case of a public subscription the sponsoring broker is probably paid a fee for his services, while in the case of an offer for sale his remuneration may be taken either partly or wholly out of a differential between the price which the company and/or vendors receive and the price at which the capital is offered to the public.

From the company's viewpoint the advantage of an issue by full prospectus or offer for sale lies in the wide publicity which it will attract, since every member of the public has an equal chance of obtaining an allotment of stock or shares. The disadvantage lies in the fact that, where the amount subscribed by the public is small, the cost is high in relation to the money involved. A variation on this method of issue, which safeguards the vendors against a very large premium on the price developing immediately after the issue, is the *offer for sale by tender*. This method has been employed for many years in issues by water companies and has been adapted for issues by industrial companies.

In the case of water companies, shares are offered for sale at a minimum issue price, but in the form of application the subscriber states not only the number of shares required but also the price, above the minimum, which he is prepared to pay. Allotments are then made from the highest price downwards until the issue is fully subscribed. As the ordinary shares of water companies are normally entitled to a maximum dividend, and since one water company does not differ vastly from another, there is ample evidence on which to tender. The price difference between highest and lowest tenders should not therefore be of great significance.

In the case of ordinary shares of companies in other fields where comparison with existing quoted shares is difficult, the tender method may be worth consideration. Allotment is made on a somewhat different basis from that in water company issues. Applications are listed at each price-level, from the highest to the lowest. Working from the highest price downwards, at some price-level the total number of shares for which tenders have been made will fully subscribe the issue.

Theoretically all tenders are accepted at this price. In practice one of the objects of the issue is to obtain a reasonable spread of shareholdings among the public and, if the method were taken to its ultimate conclusion, one application might subscribe for the whole issue at the highest price. It is also unlikely that the total number of shares tendered down to the allotment price would exactly match the number of shares to be issued. The sponsoring stockbroker must be given discretion in determining the basis for acceptance, reducing large or multiple tenders, and, if necessary, accepting a slightly lower level to increase the spread of holders, scaling down all applications accordingly.

The advantage of the tender method is that, if a very high level of public demand is expected in a share which is difficult to evaluate, the vendor receives the benefit of the popularity of the issue, and not the successful speculator who 'stags' it. The disadvantage is that the discretion which must be given in fixing the price and scaling down allotments lays the sponsor open to possible criticism from dissatisfied applicants. In addition few offers for sale by tender have proved to be very successful from the point of view of the investor, many of the issues failing to recover their opening price for some considerable time.

(ii) *Placing*. In the case of small issues or issues of shares in which there is unlikely to be much public interest, the Council of The Stock Exchange will permit a *placing*.

In a public placing it is normal for the stockbrokers sponsoring the issue to subscribe or purchase the capital to be issued and to sell it direct to their own clients. Under Stock Exchange regulations a minimum of 35 per cent of the issued ordinary shares must be the subject of the placing (which also 'uncloses' the company for tax purposes) and of that amount at least 25 per cent must be offered to the public through the medium of the jobbers in the market and their connections with other firms of brokers. This increased distribution of shares also assists in providing an orderly market when dealings commence. When there is likely to be public interest in a small issue, the Council may require that a higher proportion shall be placed through the market.

A placing has the advantage of lower cost since there is no need to underwrite the issue, and advertising, printing and bank charges will be lower, although the prospectus must still be published in at least one national newspaper. It has the disadvantage that the general public are not given the same opportunity to subscribe for shares as the clients of the sponsoring brokers, and the Council therefore does not normally permit placings of ordinary shares (or fixed-interest stocks convertible into ordinary shares) except in very small issues.

(iii) *Introduction.* Although it has been assumed that the application for a listing is linked with an issue or sale of capital to the public, there are cases where a reasonable distribution of shares already exists. The listing is required simply to establish a market or to bring the company's name before the public for other reasons. Under these conditions the Council of The Stock Exchange may permit an *introduction*. Since no capital is being offered, no prospectus is required under the Companies Act, but the requirements of The Stock Exchange provide for a similar advertisement to be prepared for circulation by the Exchange Telegraph statistical service.

No rule of thumb as to the number of shareholders or the spread of holdings which will provide eligibility for an introduction can be applied, since each case must be judged on its merits. The majority of London quotations for overseas companies, whose shares are normally widely spread in the country of origin, are by means of introductions. Since there will be a market in an overseas centre, no problem arises in the establishment of a fair price for the shares. In the case of a U.K. company, an introduction will only be allowed if it is considered that the normal supply and demand among new and existing holders will provide a satisfactory market in the shares.

(*d*) *The Terms of the Issue*

Part of the expertise of the Corporate Finance Department lies in its judgement of the price at which a placing or an offer for sale may be made. In the early stages only an indication of the terms will be given, and the meeting to finalise the prospectus is left as close as possible to the date when listing is granted, so that there is the least risk that a general movement of the stock market will upset the success of the issue. Some indication of the terms will, however, be given in the initial proposal, subject to the approval of the Council of The Stock Exchange to the basis of the issue and subject to market conditions being satisfactory at the time when the issue is planned to take place.

The value which can be placed upon a company's share capital depends upon a number of interrelated factors, including the capital structure, the denomination of the shares, the present and prospective dividends, the present and prospective earnings, etc. Reference to the *terms of issue* covers all these factors.

Gauging the terms of issue is largely a combination of experience and a statistical comparison with other quoted securities in the same field. The latter exercise can only give an approximate indication, since no two companies are ever identical, but a yardstick can usually be obtained as to terms which will attract a response from the public. Prospective investors will examine a new issue in just the same way that they will investigate shares in an existing company, so that most of the investment criteria discussed in earlier chapters will be applied in establishing a value for new shares. In addition the public must be given some temptation to attract them towards a new investment, so that the price must be slightly below that of an equivalent quoted stock. Otherwise there is no reason for the investor to take the risk on the new share rather than invest in the established concern with the long public record.

The old adage of success breeding success applies to some extent in new issues. Where investors have seen a successful original issue, they tend to support succeeding issues by the same company, provided that the terms are satisfactory. While the stockbroker sponsoring the issue will endeavour to obtain the best possible price for the shares being issued, he will probably advise the company that it usually pays, when first marketing shares, to err slightly on the side of generosity.

While The Stock Exchange requires that at least 35 per cent of ordinary capital shall end up in the hands of the public, quotation will be obtained for the whole of the ordinary share capital, even if only a part is to be marketed.

COST OF THE ISSUE

The proposal will also give some estimate of the cost of the issue. Individual expenses vary with the complexity and the amount of work carried out by the professional firms involved, so that it is not possible to give more than a general indication here. Issues of up to £1 million would attract expenses of between 7 and 9 per cent, while a study of the few flotations that took place in the summer of 1976 showed expenses of 3.8–4.5 per cent on issues in excess of £3 million. The disparity between the two percentage costs is due to the fact that certain basic expenses must be incurred, irrespective of the amount of money which the public is asked to subscribe, while others are directly, or almost directly, proportional to this figure.

THE TIMETABLE

Although much of the basic work will have been completed by the Corporate Finance Department in setting out its detailed proposal in writing, it is after the proposal has been accepted that the work begins to intensify and the snowball of paper mounts towards its peak. The main role of the department is now as the co-ordinator of a team of solicitors, accountants, printers and press agents. Every separate stage must be completed to a timetable, so that nothing is left undone for the final grant of listing and the commencement of dealing. The simplified timetable shown below (Table 8) has been constructed to apply either to a placing or an offer for sale, although the completion date may be postponed to the Friday in the latter case. It is also assumed that meetings of shareholders can be held at short notice.

Listing is normally granted by the Quotations Committee of The Stock Exchange either on a Wednesday or a Friday (D-Day in the timetable), and the days of the week have been shown in brackets in the example. In this case a Wednesday has been selected.

TABLE 8 Simplified timetable

Date	*Event*	*Action by*
About D−40	Meeting to draw up timetable and finalise procedures.	Stockbrokers, company and solicitors.
About D−40	Drafting of proofs of: (*a*) prospectus; (*b*) allotment letter or letter of acceptance; (*c*) form of acceptance; (*d*) underwriting agreement.	Stockbrokers, solicitors, accountants and company

Date	*Event*	*Action by*
About D−30	Proof prospectus and attached documents to Stock Exchange for comment.	Stockbrokers.
D−12 (Friday)	Meeting to finalise prospectus.	Stockbrokers, solicitors, accountants and company.
D−7 (Wednesday)	Extraordinary General Meeting and separate class meetings to approve capital reorganisation, adoption of new Memorandum and Articles, etc.	Company and solicitors.
	Agree terms. Board meeting to allot new shares, approve prospectus, exchange share purchase and sale agreement, etc.	Company, stockbrokers, solicitors and accountants.
	Documents filed with Registrar of Companies.	Solicitors.
	Bulk printing order given.	Stockbrokers and printers.
	Start underwriting.	Stockbrokers.
D−6 (Thursday)	Press conference	Stockbrokers
D−5 (Friday)	Underwriting completed	Stockbrokers
D−2 (Monday)	Prospectus advertised in London morning papers.	Stockbrokers through advertising agents.
	Final documents supporting application for listing lodged with Stock Exchange.	Stockbrokers.
D-Day (Wednesday)	Permission to deal and listing granted, subject to the posting of allotment letters, or letters of acceptance.	Stockbrokers.
D+1 (Thursday)	Application lists open and close.	Bankers.
D+2 (Friday)	Allotment meeting.	Stockbrokers, company and bankers to the issue.
	Press announcement on basis of allotment.	Stockbrokers.

Date	*Event*	*Action by*
D+3 (Saturday)	Allotment letters or letters of acceptance posted.	Bankers to the issue.
D+5 (Monday)	Dealings begin.	Stockbrokers.
D+42 (Wednesday)	Last day for split allotment letters.	Bankers to the issue.
D+44 (Friday)	Last day for renunciation.	Bankers to the issue.
D+72 (Friday)	Share certificates ready.	Company.
	File return of allotments.	Company through solicitors.
	Statutory declaration filed with Stock Exchange.	Company and solicitors.

UNDERWRITING

An offer for sale, whether the price is fixed before the prospectus is issued or is fixed by tender, requires to be underwritten. In other words a premium is paid to assure that the shares issued are subscribed in full. If the public fail to apply for sufficient shares, the balance is allotted to the underwriters in proportion to their underwriting commitment.

Every firm of stockbrokers specialising in new issues has its own list of underwriters, mostly the institutions and tied trusts, but possibly some private clients also. Traditionally inclusion in a list of underwriters of a firm with a reputable issue business was considered by institutions to be very profitable, since underwriters were only called upon to take up stock or shares on relatively few occasions. Experience in the early 1970s, however, has shown underwriting to be a somewhat more hazardous occupation.

The task of the Corporate Finance Department on about D–7 is to allot underwriting among the firm's clients, so that a balance is kept between the large institutions who must be offered a reasonable slice of underwriting commitment and all the other clients who must be sandwiched into an allocation, however small.

PLACING

Similarly, in a placing, the department will collaborate with the partners engaged in servicing the institutions, tied trusts and private clients in selecting firm hands to whom the shares can be offered. No brokers will accept the sponsorship of an issue unless they believe that it is a sound investment, so that they should have no difficulty in recommending the acceptance of a placing to any client for whom the investment might be suitable.

SUBMISSION OF DOCUMENTS TO THE STOCK EXCHANGE

One of the requirements of The Stock Exchange is that draft copies of almost all documents prepared in connection with the issue, particularly the prospectus itself, must be submitted to the Quotations Department for approval in compliance with The Stock Exchange's publication 'Admission of Securities to Listing'. Where the stockbrokers are acting in conjunction with an issuing house, their principal role in the initial stages is to act as a channel between the issuing house and this department.

The Quotations Department is concerned that any prospectus shall put before the public as full and fair a picture of the company and its prospects as possible. In almost every issue the department will have some comment to make or some suggested amendment to the prospectus that will be of advantage to the public.

THE GRANT OF LISTING

The finalised documents must be submitted to The Stock Exchange two clear days before the date when permission is given to deal in the new shares and when listing is officially granted. By this time all the problems regarding the issue will have been resolved, and it is only rarely that the Quotations Committee will want to make a last-minute enquiry. Nevertheless, a partner of the firm must attend to answer any questions that may arise.

COMMENCEMENT OF DEALINGS

It will be seen from the timetable that between the grant of quotation and the commencement of dealings about five days have elapsed, including a weekend. In the case of an introduction where there is no listing elsewhere, two clear days must be allowed to elapse, so that some estimate of the demand for shares may be obtained through the jobbers, in order to establish a fair price at the commencement of dealings. In a placing, dealings may begin the day after the grant of listing.

One of the duties of the stockbrokers to an issue is to obtain the confidence of the market in the issue. They will hold meetings with the relevant firms of jobbers prior to the first day of dealing, to fill in any additional information which may be required. Sometimes the

Corporate Finance Department will prepare a précis of the information published, together if necessary with some comparative statistics drawn from companies in the same field.

Every new issue requires a certain amount of nursing in its early stages, until the market in the shares settles down.

COMPANIES ALREADY LISTED

Companies which already enjoy a listing may make two different types of issue to their ordinary shareholders:

(*a*) Capitalisation issue.
(*b*) Rights issue.

(*a*) *Capitalisation Issues*

Where a company has built up substantial reserves and where the capital employed by the company is large compared with the issued ordinary capital, a strong case exists for bringing the two more closely into line. For example, a company with an issued ordinary capital of £500,000 may have reserves of perhaps £1,500,000. The dividend on the ordinary shares may be 40 per cent and the £1 ordinary shares may stand at 800p to give a dividend yield of 5 per cent. The company has fully adequate reserves to capitalise £500,000 by giving a capitalisation issue of one new £1 share for every old £1 share. This is, in fact, nothing more than a book entry. The issued share capital will rise from £500,000 to £1 million, and the reserves will fall equivalently from £1,500,000 to £1 million. Unless otherwise stated the dividend would be likely to drop from 40 per cent to 20 per cent and the share price would halve from 800p to 400p.

What then are the advantages of the issue? There are several:

Marketability. By doubling the number of shares in issue, the marketability improves. Similarly, by reducing the share price from the very 'heavy' 800p to a more reasonable 400p, a new class of investor is interested in them. At the same time (in this particular example) the £1 shares might be reduced to a nominal value of 25p., increasing the number of shares by a further three times, reducing the price to 100p, and increasing both the marketability and the number of prospective investors accordingly.

Rate of Dividend. The rate of dividend is reduced from 40 per cent to 20 per cent. Politically this is a sound move, for there are still unsophisticated members of the public who believe that, by buying a share which pays a dividend of 40 per cent of nominal value, the capitalist will recoup his investment by way of income in only two-

and-a-half years. A lower rate of dividend defeats this objection.

Eligibility under the Trustee Investments Act, 1961. The provisions of this Act limit investment in ordinary shares to those companies whose issued share capital is £1 million or more. The increase of the issued capital to this figure, therefore, makes the shares eligible to another class of investor.

For many years press reference to capitalisation issues was made under the misleading title of 'bonus' shares, as though the shareholder were receiving something for nothing. It should be stressed that such shares can only be issued by the capitalisation of reserves which have been built up over the years, either as earnings which have suffered tax and been ploughed back into the company, or from the improved value of the assets. The term 'plough-share' which has been adopted by certain popular newspapers is much more descriptive of the true nature of the issue.

The paperwork of a capitalisation issue is carried out between the company, their solicitors, the stockbrokers and The Stock Exchange. Draft documents must again be sent to the Quotations Department for approval and the necessary resolutions passed by shareholders in general meeting. The work involved, however, is largely formal.

(*b*) *Rights Issues*

Where a company requires additional funds, it may obtain these either from the public at large or from its own shareholders. In the case of loan capital or preference share capital, where the rights of existing ordinary shareholders are not affected, shares may be offered to the public at large. In the case of ordinary shares or loan capital which may be converted into ordinary shares, except under special circumstances (such as the purchase of an asset, a trade link-up, etc.), such funds must be obtained (under Stock Exchange rules) by an issue of capital to ordinary shareholders in proportion to their existing holdings unless shareholders in general meeting agree otherwise.

The term 'rights' therefore refers to the entitlement of the shareholder to a participation in the new issue.

Rights issues of ordinary shares are somewhat more complicated than capitalisation issues, for a decision must first be reached as to whether an ordinary share issue is the best means of obtaining finance at the particular time. Then the terms of the issue must be established.

The new shares must obviously be issued at a price somewhat lower than the price of the existing ordinary shares in order to make them an attractive investment. A decision has to be taken as to whether this price can be so reduced that, allowing for fluctuations in the market during the period of subscription (usually about three weeks), all the shares will be subscribed by shareholders or any left over can be sold in the market without loss; otherwise the issue must be underwritten. The criticism of underwriting such issues is that the discount which could have been offered to the shareholder is being paid away to a third party.

Shares not subscribed by those to whom they have been offered are (unless shareholders in general meeting have agreed otherwise) normally required by the Council to be dealt with by one of the following methods:

(i) sold for the benefit of the shareholders entitled to them;
(ii) offered to existing shareholders by the provision of application forms for excess shares;
(iii) sold for the benefit of the company.

On occasions a combined capitalisation issue and rights issue is made, and the rights issue may be underwritten. Under such conditions the advantages of reducing the two issues to a larger rights issue, at or near par, may be considered. In Australia and Japan particularly, regular rights issues are made at par. If the rate of dividend is maintained and the price of the shares continues to stand substantially above the nominal value, the shareholders, while contributing new capital to the company, are obtaining an improvement in both capital and income.

The imposition of dividend limitation has raised an additional advantage to shareholders in those companies raising new capital by way of rights issues. In order to reduce the cost of new finance, the Treasury has taken a sympathetic view of dividend increases above the statutory 10 per cent forecast at the time of a rights issue or at the time of an acquisition of another business by way of issue of ordinary shares. Any rights issue at a discount greater than 25 per cent of the market price must also be approved by the Treasury.

ISSUES OF LOAN CAPITAL

Types of loan capital were discussed in Chapter 6 from the point of view of the investor. Somewhat different criteria apply from the point of view of the company issuing the security.

Mortgage debentures (loans secured upon a specific part of the assets of the company, normally its land and buildings) are most suitable for companies where the freehold or long leasehold element is large. Property companies, retail outlets, breweries, etc., can usually provide the specific assets for such securities, although in recent years many companies have preferred not to create a charge over specific assets, but to issue debenture stocks.

Debenture stocks (normally secured by a floating charge on all the assets of the company remaining after meeting any prior claims) have been a favourite form of investment for insurance companies and pension funds. As a form of loan capital the debenture with final redemption dates is probably the most suitable form of fixed-interest issue for the majority of companies.

Unsecured loan stocks (having no specific security other than the recognised financial strength of the company concerned) are appropriate only for larger companies. The majority of institutional investors do not view unsecured loans of smaller or lesser-known companies with approval, since, if loan capital is required, the security should be available. The various restrictive covenants which are substituted for the security are often such that a small company cannot prudently accept them without too great a surrender of flexibility.

Convertible stocks (covering all loan capital with the additional right that the holder may elect to exchange the stock for ordinary shares at certain specified dates and in certain proportions) may provide a useful means of raising finance on the best terms from the point of view of the company. The interest rate is not normally as high as would have been necessary for a loan stock without the attraction of a future stake in the equity of the company, and the conversion terms are usually at a premium above the price of the ordinary shares at the time of issue, thus providing finance which would not have been available on the basis of a rights issue of ordinary shares. Convertible issues are particularly suitable either when market conditions do not permit a rights issue of ordinary shares, or when there may be some delay between the raising of the finance and the eventual effect upon the profits of the company.

Issues of loan capital have two advantages to the borrower. First, interest payments are met out of earnings before the charging of corporation tax, so that, in the majority of cases, they provide a cheaper form of fixed-interest capital than preference shares. Second, where a company is earning a reasonably high rate on the capital it employs, the difference between the earnings on the loan capital and the interest payments accrue to the benefit of the ordinary shareholders.

The disadvantage of loan capital lies in the creation of a charge or some other restriction on the assets. Many companies are reluctant to entertain this, since it may affect the scope of their existing overdraft facilities with their banks.

The issue of loan capital does not, however, limit the company to a further issue of additional stock of the same class in the future. Most debenture issues are made on a 'formula' basis. The formula permits further issues, providing that the relation of the total amount of debenture in issue to total assets and earnings is maintained.

Since the Finance Act 1976 corporate issues of all loan stocks have been exempt from *ad valorem* stamp duty. The high rates of interest currently ruling, however, have reduced the amount raised by such issues to a negligible figure.

METHOD OF ISSUE

Loan capital may be issued by any of three methods:

(*a*) As an offer for sale;
(*b*) As a placing;
(*c*) As an offer restricted to shareholders.

(*a*) *Offer for Sale*

The offer for sale has the advantage that close terms can usually be obtained, but this is counterbalanced by the expenses of the issue, which are high. A full prospectus is required, with the high cost of advertising, underwriting, bank charges, etc. Preferential treatment may be offered to applications from existing shareholders.

(*b*) *Placing*

Unlike equity issues The Stock Exchange puts no limit on the size of fixed-interest issues which are the subject of a placing, since there is a limited class of investor (primarily insurance companies and pension funds) interested in this type of security. However, at least 30 per cent of the stock subject to placing must be distributed in a reasonable number of hands. Where the amount placed does not exceed £1.5 million, not less than 20 per cent must be offered to the market for distribution through other firms of brokers. For amounts in excess of £1.5 million but less than £15 million, 10 per cent of issue must be offered to the market and a further 10 per cent must be at the call of the market until noon on the day after the particulars appear in the press. For amounts in excess of £15 million special requirements may apply and The Stock Exchange request early consultation.

Placing of fixed-interest securities, in particular loan capital, are frequently more advantageous to the borrower, despite the fact that a narrower section of the public may be able to participate. Not only are the costs of the issue lower than for an offer for sale, but the terms (price and life of the security) need not be fixed until about a few days before the placing, as opposed to three or even four weeks before a public offer. In 'crash programmes' for loan issues the terms are fixed on the day before the placing. Consequently the borrower (or the company) secures terms most closely in accord with current market conditions.

(*c*) *Offer to Shareholders*

The cost of an issue to shareholders is again reduced, but it requires to be underwritten, since it is unlikely that existing shareholders will fully subscribe most debenture issues, unless they contain some conversion terms. Underwriters will thus expect to be left to take up stock, so that the terms must be relatively attractive.

In the majority of cases, therefore, a placing will probably be found to be the most satisfactory method. At least 30 per cent of any class of fixed-income capital for which quotation is sought must end up in the hands of the public.

ADDITIONAL ADMINISTRATIVE MATTERS

Issues of loan capital require additional administration in a number of directions. Trustees must be appointed to ensure that the company adheres to its various undertakings. Usually one of the insurance companies, often the office which undertakes the company's own insurance, will accept the appointment. The trust or mortgage deed must be prepared, and the prospectus will contain a number of new paragraphs, the principal of which are given at the end of Appendix 5.

QUOTATION OF FOREIGN COMPANIES

In recent years a number of overseas companies have realised the value of a quotation in London, just as a number of leading British companies have taken steps to arrange quotation for their shares in the United States and in leading European centres.

Normally the initiation of an overseas issue will come to the Corporate Finance Department through the Foreign Department of the firm, and one of the duties of the partner in charge will be to explain the advantages of a London quotation and the requirements of The Stock Exchange to the overseas client.

ADVANTAGES OF A LONDON QUOTATION

The general advantages of a quotation have already been discussed, but for the foreign company two factors are of the greatest importance.

(*a*) *An Additional Source of Finance*

London provides the largest source of investment finance in Europe and, next to New York, in the world. The investment trusts provide the largest closed-end trust organisation in the world, and their traditional outlook has caused them to place a relatively large proportion of their investments in overseas securities. The insurance companies also have tended to hold a higher proportion of their investments in ordinary shares than have insurance companies in other countries, and, although they may not have liabilities in certain overseas countries, many offices have considered it wise investment policy to give their portfolios a global spread.

The foreign company which, by reason of its London listing, publishes its reports in English and produces its accounts in a form with which U.K. investors are acquainted thus has a distinct advantage as a recipient of British institutional funds over its counterpart who does not have a listing.

Institutions are forced to rely on the advice of bankers or brokers close to foreign companies as to the progress of the concerns and their outlook for future growth. Where a London merchant bank and a firm of stockbrokers have been engaged in introducing shares to the London market, institutions are able to make enquiries from people with whom they are probably in daily contact, and, other factors being equal, will prefer to invest in the concern with which they can keep in the closest touch and whose share price they can follow daily in the financial press.

(*b*) *Publicity Value*

Compared with the cost of mounting even a fairly small advertising campaign in the British press, the cost of a listing on The Stock Exchange gives remarkable value. The names of the leading foreign stocks are still relatively unknown in Britain and the number of quotations relatively few, so that any innovation receives very considerable editorial coverage in the press. A quotation in the leading national financial papers also provides a regular reminder of the company's existence to a wide range of executive and professional men who read these journals.

REQUIREMENTS FOR A LISTING

The requirements for the listing of the shares of a foreign company do not differ much from those of shares in companies incorporated in the United Kingdom, since it is the policy of The Stock Exchange that, if a company wishes to enjoy the facilities provided by London, it must provide investors with the same information and undertake the same pledges as a domestic concern. The requirements are sufficiently flexible, however, for there to be no absolute limitation on the listing of a foreign security which cannot for good reason comply with every requirement of the regulations. The Council are also prepared to consider some slight amendment to the requirements of the Listing Agreement which would obviously be either unduly burdensome or inapplicable to overseas companies.

The principal difficulties arise in connection with the publication of consolidated accounts, with the qualifications of the auditors and with the paragraph entitled 'Profits, Prospects and Dividends' in the prospectus.

In order to make clear the requirements of The Stock Exchange to companies incorporated outside Great Britain, the Quotations Department has published a 'Foreign Companies Memorandum' on the subject.

PROFITS, PROSPECTS AND DIVIDENDS

One of the requirements of The Stock Exchange is that a paragraph on the current profits, the future outlook for the company and the directors' intention with regard to dividends shall be included in the prospectus at the time of an issue. This may conflict with the regulations in the country in which the company is incorporated. It may be found desirable, therefore to seek a London listing immediately after the end of an accounting period, when up-to-date figures will be available for the prospectus and when the 'Profits, Prospects and Dividends' paragraph can be drawn from the statement recently made to the company's shareholders.

EXPENSES

Since listing of a foreign company's shares is often undertaken partly for advertising and prestige, it is normally advisable to utilise the services of an issuing house, and preferably one with a reputation for international coverage. The translation of documents and the preparation of accounts in the form required for listing, together with the travelling expenses of members of the issuing house and possibly of the reporting accountants, may increase the expenses over those which would be applicable to a similar introduction of a company incorporated in the U.K.

TAKE-OVER BIDS

The most exciting part of a stockbroker's life comes when he is concerned with either an attempt to take over a company or the defence of one of the companies which he represents in the face of a bid. Unlike the sole responsibility of a new issue, however, stockbrokers are not normally given sole charge of advising a company in a take-over situation, unless both managements have agreed to recommend the terms to their shareholders. Where a bid is likely to meet opposition, one of the issuing houses with considerable experience in this field is likely to be employed. The duties of the stockbroker are largely confined to market operations where shares have to be acquired, to advising on whether the terms of the bid or the counter-bid moves will be acceptable to the public or not, and to advising on the attitudes likely to be taken by institutional investors and the Quotations Committee.

The regulation of the conduct of take-over bids lies with the Take-Over Panel, a body supported on a voluntary basis by all the principal components of the securities industry. The stockbrokers will consult the executive of the Panel for guidance on any doubt they may have, either on the course of the bid or the interpretation of the Rules and Practice Notes published in the Take-Over Code.

The first essential in the planning stage is security and the second to ensure, if possible, a bid acceptable without contention. In a defended bid much time, effort and expense can be wasted in an abortive attempt, and the effect on the morale of the acquired company, if the bid is successful, can be substantial. Where a bid is opposed, both sides will want to keep the initiative in the battle. The classical attack is the offer of either cash, loan stock or shares very considerably above the current market price, with some indication of the progress of the bidder company and the benefits of the merger of interests. This may be matched by the defending company forecasting an increase in profits and dividend, and often showing some dramatic change in management to prove that the lethargy of the past has been shaken off. Private shareholders tend to be loyal to their boards of directors and their sympathy is often with the under-dog. Institutional holders, being more professional, are concerned with obtaining the greatest possible long term financial advantage for their own shareholders or policy-holders, but they too will normally stand behind existing management unless the case for accepting a bid is irrefutable.

During the course of the battle both sides may be operating in the market, making daily disclosures of their transactions in accordance with the Take-Over Code. As the date for acceptance of the bid approaches, the excitement becomes intense. The life of the partner concerned is very different from the quiet City existence imagined by the public.

CONCLUSION

I may have been guilty of devoting too much space to the work of the Corporate Finance Department, which is essentially a specialised part of any stockbroker's office. Little appears to have been written about it in the past and the mechanics of an issue are still shrouded in mystery for most people. It also happens to be one of the departments which I myself find the most fascinating and the most exciting.

8 Foreign Securities

Much of the success of the investment policies of British institutions has been due to their foresight in spreading their interests throughout the world. At 31 December 1976 investment and unit trusts alone held securities in overseas companies worth £2976 million out of total assets of £5292 million. Comparative figures from insurance companies are not easy to establish since they are not segregated in the official statistics. In view of the high proportion of business carried out in the United States and the many years during which regular investment abroad has been carried out, the market value of insurance company holdings is likely to be considerable.

Among the firms of stockbrokers in London a number have acquired the reputation of being specialists in some particular area—usually Canada, America, Europe, South Africa, Austrialia or, in more recent years, the Far East and South America. U.K. firms now (end–1977) operate 39 branch offices in 17 countries. On the other hand no less than 28 firms of overseas stockbrokers have offices in London, 13 from the United States, 11 from Canada, 4 from Japan and 11 from the E. E. C. A firm which does not possess a specialised department dealing with foreign securities is thus able to obtain information at first hand from one of these branch offices.

In recent years the foreign departments of London firms have prepared the way for a two-way traffic, recommending overseas investments to U.K. investors and recommending British securities to foreign investors. The economic problems of the U.K. in the early 1970s and the weakness of sterling in international currency markets, however, sharply reduced foreign portfolio investment in the shares of British companies.

Overseas investments currently offer three advantages over domestic securities to U.K. residents. First, it is possible to select those economies or industries which are growing at a faster rate than in Britain. By exercising a flexible policy, investments may be switched from countries that are riding on an economic boom to those which are currently depressed. For example, in recent years it has been possible to switch investment between France, West Germany and Japan, to considerable advantage. Second, it is possible to invest in certain industries which have no investment counterpart at home. The gas and electric utilities of the United States have given possibly the best example, but in various areas coal, railroads, mining and other commodity shares offer interesting investment opportunities. Finally, at times when the outlook for sterling appears to be weak, certain other currencies, notably in recent times the American dollar, yen or the German DM, offer a safer haven than sterling.

Overseas investments are not, however, without their disadvantages also. With the exception of America, where accounting requirements are of a very high order and where disclosure of such important figures as turnover is obligatory, the accounts of few foreign companies give sufficient information to be of real value to an investment analyst. In many countries the accounts of parent and subsidiaries are not consolidated, so that transfers between the two parties can make the figures virtually meaningless. In some the auditor is in fact an officer of the company and not an independent inspector of the accounts.

In many centres the marketability of the shares of even the major companies is very restricted. As a result a purchase of a unit of investment that might be appropriate for an institution can take several days or even weeks to execute, and the possibility of selling the shares easily at a later date is remote.

There is also the difficulty of keeping in close touch with an investment when made. In the case of domestic securities any announcement of importance will be seen through the medium of the press. Alternatively the stockbroker to the company will normally be well informed about current progress. Overseas stockbrokers have not developed the same after-service to their clients, and on this situation many British stockbrokers have capitalised. A number of institutions prefer to deal through the medium of a British firm, although this may be more expensive because of the additional commission charged, since they feel that they will be kept in closer touch with their investment as a result.

INVESTMENT CURRENCY

Investment in overseas countries requires a supply of currency for the purpose. In practice the Bank of England does not make currency available at the time of each investment, but a buyer of foreign securities purchases dollars from the pool. Because the pool is limited in size, where there is an excess of demand over supply a premium is established. The *Financial Times* quotes the premium daily as a footnote to 'Americans' on the last page but two. (On 22 April 1977 the footnote read: 'S. E. List Premium 45¾% based on $U.S. 1.7187 per £.') Investment dollars purchased may be exchanged into any other investment currency.

All securities in Common Market countries can be purchased through the medium of the investment dollar, but in Scandinavian countries, such as Sweden, local regulations affect the premium paid for the currency.

A slight complication arises in understanding the quotation of Canadian securities. Since the U.S. and Canadian dollars are not in parity the same premium is applied to the dollar at the Montreal rate. (On 22 April 1977 the *Financial Times* footnote under 'Canadians' read: 'S. E. List Premium 45¾% based on $1.8047 per £.')

The sale of an overseas security was complicated by the provisions of the Finance Act of 1965. This Act included the requirement that, whenever a sale of such a security was made, one-quarter of the investment dollar proceeds must be returned to the Bank of England at the par rate. As a result any switching operation attracted an additional cost of one-quarter of the premium overall. Originally imposed as a temporary expedient to improve the U.K. balance of payments the '25 per cent surrender' almost destroyed the position of London as an 'entrepôt' market in foreign securities and was finally repealed in 1978.

SALES-AND-SERVICE

One of the problems of operating an effective Foreign Department lies in the immensity of the area to be covered. No firm can expect to be expert on every country which offers investment prospects, or on more than a limited spectrum of the security market in any one country. The first essential is to establish relations with reliable and well-informed correspondents or agents in the areas concerned, particularly those who are trained to present their material in a manner acceptable to British institutions. American, Canadian,

Australian and Japanese stockbrokers, in particular, present a wealth of statistical and other research material. To a lesser extent, but of an extremely high quality, reports are published by some of the leading banking houses in France, Belgium, Holland, West Germany and Switzerland.

The second essential is to select the areas on which the department is planning to concentrate and to maintain a service on industries and companies within these areas. It is painfully easy to develop an interest in a country when the market is rising and prospects appear rosy, only to lose interest and contact when things go wrong. The only advantage enjoyed by the London stockbroker over his foreign counterpart is the close association with his institutional client. If the service is good enough, the client will prefer to pay the additional expenses involved in dealing through the London broker.

The U.S. is traditionally the home of the greater part of U.K. overseas investment. The information disclosed by companies is more detailed than in other countries, accounts of parent and subsidiaries are consolidated, and conditions of audit provide adequate protection to the shareholder. Boards of U.S. companies are more conscious of the importance of their shareholders as owners of the business than in most other countries and are free with their information at meetings or on visits. In addition the U.S. dollar has been one of the most freely traded of world currencies, certain areas have shown continued growth over many years, and there is a ready market in many of the shares of the leading concerns.

Outstanding growth, however, has been shown in the last twenty years by a number of other countries, particularly West Germany, Hong Kong and Japan.

ARBITRAGE

Where securities are listed both in London and an overseas centre price anomalies can occur due to greater demand or supply in one of the centres. Certain firms, therefore, maintain a close watch on share prices in both countries, buying in one centre and selling in another with the object of making a profit on the transaction. This operation is termed 'arbitrage' and the firms or individuals operating it 'arbitrageurs'. Complications arise in arbitrage due both to the time differential and to fluctuations in the rate of exchange or the dollar premium. The true arbitrageur will have to take a position in a security between the time he deals in London and the time he is able to carry out the second half of the operation on the opening of the overseas market. New York, for example, opens at 3 p.m. G. M. T., Tokyo opens at midnight London time, Johannesburg at 8 a.m. The risks of being unable to complete the operation at a profit can thus be considerable.

Arbitrage is not undertaken by all firms who maintain foreign departments, but is confined to specialists. It is more akin to a form of jobbing than the normal stockbroking business, and firms engaged in arbitrage are permitted to open joint accounts with their overseas partners, buying and selling securities as principals, and thus reducing the margins that would have been necessary if they had treated the overseas correspondent as an agent and had charged commission at the minimum rates.

PRODUCTION

It is not possible to discuss in detail the peculiarities of each of the foreign markets in which U.K. investors may be interested. Appendices 7 to 23 give a brief summary of the principal markets listed in the *Financial Times* at the present time. Since the earlier edition of this book Brazil and Spain have been added. There are, however, some general points which can conveniently be discussed here.

(*a*) DEALING

When dealing in overseas securities, the Foreign Department will check whether it is to the advantage of the client to deal in the London market or in the overseas stock exchange. A purchase of a security requires a series of calculations: the calculation of the net price in the country concerned (the offered price of the security plus expenses); the conversion of this price to dollars at the official rate; the conversion of dollars to sterling at the premium quoted by a dealer in the foreign exchange market; a comparison with the offered price of the security in London.

If it is to the advantage of the client to deal overseas, the department will instruct the agents in the country concerned to make the purchase. The currency must then be covered through the foreign exchange market, with instructions given for payment and delivery of the security.

(*b*) DELIVERY AND REGISTRATION

Foreign securities may be delivered in a variety of ways. Some are registered in a central nominee company (French and West German). Some are delivered by renounceable certificates (American common stocks). Some are bearer. A decision must be made as to whether the security is to be brought home for safe custody in the U.K. or left in the country where it has been purchased. In the former case there may be insurance and shipping charges; in the latter bank safe-custody charges. Where securities are registered, in most cases it will prove most economical to have shares put in the name of a nominee company in the country concerned. Where a substantial investment has been made in shares delivered by bearer document or renounceable certificate, it is probably most economical to bring the scrip home for safe custody in the U.K. Under British Exchange Control Regulations, such securities must be held in safe custody by an authorised depositary (such as a bank).

Renounceable certificates of foreign shares traded in the London market are normally in 'good marking names' and as such are termed 'good delivery'. A list of marking names is set out in *The Stock Exchange Official Year Book* and a member need not accept delivery of shares registered in any other name. In fact the seller of shares not registered in a good marking name is liable to receive a lower price. The reason for this regulation lies largely in the complications that occur in North America when the registered owner of shares dies and it is necessary to prove the estate. The delays and legal fees can be considerable.

(i) *Overseas Deliveries*

On a number of occasions transactions in foreign securities will be carried out by brokers with the jobbers in London, although the security is held abroad. In the case of a sale the Foreign Transfer Department will ascertain where the security is held and to whose order. The jobber or overseas agent will provide the information as to where the security is to be delivered and to whose order, and this information, together with authority to release the security, is arranged. In the case of a purchase for delivery abroad the Foreign Transfer Department will check where the stock is required and to whose order it should be held. This information is given to the jobber, or overseas agent, who arranges to deliver the security accordingly. Payment is made in either case on confirmation from overseas that the stock has been delivered.

(ii) *Deposit Receipts*

A number of foreign shares are quoted in London as E.D.R. (European Deposit Receipts) or B.D.R. (Bearer Deposit Receipts). Usually the deposit receipt represents either a fraction or a multiple of the shares quoted in the foreign centre. For example General Motors are quoted in London both as shares of U.S. \$$1\frac{2}{3}$ par value and also as B.D.R. of $\frac{1}{20}$ share. The reason for quoting a different unit lies in the price. At the end of 1976 the price of General Motors shares was over £67. The U.K. private investor dislikes 'heavy' shares, of which he can afford to buy only a few, preferring lower-priced units. The market in the B.D.R. is therefore wider.

Renown (Kabushiki Kaisha Renown), on the other hand, is quoted in E.D.R.'s of 1000 shares each, since the price of each share in Tokyo is low by London standards. Shares of too small a price are suspect, so that the happy medium of somewhere over 50p and under 300p appears to satisfy the requirements of the public.

(*c*) FOREIGN DIVIDENDS

(i) *Stocks in Own Marking Names*

Most of the brokers with specialist departments dealing in foreign securities are included in the list of 'good marking names'. The name of the firm is thus included in the register of shareholders in the books of the foreign company. For each such company the Foreign Dividend Department will open an account, showing for each dividend distribution (usually quarterly) the dates the books closed, the dividend payable, the rate of the dividend, the date the dividend is received in London, the ex-dividend date and the 'Stock Exchange valuation'.

All but the final entry are self-explanatory. The Stock Exchange valuation is the value of the dividend in sterling, calculated at a rate of exchange published weekly by the Stock Exchange Marking Names Committee. The rate is based on the average \$ rate for the week, taking into account also an allowance for the costs of collecting and distributing the dividend which is due to the firm. (It should be noted that the premium on the investment dollar does not enter into calculations on dividends, which are paid at the spot rate.)

Where marking names leave mandates with companies to pay dividends to their foreign banks, these are transferred to the London branches and credited to the firm's account in sterling. The authorised depositaries who hold the securities, usually the banks of the clients who own the stock, claim on the marking names for dividend payments, which are made in sterling.

(ii) *Stocks in Other Names*

The Foreign Dividend Department will examine all foreign stock passing through the office, either bought or sold. Where a dividend is due to be claimed, either from the selling client or on behalf of the buyer, the Foreign Dividend Department stamps the back of the renounceable certificates 'Dividend due on (date) claimed by . . .' and despatches the claim accordingly.

INFORMATION

(*a*) COMPARISON OF DIFFERENT AREAS

In addition to the statistics for comparison of past and prospective growth, many foreign departments maintain charts of the stock-market movements in the countries in which they specialise. These give the historical price record (and often the record of price/earnings ratios) of the indices in each of the major areas. An assessment can be made as to whether prices in one centre over-discount future prosperity, indicating a switch in emphasis to an area of prospective recovery.

(*b*) CURRENCY COMPARISONS

In the last decade, following the floating of some currencies and the revaluation of others, fluctuations in currency rates have been as important a factor as movement of security prices. A number of firms, therefore, have acquired experise in comparing the economic factors in different areas which could cause currency movements to occur.

(*c*) SELECTION OF INDIVIDUAL SECURITIES

The selection of shares is little different from that in the United Kingdom, with the exception that accounts of companies in many overseas areas are less detailed and less revealing than those of their British counterparts. A personal visit to an overseas company is almost always worth the trouble and expense, and some arrangement for a continuous flow of information about the company is essential. Most of the stockbrokers who specialise in a particular area send a partner on a visit at least once a year, and sometimes more often. In European countries a knowledge of languages is important, but in such countries as Japan the British broker inevitably has to accept an interpreter's translation both at verbal interviews and of written reports.

NEW ISSUES

The listing of foreign companies' shares in London has already been discussed in Chapter 7.

CONCLUSION

There seems little doubt that, as methods of communication improve and as countries become more sophisticated in the publication of essential information and the preparation of accounts, increasing interest will be shown in overseas securities. Firms which have established a reputation in this field should reap a future harvest.

9 Stockbroking as a Profession

I HAVE endeavoured, in the preceding pages, to give some indications of the operations which take place in a stockbroker's office today. A young man who is considering stockbroking as a profession will want to know the answers to other and broader questions. What is the future of stockbroking? What are the advantages and disadvantages of the profession? What qualifications does he require? How do firms recruit their new entrants? What will it cost him to become a member of The Stock Exchange?

THE FUTURE OF THE STOCK EXCHANGE

In answer to the first question, I can only express my personal opinion. The final chapter of this book includes some brief comment on the outlook for stockbroking and a more detailed study will be contained in a successor volume. In summary, while capitalism exists, some market for the exchange of securities must also exist. The Stock Exchange, although its structure has already changed radically since the first edition of this book was published and will continue to change in the future, should still provide a reasonable livelihood for forward-looking stockbrokers.

ADVANTAGES AND DISADVANTAGES

The advantages and disadvantages are more easily enumerated. I shall deal with the disadvantages first. Stockbroking is an uncreative profession. The engineer or the architect can look at some physical result of his labour. Even the doctor can be certain in his own mind that he has saved a life or cured an illness. The stockbroker may make a great deal of money for his clients, but he rarely receives much praise for it and can never boast about it. It is a worrying profession, particularly for those who deal with the affairs of private clients. Duodenal ulcers are a common occupational hazard among stockbrokers, caused during busy times by rushing meals, worrying over clients' affairs and by the demands of the non-stop telephone. And the stockbroker, like the doctor, carries his work with him out of office hours. Certain clients will wait until the comparative calm of the evening to discuss their own investment problems on the telephone. A stockbroker is always fair game for free advice at a cocktail party.

Stockbroking is also a precarious profession. The swings of fortune can be very wide and sharp. The Stock Exchange is the barometer of the country's economic strength, a target for left-wing politicians, and it is not uncommon for firms who have enjoyed boom conditions in one year to experience heavy losses the next. During the sharp recession of 1974/5 the stockbroking industry contracted from 357 to 285 firms, with a reduction of almost one-third of the total employees. Unfortunately the training of a stockbroker does not fit the individual for any other profession. The accounting procedures are peculiar to the industry, and even the examination syllabus does not fit the successful candidate for alternative employment.

Finally, in common with the professions as opposed to trade, stockbroking gives less opportunity for the build-up of capital through the business itself. The man who expands a small company into a large concern is rewarded by the increase in the value of his shares. A stockbroker leaving his firm may well take out of it only the capital which he put in, since few succeeding partners nowadays are prepared to make a substantial payment for goodwill, and no corporate member firm of brokers has yet achieved a Stock Exchange listing. There is also a widespread impression that, as a stockbroker works close to the centre of investment, he is in a privileged position, able to take advantage of much secret information which is not available to the public. Any stockbroker worth his salt should be able to invest his own funds with reasonable success, but this is a far cry from making a large personal fortune. On the few occasions when he is in possession of guaranteed information, such as a take-over bid, he is rightly prevented from using the information to his own advantage by being professionally involved in the case and classed as an 'insider'.

The advantages, in my opinion, far outweigh the disadvantages of the profession. Possibly the variety of the work is one of its chief attractions. No two days are ever the same. No one, on arriving at the office, has the faintest notion of the business of the day, the surprises, disappointments and the successes to come. In every department the daily contact is with people and all stockbrokers have a wide circle of acquaintances, many in every quarter of the globe. In the smaller firms, where the control is more centralised, the stockbroker is like a general practitioner, having to deal single-handed with every facet from the book-keeping in the office to the whole range of the sales-and-service departments. He may be advising a widow with two children to support on a small pension at one moment of the day and discussing the best means of defence against a take-over bid an hour later. When actual trading is slack, it is still impossible to leave the office altogether for a day or two each week. It is a job in which keeping abreast of events is vitally important and endeavouring to predict the outcome of events wholly fascinating.

The financial rewards of stockbroking are considerable. While it may be difficult to create a large capital, a partnership in a successful firm may produce a very sizeable annual income. In comparison with positions of equal responsibility in industry, these rewards are often considerably greater. But the risk of greatly diminished profits in bad times compensates for the high earnings during boom periods.

The Stock Exchange, in common with Parliament, has often been called a first-class club. This phrase has something of the pre-war ring of the Establishment about it, the closed shop of the moneyed ranks. In fact it means something totally different. Working within the confines of the City, a communal influence embraces all firms and all employees of them. Every sort of sport and interest is encouraged by someone, who voluntarily organises an association to cater for it. Cricket, football, rugby, hockey, athletics, skiing, swimming, tennis, golf, boxing, rifle clubs are all available as well as the chess, darts, billiards and bowls clubs. The London to Brighton walk is an annual feature in the nation's athletics calendar. For those with artistic interests, there are societies devoted to art and drama, with an orchestra and a male-voice choir. And so wide-spread are the interests of the members that, however unusual a hobby a new member may have, someone else is likely to be either interested, or even expert, in the same field.

The very fact of having one central place of business, the House itself, instils a certain comradeship between members of The Stock Exchange, although this spirit has become sadly reduced as the technician, working from the confines of his office, has overtaken the old-time stockbroker who operated almost exclusively on the floor of the House. Nevertheless it still remains. Most members will count other members, not necessarily of their own firms, among their closest friends. A member signifies to another member someone whom he can trust, for his business is based on trust.

Lastly, for the member who falls on difficult times, The Stock Exchange Benevolent Fund was formed over 150 years ago. It caters for those members or their dependants who are in need of financial help, and operates in addition a residential home in Surrey.

Even in the deepest financial gloom of 1974 the stewards of this fund raised over £80,000 from the membership in their annual collection, the highest figure reached at that time.

RECRUITMENT

Different firms have different methods of recruiting new members of their staff, but in practice three doors are open to a young man seeking employment in stockbroking: to the general office, working his way up the clerical tree; to one of the specialist departments, depending upon his qualifications and experience; and the traditional entry, to one of the sales-and-service departments, depending upon his business connections.

(*a*) TO THE GENERAL OFFICE

Stockbrokers require, in their clerical staff, just the same qualities that are demanded from clerks in any walk of life. No particular mathematical ability is required, provided that the man is accurate and neat with figures. Any complicated sums are worked out on machines. A young man with ambition, a reasonable level of intelligence, and a conscientious approach to his work can rise through the production departments to the partnership. In the history of my own office several of the partners have started their business life as an office boy.

Vacancies are filled either through the medium of the press; the register of those desiring employment kept at the Stock Exchange Employments Bureau, for the higher grades; the Stock Exchange

Clerks Provident Fund, for existing employees and the more junior grades; or, usually as a last resort, through the City Employment Exchange.

The fluctuating fortunes of stockbroking, coupled with the rather unwieldy procedures that have held back the progress of automation, have resulted in severe shortages of staff during boom periods. Both men and women found it easy to move from job to job at increasing salaries as one firm bid against another to maintain its staff in active conditions.

Owing to these severe fluctuations in profits, salaries in stockbroking offices were traditionally low, with a high level of profit-sharing bonus added. As a result, in the past, over 100 per cent of salary might have been received by the older and more responsible members in particularly good years. This situation has materially changed in recent times, and salary levels are now more closely comparable with those in other financial institutions, the bonus or profit share element being relatively small.

In addition employees may be entitled to a share of the commission charged on business which they introduce. The maximum proportion which can be allowed to a clerk is one-third and to a member of The Stock Exchange it is normally one-half, with a minimum commission of £10 before sharing is permitted. With the increase in overheads during the last decade, however, some firms have abolished the sharing of commission with employees, while others have reduced the maximum to members to 40 per cent or a lower figure, or made a charge for the firm's services which effectively brought down the proportion allotted to the employee.

(*b*) TO ONE OF THE SPECIALIST DEPARTMENTS

With the increasing emphasis on technology, the man with suitable qualifications is now actively sought by the larger firms. The chartered accountant is probably the most suitably qualified individual, since his training enables him to seek employment in the production side of the office, in the Research Department where a knowledge of company accounts is essential, in the sales-and-service departments, or in the corporate finance side of the business. Of somewhat more specialised knowledge is an actuarial qualification, the examination for which alone contains the papers on investment. The investment managers of many insurance companies have actuarial qualifications, so that the ability to talk and think on the same lines can be of advantage both in presenting the case for investment and in selecting the security. The precise mathematical techniques of gilt-edged switching have also proved to be fields where actuaries can use their talents to advantage.

In the research departments economists and statisticians are also required, for the long-term prediction of economic trends and the interpretation of particular statistics. In recent years a number of financial journalists have left their earlier calling to join research departments. They have not only the flair to write their material in simple straightforward language and a knowledge of presentation, but many of them have developed close connections in industry which can be invaluable as sources of background information.

Managers or assistants in the investment departments of institutions such as insurance companies and investment trusts have also been tempted to cross over from customer to salesman. They have the advantage of possessing the knowledge of how the institutional investor likes the case for a purchase or sale presented to him. The more senior managers have been given exemption from certain examinations and granted a reduced period of training.

A number of firms make a regular policy of interviewing graduates from the universities, in the hope of finding those who may prove to be outstanding material. Some are assisted financially to broaden their viewpoint by being sent abroad for a few months before they join the firm. Other firms offer undergraduates holiday work during the summer vacations, thus saving the problems of carrying too excessive a staff, and offering future employment to those young men who seem particularly suitable. The importance of some recognised qualification is becoming more and more important in obtaining employment in the City.

Finally, the growth of data-processing both as an aid to investment and as a tool in the accounting departments has opened the field to systems analysts and programmers.

(*c*) TO THE SALES-AND-SERVICE DEPARTMENTS

In common with most walks of life where no particular qualifications are obligatory, opportunities in The Stock Exchange are still open to young men whose personal connections can guarantee substantial business to the firm. The guarantee, however, is much less easy to secure than it has been in the past. Neither private clients nor institutional investors are prepared to spoon-feed a young man because of his family connections. Business is placed primarily in recognition of the investment service provided. It would, however, be blinking the obvious if it were denied that good connections can still assist in providing a reasonable livelihood in stockbroking.

TRAINING

The size of most firms on The Stock Exchange makes it difficult to arrange any formal training during the early years, nor is there any joint training college under Stock Exchange control. A number of colleges provide special courses for those intending to sit the Stock Exchange examinations and The Stock Exchange publishes a substantial volume of lecture notes on 'Stock Exchange Practice'.

Most firms lay out a two-year course of apprenticeship for the promising young man who may eventually come into their partnership stream, so that he spends sufficient time in each of the departments to become proficient. At the end of this period it should be evident, from the progress reports of the heads of the departments, where his ultimate future lies and how valuable a member he is likely to be.

In the future I believe that, if stockbroking is to progress in step with the more advanced sections of industry, the larger firms will have to engage men who are specifically trained in management skills to ensure that the best output is obtained from the individual and that communication from the partnership to the lowest member of the departments is rapid and complete.

The conclusions which can be drawn from these few paragraphs can be summarised in a few words. The opportunities for a nice chap, without connections and with no particular qualifications, are becoming fewer and fewer. The opportunities for the qualified man are, I believe, considerable.

ELIGIBILITY FOR MEMBERSHIP

Three methods of entry into the membership of the London Stock Exchange existed in the past: through long service as a clerk, which was limited to a few vacancies each year; through serving a normal apprenticeship; or, by paying higher entrance fees and subscriptions, it was possible to achieve immediate membership.

The rules covering membership have been altered from time to time, but now the emphasis is placed on professionalism as well as integrity. Rule 31(1) includes the following provisions:

(*a*) A candidate for membership must be at least twenty-one.

(*b*) He shall have completed not less than three years' training with a firm, although partial remission may be given for special experience or qualifications.

(*c*) He shall have attained a minimum standard in a written examination.

(*d*) He shall be separately proposed and seconded by two members who can satisfy the exchange committee that he is a fit person to become a member.

EXAMINATIONS

These are held in June and November of each year and, unless exempted by reason of other professional qualifications, candidates are required to pass four papers:

Interpretation of Accounts
Taxation
Technique of Investment
Stock Exchange Practice

Papers failed at one attempt may be retaken at subsequent sittings. Pocket calculators are permitted.

COST OF MEMBERSHIP

A new member of The Stock Exchange has two separate costs to bear:

(i) A payment of £1000 to the Trustees of the Nomination Redemption Fund.

(ii) The annual subscription, currently £350.

The payment to the Nomination Fund is usually borne by the member himself, while the annual subscription may be paid each year by his firm. A total of approximately 3000 nominations are currently in existence and those members possessing them will be reimbursed from the Redemption Fund at £1000 a nomination at the time of retirement or resignation.

PARTNERSHIP

The ultimate aim of most young men after achieving membership is to be taken into partnership. Owing to the amalgamation of stockbroking firms into larger units, competition for a place in the partnership of the larger firms is becoming increasingly fierce. A first step to partnership may therefore be the inclusion of the name of the member on the writing-paper and other of the firm's documents, as an associate member 'below the line'.

Different firms use this facility for different purposes. Those who have a number of members, operating for their own clientele on a commission basis, may insert their names to add to their prestige. Others may show recognition of the managers of their specialist departments, such as Research or Foreign. It can therefore either be a step towards partnership or a recognition in lieu of it.

It has already been mentioned (Chapter I) that the names in the partnership of stockbroking firms may not all be profit-sharing partners. Some may be salaried, some paid on a commission-sharing basis, and some may directly share a proportion of the profits. Very often young men being accepted into partnership may start on a purely salary basis, with some form of bonus or commission-sharing payment, graduating to profit-sharing at a later date.

It should be stressed at this point that a partner, whether he derives his remuneration from salary or a share of the profits, is liable for the whole of his personal assets in the event of a failure of his firm. This factor is too often disregarded by young men, accepting partnerships with firms who undertake speculative business, and proved disastrous to a number of individuals, who were in no way connected with the management or viability of their firms, in the 1974 recession.

The cost of becoming a partner will obviously vary from firm to firm. The Stock Exchange regulations state that every firm shall at all times maintain a minimum liquidity margin, which for partnerships is presently calculated by multiplying £5000 by the number of partners or the aggregate of associated members and attachés, whichever is the greater (Rule 79(a)). Many firms have appreciated the difficulty of attracting the best young men into their partnerships if a large amount of capital must be put up at the time of entry. As a result it is now commonplace for incoming partners to be given a period of some years to contribute their full requirements of capital and tax reserves, while those partners whose shares are being reduced to make room for the newcomers accept repayment in instalments over the period.

One final word of advice. Having started life myself in a small firm, with a total complement including partners of only eight, and having then been particularly lucky in being offered a partnership in a larger firm, I would advise any other prospective stockbroker to enter the business in the reverse order. A young man who has been trained with one of the larger firms has a valuable background to investment. He has experience of research methods, possibly personal connections with institutions, and the overall outlook that only a widespread business can give. If, after he has worked with the larger firm for some years, he then decides that his future there is uncertain, he has something to offer to the smaller firm. There is also the possibility that the larger firm will not want to lose him and will offer him some additional incentive to stay.

10 Stockbroking Tomorrow

The first edition of this book contained two parts, the first bearing the title 'Stockbroking Today' and the second, smaller section 'Stockbroking Tomorrow'. In the final three chapters, an attempt was made to review the pressures and opportunities facing the securities industry and to identify the changes that might take place.

Ten years have now elapsed since publication and almost twelve since the first words were written. During this period the City as a whole has been under increasing attack, not only from the politically motivated, but also from those in industry with whom communication had been allowed to lapse. The pressures for change have therefore increased, but the opportunities have not diminished. It would seem appropriate, therefore, to try and do more justice to the future by engaging in a completely new volume on the prospects for tomorrow and limiting this chapter to a review of the successes and failures of the previous predictions. This decision also has the secondary advantage of allowing the publishers to price this volume at a level which most students should be able to afford.

THE INVESTOR OF THE FUTURE

In looking to the investor of the future, the points were made that '. . . *if we are to see the small client becoming an economic factor in stockbroking, then the costs of sales and service—and more particularly the cost of production—must be reduced. Reduction in production costs depends to some extent upon a united move by all stockbrokers. Costs of sales and service are much more directly under the control of the individual firm. . . .*'

'*The future outlook of stockbrokers towards the smaller private clients may therefore be to limit their specialist advice to perhaps two hundred securities.*'

'*It seems more important to me to leave the question of individual advertising to a time when the procedures of transacting business in The Stock Exchange have been so streamlined that small business is economic.*'

All these points still hold good to-day. The introduction of the new central settlement system, discussed later, may ultimately sound the death-knell of the share certificate as it is known today and bring to reality a low-cost system of transferring securities.

'*One of the great criticisms levelled against stockbroking firms . . . is that they fail to look after their clients, by leaving their portfolios static for long periods of time*' is less true in the seventies than it was in 1968. More and more firms have set up discretionary services for their clients, giving the brokers authority to deal without reference and thus encouraging them to stand or fall on their investment judgement. '*It seems to me, therefore, that a more active approach will be given to private clients, with action taken to take advantage of opportunities and not just to make sporadic reviews and recommendations.*' This attitude is certainly a reality today.

What of the client in the 1980s? Certainly statistics published by the building societies and the savings banks indicate that two new groups of saver have arrived: the younger generation and the skilled artisan – the young because the differential between the apprentice and the skilled worker has sharply diminished and much of the living expenses of youth are borne by their parents: and the skilled artisan in recent years has earned more than he required for the basic essentials of life, while the high levels of unemployment in the middle 1970s persuaded him that a nest-egg for the future was a prudent precaution. How best to persuade these two groups to invest their savings in securities is a more difficult problem. It seems likely that the majority will hold monetary assets through the final years of double-figure inflation, only joining the rush into ordinary shares as the next bull market reaches its peak.

JOBBERS AND BROKERS

'*It seems likely that the contraction in the number of firms of jobbers will continue in the future, possibly at a higher pace than in the past, and the market may be reduced to only four or five firms in the gilt-edged market, a dozen or so in industrials and three or four in each of the other markets.*'

The number of jobbing firms has indeed fallen from 36 in 1968 to 15 London firms and 5 country jobbers at 31 December 1976. What was not foreseen was that half-a-dozen major firms would emerge, represented in all markets. This development has enormously strengthened the finances of the larger jobbing firms and helped to alleviate the problem forecast of risk capital. '*But there is a shortage of* risk *capital, the equity of the jobbing firms, and this problem is likely to become more acute as younger and less well-endowed members take the places of the older generation.*'

The two-tier market which was forecast in that chapter may yet come to pass in the future. '*Too many jobbers have been acting in certain leading securities, with cut-throat competition and losses to all in some stocks, while in others there have been too few. . . . My own view is that, sooner or later, the London market must be divided into two sections, the first and the second floor. The first floor should contain a limited list of major securities, in which there is a ready market. The second floor should contain all other securities. From time to time a security may be up-graded from the second to the first floor and vice versa.*'

I still maintain the opinion that a two-tier market could offer certain advantages to the system. But now I believe that the weight of institutional investment, limited largely to the market leaders, demands something akin to a 'trading post' or 'specialist' market for the first floor, allowing the traditional jobbing system to continue in the second tier.

'*In chapter 1 the number of stockbroking firms* [for London only at 28th March, 1967] *was given as 255. It does not require much imagination to see this figure falling to one-half, or less, within the next five years.*' In fact, after almost ten years, the figure had fallen by exactly this proportion to 112, but the time-scale was longer than anticipated. '*The take-over of provincial firms by London stockbrokers will not be confined to a one-way traffic, and a number of the larger provincial firms would willingly absorb a smaller London firm to provide a London sales office and a medium of dealing direct on the London market. The advantages of having the bulk of overheads in a lower-cost area than the City might even put these firms at an advantage.*' In 1976, 15 provincial firms had offices in London and 22 London firms operated 30 out-of-town facilities for sales or processing their transactions.

'*In my own view (and this is entirely a personal opinion), the time is not too far distant when merchant banks should be offered a direct equity stake in stockbroking firms. If the United Kingdom eventually joins the Common Market, the traditional lead that London has developed in providing a capital market must be developed with all the resources at our disposal. The financial strength of the issuing houses, in partnership with the technical expertise of firms of stockbrokers, would provide a formidable combination.*'

In 1969, the Council passed a Rule permitting member firms to adopt limited corporated structure. No individual institution was permitted to hold more than 10 per cent of the voting capital and no consortium to hold more than 30 per cent. The leading firms, however, have not yet found it necessary to introduce institutional funds, since the partners feel that this would dilute their equity and weaken their autonomy. The prospect of partnership in the wider international markets which will develop in the future is still a very real possibility.

FINANCING THE STOCK EXCHANGE INSTITUTION

As far back as 1958 I was the joint author with Michael Bennett of an article for the summer edition of the *Stock Exchange Journal*. At the time the plans for rebuilding The Stock Exchange had just been postponed, possibly for a period of twenty years, and we wrote:

> The House itself is probably one of the greatest wastes of valuable space in the City of London, but plans for rebuilding are well under way—in twenty years' time. . . . The traditional techniques continue unabated; Members still queue for telephones in busy times; the clearing house still issues impassioned pleas to firms either to deliver names earlier or collect them later . . . there has been no specialist work-study, to the public knowledge at least, to improve this situation. . . . Advertising—well the gallery undoubtedly has been a step in the right direction, although it seems a pity that the only time the Stock Exchange gets a full-scale press is when a firm has been hammered or a Bank rate leak alleged.
>
> We said that Finance was the key to most of our problems, and there's been a rare old hubbub about the increased subscriptions announced recently, not to mention the new issue charges. When the small firms find it difficult to make ends meet in bad times and the big ones have permanent institutional investment to tide them over, even a small increase in subscriptions hits the small firms very hard. Why should the big firms get a relatively greater advantage when the improved facilities will be available to all? Be that as it may, suppose in fact the big firms were made to pay the greater part of the cost. How would the members react to a levy on net profits before tax . . . say, at a guess, of as little as ½ per cent or 1 per cent on the profits over £5,000 of all firms? The

figures are a cockshy, but the proceeds should be pretty considerable. If you wanted, you could make it a heavier tax for a limited number of years . . . nasty medicine but soon over.

Then we could think about rebuilding the House in earnest. We might consider an electronic department that centralised all broker-jobber accounting. If jobbers could be persuaded to report bargains into this machine as they were carried out it would clear all stocks automatically and, not only that, it would give a running record of dealing prices in every broker's office, reducing the staff required in boxes and order rooms and the House itself. And if sufficient finance were available we could begin to advertise the House as a serious place of business to attract new classes of investors. We might even manage to reduce the costs to such an extent that small orders became profitable and the ideal of the Cloth Cap Investor at last became a reality.

By 1976, virtually all these criticisms had been answered and the suggestions brought into practice. The new Stock Exchange building, a massive 24-storey office block adjacent to a vast domed single-storey market-place, had been constructed. The central telephone system, with the capability of linking both London and provincial members to the centre, contained an automatic exchange suitable for a medium-sized city. The central settlement system was gradually evolving into the most advanced computer-based operation in the securities industry anywhere in the world; McKinsey, the business consultants, had examined the plans in this connection and agreed that they were both viable and should produce the desired degree of savings. In the new building, the Visitors' Gallery had developed into a massive public relations operation, with charming and beautiful guides, a cinema, an exhibition room where commentaries could be heard in five languages and a private television studio for interviews and training. Advertising by member firms had begun in a small way and had been approved and encouraged by a report from the Monopolies Commission. The Market Price Display Service, covering price movements on 700 securities, together with currencies and security indices and four pages of general news, was transmitted to 127 member firms and 99 non-member organisations in London and 34 members and six others in provincial centres. A major investigation had even been carried out into the possibility of reporting bargains directly from the jobbers' pitches into the central system, but found to be impracticable.

Even finance had been moved away from the bias towards individual subscriptions and a general charge imposed on firms—not the ½ per cent or 1 per cent of profits over £5000 but, more equitably, at first 0.6 per cent of all income, rising to 2 per cent as the development of the settlement system began to grow nearer completion.

This central settlement system – TALISMAN (Transfer Accounting, Lodgement for Investors, Stock MANagement for Jobbers)—is unlikely to commence operations for at least two years. While the detailed plans for its operation are very far advanced, many changes may take place in the interim period. As explained in Chapter 3, therefore, only a brief outline of its likely effect is given here.

The basis of the TALISMAN system lies in the establishment of a central nominee company—SEPON Limited (Stock Exchange POol Nominees)—which will be granted an account in the register of every listed security, excluding gilt-edged issues. Under the present system, described in Chapter 3, for each purchase transaction a ticket is issued which is used by the buying brokers to identify the delivery of stock from brokers acting for sellers or from the jobber. TALISMAN operates a pool system, whereby all stock sold is transferred from the seller into the central pool and purchasers receive their deliveries out of the name of SEPON in one transfer of exactly the number of shares they have purchased.

While the system sounds simple and obvious enough in its conception, a number of complications arise in practice. A change of law has been necessary to permit the operation of the single undesignated account for SEPON, and The Stock Exchange (Completion of Bargains) Act received Royal Assent in 1976. Jobbers must have separately designated accounts within the pool so that stock belonging to one firm cannot be used to satisfy claims on another, and so that a statement of his holding in the name of SEPON is recognised as sufficient collateral on which a jobber may borrow from his bank to finance his business. The sheer volume of business passing through the central system and the time factors involved make it impossible for an institution to continue its present practice of delivering a sold security against simultaneous receipt of the sale proceeds. For brokers (or The Centre) to finance such transactions for twenty-four hours would be prohibitively expensive, so that institutions have been asked to agree to accept a receipt for stock delivered, guaranteed by The Stock Exchange, and receive payment the following day.

Advantages from the point of view of broking firms are considerable.

For sold transfers there will be no ticket processing, no stamping of transfers (*ad valorem* stamps will be applied centrally), fewer deliveries and virtually no splitting, with residual certification of balances only.

For purchase transfers the ticket will be eliminated, registration will be carried out centrally from details supplied by the brokers, and many of the brokers' internal controls will be unnecessary.

The accounting work should be considerably reduced with the abolition of ticket accounts, and dividends and rights will be claimed centrally, which should reduce the work necessary to protect clients' interests.

From the clients' point of view, there are also a number of advantages. Certificates, which currently may be received several months after a purchase, should be available within two or three weeks from Account Day. Delays in claims for dividends, which sometimes are made after the client has completed his tax return for the year, should be much reduced. Queries and complaints regarding settlement are likely to be less frequent.

There are, of course, attendant disadvantages as well. Much of the work currently carried out within the production departments of member firms will henceforth be centralised, not only reducing the control which partnerships have over their expenses but also placing a greater degree of risk on industrial action at the centre. The organisational structure of firms' production departments will require a significant change of direction, towards client orientation and away from the existent sectional structure, although the necessity will remain to check for errors at The Centre. Theoretical savings are difficult to attain in practice and in the smaller firms, where during times of low activity the partners themselves may do much of the general office work, savings may be small and costs possibly even increased. Much depends on the final charging structure, the weighting of charges on the size of the bargain, the division between broker and jobber and the countrywide operation of the system.

The future potential of TALISMAN is almost more exciting than the immediate effect of its introduction. While in the short term the system will be seen to have its greatest effect in coping with substantially increased volumes of business without the attendant bottlenecks and staff problems, in the longer term it might well be developed to handle very large quantities of small business with the minimum of expense. The new Act permits a 'certificateless society'. As the computer print-out from SEPON is sufficient evidence of ownership to justify a bank loan on the holding as security, the small man's share shop might well result from this facility, with a relatively minor extension to the TALISMAN configuration.

The concept of a central registrar for the 200 or so companies which make up some 70 per cent of the turnover in the shares of listed companies may be considered as a further extension of the TALISMAN initiative.

FIXED-INTEREST SECURITIES

At 31 March 1964, institutions held just over two-thirds of outstanding debenture and loan stock issues by market value and almost 40 per cent of preference shares. New issues of debentures since that date have been subscribed primarily by pension and insurance funds. Between 1970 and 1976, out of a total of £5149 million raised for companies by way of new issues, only £165 million were in preference shares. The comment '*it seems likely, therefore, that the debenture market will remain largely institutional and that preference issues will become less frequent in the future*' has undoubtedly proved correct.

At the same time, the amount of capital raised for industry by means of sterling debenture issues has been declining rapidly, primarily due to the high interest rates caused by the substantial demands of Government. In an endeavour to increase the attraction of corporate debenture issues, The Stock Exchange made repeated requests to the Chancellor of the Exchequer to reduce or abolish the *ad valorem* stamp duty. The duty was finally eliminated in the Finance Act, 1976.

When long-term interest rates fall to a level at which companies can anticipate a reasonable degree of profitability from money borrowed in this way, it is likely that the debenture market will return to prominence as a means of raising finance for industry and commerce.

RESEARCH

Two points were made in this connection. *'Firms of stockbrokers will tend to become less and less general practitioners to their institutional clients and more and more specialists in one or two industrial sectors in which they gain a particular reputation. . . . It seems likely that the larger firms, with their computers or sharing them on a co-operative basis, will devote more of their research effort towards improving computer techniques.'*

The prime example of the development of computer systems for research has lain in the creation of DATAstream by a firm of stockbrokers—Hoare, Govett & Co. This system has now been sold to a commercial syndicate, so that its services are available to all firms of stockbrokers and to industrial, academic and Government subscribers.

NEW ISSUES

Attention was drawn to the role of the clearing banks, developing into the areas normally occupied by issuing houses in the provision of long-term capital for their customers. Just prior to the publication of the first edition of this book, the Westminster Bank sponsored its first industrial issue. Since then three of the major clearing banks have acquired or set up merchant banking subsidiaries—National Westminster (County Bank); Midland (Midland Montagu); and Barclays (Barclays Merchant Bank).

There is also a growing trend by companies towards using the services of not one firm of brokers but two or, in the case of very large concerns, three. Firms who specialise in the raising of capital for companies are sometimes deficient in the other services which their client corporations demand, and the joint broker concept may well accelerate in the future.

FOREIGN SECURITIES

Two misjudgements are now apparent in the emphasis placed in the section dealing with this area of activity. Although, in 1961, my own firm had arranged for a senior director of one of the leading Japanese firms to give a series of lectures in London and Edinburgh on the prospects for the Japanese market and had acted as one of the sponsoring brokers to the introduction of Honda Motor shares to the London market, I foresaw a much quicker and more dynamic future in the immediate absorption of the U.K. into the Common Market than in the development of the Far East. In the event, the U.K. was destined to remain outside the E.E.C. for almost a decade and the growth of the Japanese and Hong Kong markets over the period was far more dramatic.

The second misjudgement was to believe that New York would remain the traditional and sole financial centre for the floating of foreign bonds. Few people, I believe, could have foreseen the growth of the Eurocurrency market in London and the astonishing development of the Eurobond market. The imposition of the Interest Equalisation Tax in the U.S. under the Kennedy regime virtually closed the doors of New York to foreign borrowers and the bankers of London were not slow to take advantage in establishing an alternative.

FUTURE DEVELOPMENTS

So what of the future now? At the beginning of this chapter I stated that a detailed look at the pressures and opportunities demands a volume to itself. Political influences will so shape our future development that they require some analysis – self-regulation or a statutory body; the E.E.C. regulations on the Right of Establishment and the harmonisation of security markets; the opening of the New York Exchange to foreign membership; the examination of the Rules and Regulations of the Stock Exchange by the Office of Fair Trading; the declining role of the private saver and how the trend can be reversed. All these general questions deserve debate and discussion.

Technical advances in the securities industry also deserve a closer scrutiny: the operation of the Eurobond markets and how the stockbroker can fit into this market, which is dominated by the banks and international houses; the establishment of a European market in Traded Options in Amsterdam and the extensions to the existing options market in London; the use that can be made of options both by the private investor and by the institutions; money broking, and how this facility improves the liquidity of the London market; the management of liquidity for companies as an additional service offered by corporate finance departments.

Within the stockbroking industry itself, the lessons to be learnt from experience in merging disparate or complementary partnerships should at some time be put on record. The precarious balance between present happiness and the prospect of greater profitability, and the methods by which both may ultimately be obtained, is a crucial study in itself.

In the developing world, new Stock Exchanges are in the course of establishment. The Tehran Stock Exchange, with which I was involved at the planning stage, was elected an Associated Member of the Fédération Internationale de Bourses de Valeurs (FIBV) in 1976 and The Stock Exchange was pleased to be one of its proposers. For some years I have been involved in advising on the establishment of the Stock Exchange in Kuwait, and consulted on the reopening of a Stock Exchange in Djakarta. New Exchanges are planned in a number of different areas.

Stockbroking on an international scale seems destined to be one of the growth industries for the remainder of this century. London, with its tradition of trust and its fund of expertise, has an unparalleled opportunity to exploit its position in this field.

APPENDICES

Appendix 1a
Institutional Share of Market in U.K. Listed Ordinary Shares

	Holdings of listed ordinary shares in U.K. companies at 31 December 1973[1] *(market value)*		*Turnover (1st quarter 1974)*		*Turnover (2nd quarter 1976)*	
	£m.	%	£m.	%	£m.	%
Insurance companies:						
long-term funds	5760	14	370[2]	8	360[2]	9
general funds	790	2	70[2]	1	100[2]	3
Pension funds	4950	12	365[2]	8	685	17
Investment trust companies	2640	7	360	7	205	5
Unit trusts	1390	3	285	6	350	9
Total Institutions	15530	38	1450	30	1700	43
Other	24990	62	3365	70	2275	57
Total	40520	100	4815[3]	100	3975[3]	100

[1] *Source*: *Second Report of the Royal Commission on the Distribution of Income and Wealth* (1976).

[2] Estimates.

[3] Total Stock Exchange turnover in ordinary shares plus net issues of ordinary shares by U.K. listed public companies.

Appendix 1b
Institutional Assets and Share of the Market

(Assets held at end-1975)

Values	Insurance companies Life (Book)	Insurance companies General (Book)	Pension funds (Market)	Building societies (Book)	Investment trusts (Market)	Unit trusts (Market)	Property unit trusts (Book)	Trustee Savings Banks' special investment depts. (Market)	National Savings Bank investment account (Market)	Finance houses (Book)	Other[1] (Book)	£million Total
Cash and short-term assets (partly net)	950	817	1100	1683	323	251	87	131	57	–[2]	544	5943
British government securities:												
0–5 years	395	454	401	1746[3]	46[3]	9[3]	–	146[3]	52[3]	–	83	3333
over 5 years	5211	438	1766	382[3]	177[3]	22[3]	–	534[3]	323[3]	–	5	8858
U.K. local authority securities:												
Quoted }	559	119	{ 116	188	11	3	–	308	92	–	2 }	4061
Unquoted }			{ 201	1381	–	–	–	994	87	–	– }	
Overseas government, provincial and municipal securities	104	71	38	6	7	1	–	2	–	–	–	229
Company securities:												
Debenture and Loan	2617	167	835	–	167	24	–	–	–	–	32	3842
Preference	166	149	30	–	71	39	–	–	–	–	–	455
Ordinary	5062	963	7268	–	4847	2195	–	–	–	97[4]	98	20530

Values	Insurance companies Life (Book)	Insurance companies General (Book)	Pension funds (Market)	Building societies (Book)	Investment trusts (Market)	Unit trusts (Market)	Property unit trusts (Book)	Trustee Savings Banks' special investment depts. (Market)	National Savings Banks investment account (Market)	Finance houses (Book)	Other[1] (Book)	£million Total
Unit trust units	454	1	15	–	–	–	–	–	–	–	–	470
Loans and mortgages	3016	182	248	18882	–	–	–	–	–	153	915	23396
Land, property and ground rents	4350	437	2255[5]	308	–	–	292	–	–	–	22	7664
Hire-purchase debt	–	–	–	–	–	–	–	–	–	658	–	685
Other	459[6]	750[6]	149[7]	13	117	–	12	48	14	264[8]	94	1920
Total	23342	4548	14422	24589	5766	2544	391	2163	626	1199	1795	81385

1. Includes the Central Trustee Savings Bank, the Crown Agents, and the Special Finance Agencies.
2. Not available.
3. Nominal values.
4. Includes trade investments.
5. Includes £323 m. investment in property unit trusts.
6. Includes working capital of companies' agents.
7. Includes £84 m. investment by local authority pension funds in the Local Authorities Mutual Investment Trust.
8. Leased assets.

Appendix 1C
Acquisitions of assets during 1975

Values	Insurance companies Life	Insurance companies General	Pension funds	Building societies	Investment trusts	Unit trusts	Property unit trusts	Trustee Savings Banks' special investment depts.	National Savings Bank investment Account	Finance houses	Other[1]	£million Total
Cash and short-term assets (partly net)	−250	1	−314	−28	−281	−133	52	4	−9	−2[2]	158	−802
British government securities												
0–5 years	138	249	118	501	−8	−3	–	9	1	–	72	1077
Over 5 years	1011	205	812	140	84	6	–	22	–	–	–	2280
U.K. local authority securities:												
Quoted	} 53	25	{ 32	85	−14	–	–	−13	−1	–	1 }	901
Unquoted			{ −33	571	–	–	–	148	47	–	– }	
Overseas government, provincial and municipal seurities	14	14	18	–	−15	−1	–	–	–	–	–	30
Company securities:												
Debenture and loan	32	23	−11	–	15	–	–	–	–	–	−2	57
Preference	−3	23	16	–	2	13	–	–	–	–	−1	50
Ordinary	214	125	1187	–	182	329	–	–	–	13[3]	−2	2048
Unit trust units	75	–	–	–	–	–	–	–	–	–	–	75
Loans and mortgages	60	20	−15	2768	–	–	–	–	–	18	93	2944

Values	Insurance companies Life	General	Pension funds	Building societies	Investment trusts	Unit trusts	Property unit trusts	Trustee Savings Banks' special investment depts.	National Savings Banks investment Account	Finance houses	Other[1]	£ million Total
Land, property and ground rents	371	35	427	38	–	–	34	–	–	–	–	905
Hire purchase debt	–	–	–	–	–	–	–	–	–	−45	–	−45
Other	53	36	−1	–	−2	–	4	–	–	−3[4]	2	89
Total	1768	756	2236	4075	−37	211	90	170	38	−19	321	9609
(Rate growth % during 1975)[5]	(8.5)[6]	(20.8)[6]	(24.3)	(20.1)[6]	(−1.0)	(15.0)	(29.8)	(9.9)	(8.9)	(−1.7)[6]	(21.8)[6]	(15.0)

1. Includes the Central Trustee Savings Bank, the Crown Agents and the Special Finance Agencies.
2. Partial figure.
3. Includes trade investments.
4. Leasing.
5. Net acquisitions at cost as a proportion of total assets held at the beginning of 1975.
6. Calculated on book value of assets held at the beginning of 1975.

Appendix 2
Scale of Minimum Commissions

A. Securities quoted under the following headings in the Official List or the Official List—Irish:

(i) British Funds, &c.
Irish Government Funds

(1) Securities having no final redemption date within ten years

0.625%	on the first	£2,000 consideration
0.25%	on the next	£12,000 consideration
0.125%	on the next	£986,000 consideration
0.1%	on the next	£3,000,000 consideration
0.05%	on the next	£6,000,000 consideration
0.03%	on the excess	

(2) New Issues of British Funds

0.625%	on the first	£2,000 consideration
0.125%	on the next	£2,000 consideration
0.0625%	on the next	£996,000 consideration
0.05%	on the next	£9,000,000 consideration
0.03%	on the excess	

(3) Securities having ten years or less to final redemption

0.625%	on the first	£2,000 consideration
0.125%	on the next	£2,000 consideration
0.0625%	on the next	£996,000 consideration
0.05%	on the next	£3,000,000 consideration
0.025%	on the next	£6,000,000 consideration
0.015%	on the excess	

(4) Securities having five years or less to final redemption and not in default
At discretion

(ii) Securities issued by the International Bank for Reconstruction and Development
Securities issued by the Inter-American Development Bank
Corporation and County Stocks—Great Britain and Northern Ireland
Public Boards, &c.—Great Britain and Northern Ireland
Commonwealth Government and Provincial Securities
Commonwealth Corporation Stocks
Irish Land Bonds
Irish Corporation Stocks and Public Boards

(1) Securities having no final redemption date within ten years
0.625% on the first £2,000 consideration
0.25% on the next £12,000 consideration
0.125% on the excess

BARGAINS SUBJECT TO RULE 208
0.1% on the consideration over £1,000,000 up to £4,000,000
0.05% on the consideration over £4,000,000 up to £10,000,000
0.03% on the excess over £10,000,000 consideration

(2) Securities having ten years or less to final redemption
0.625% on the first £2,000 consideration
0.125% on the next £2,000 consideration
0.0625% on the excess

BARGAINS SUBJECT TO RULE 208
0.05 on the consideration over £1,000,000 up to £4,000,000
0.025% on the consideration over £4,000,000 up to £10,000,000
0.015% on the excess over £10,000,000 consideration

(3) Securities having five years or less to final redemption and not in default
At discretion

B. Debentures, Bonds, &c.

Debentures and Bonds and any other securities representing loans (Debenture Stocks, Loan Stocks, Notes, Annuities, &c.) other than those included in Section A above

(1) Registered*

0.75%	on the first	£5,000	consideration
0.375%	on the next	£45,000	consideration
0.325%	on the next	£50,000	consideration
0.3%	on the next	£150,000	consideration
0.25%	on the next	£500,000	consideration
0.2%	on the next	£1,000,000	consideration
0.125%	on the excess		

* Including New Issues passing by delivery in scrip form or by letters of renunciation.

(2) Bearer

0.5%	on the first	£5,000	consideration
0.25%	on the excess		

(3) Euro-Currency Bonds i.e. Fixed Income Securities (excluding Preferred Stock and Preference Share Capital) including Convertible Securities carrying a fixed rate of interest issued after 1 January, 1963, on which capital moneys are payable in a foreign currency listed below and, except in the case of Japanese issues, the interest on which is payable without deduction of tax at source.

U.S. Dollars (external)	French Francs
Dutch Florins	Luxembourg Francs
Italian Lire	Belgian Francs
Deutsche Marks	Swiss Francs
Sterling/Deutsche Marks	E.U.A. (European Units of Account)

At discretion

(4) Fixed Interest securities issued by or guaranteed by any Foreign Government, Government Institution or Public Authority, payable in the currency of the country of the borrower

0.6%	on the first	£5,000	consideration
0.25%	on the next	£15,000	consideration
0.2%	on the next	£5,000	consideration
0.15%	on the next	£75,000	consideration
0.125%	on the excess		

provided that

In the case of an individual order specified at the time of origin and exceeding £250,000 consideration for the same Principal a Broker may in transacting such order charge commission at 0.125% on the entire amount.

(5) Other Loans quoted in London expressed or optionally payable in a foreign currency other than that of a Scheduled Territory
0.25% on consideration

C. Stocks and Shares

Stocks and Shares Registered or Bearer (other than those in Sections A, B or D) whether partly or fully paid

1.5%	on the first	£7,000 consideration
0.5%	on the next	£93,000 consideration
0.4%	on the next	£150,000 consideration
0.3%	on the next	£500,000 consideration
0.2%	on the next	£1,000,000 consideration
0.125%	on the excess	

D. American and Canadian Shares

Shares of Companies incorporated in the United States of America or Canada (whether dealt in in London on a Dollar or Sterling basis), with the exception of Shares which are deliverable by Transfer

0.9%	on the first	£5,000 consideration
0.4%	on the next	£5,000 consideration
0.3%	on the excess	

E. Short-Dated Securities

Securities having five years or less to final redemption and not in default
At discretion

F. (1) **Unlisted units of Unit Trusts**
At discretion

(2) **Listed Units of Unit Trusts except those marked ◪ in the Official List**
(a) Purchases
(i) From the Market
1.25% on the first £7,000 consideration, and thereafter at the rates laid down in Section C
(ii) From Managers of Unit Trusts
At discretion

(b) Sales
At discretion.

(3) **Listed Units of Unit Trusts marked in the Official List with the following symbol ◪**
All purchases and sales—At the rates laid down in Section C

G. Options

'Givers' of option money for more than one Account
As laid down in Rule 210 (1)
'Takers' of option money for more than one Account
As laid down in Rule 210 (5)
Options for one Account or less
At discretion

H. Small Bargains	Securities in SECTION A	Securities in all other Sections
The minimum commission to be charged shall be	£4	£7
except in the case of		
(1) Transactions on which the Commission may be	at discretion	at discretion
(2) Transactions amounting to less than £200 in value on which commission may be	at discretion	at discretion

I. Valuations

(1) Probate Valuations
Under £5,000
At discretion
£5,000 or over
0.05% on the Probate value up to £100,000
0.0125% on the balance, subject to a minimum charge of 50p per item.

(2) All other valuations
At discretion

Appendix 3
Listings on The Stock Exchange

	All securities officially listed at 31 March 1977			Applications for listing granted in the year to 31 March 1977		
	Number of securities	*Nominal amount (£m.)*	*Market valuation (£m.)*	*Number of securities*	*Nominal amount (£m.)*	*Proceeds received by issuing undertaking (£m.)*
1. British, Irish and Government and Government-guaranteed	150	44,129	38,321	10	8,300	8,103
2. Local authority and public boards	866	3,108	2,748	1,671	1,145	1,137
3. Commonwealth Government, provincial and municipal.	73	418	302	–	–	–
4. Foreign stocks, bonds and corporation stocks	432	4,316	3,703	61	1,374	813
5. Loan Capital	2,257	6,924	4,763			
6. Preference and preferred	1,531	1,255	812	1,391	3,321	1,626
7. U. K. ordinary and deferred	2,597	13,523	48,538			
8. Overseas ordinary and deferred	473	14,681	194,128			

Source: The Stock Exchnage.

Appendix 4
Charges for Listing on The Stock Exchange

Initial Charges

(No charge is made for applications for conversion into stock units, unnumbering, or applications arising out of change of name, denomination, dividend rights, or exercise of conversion or option rights.)

1. A charge will be made for securities to be admitted to the sections of the Official List set out below in accordance with the following scale:—

   British Funds.
   Corporation and County Stocks.—Great Britain and Northern Ireland.
   Public Boards, etc.—Great Britain and Northern Ireland.
   Commonwealth Government and Provincial Securities.
   Commonwealth Corporation Stocks.

   (a) Having a life of two years or less . . . . Nil
   (b) Having a life of over two years but not over five years: . . . . One-half of Scale (c)

   (c) Having a life of over five years:

Money value not exceeding	£1,000,000	. .	£400
,, ,, ,, ,,	£5,000,000	. .	£750
,, ,, ,, ,,	£10,000,000	. .	£1,000
,, ,, ,, ,,	£50,000,000	. .	£1,500
,, ,, ,, ,,	£100,000,000	. .	£2,000
,, ,, exceeding	£100,000,000	. .	£3,000

2. In the case of securities having a money value not exceeding £100,000, a charge will be made for securities to be admitted to the Official List (other than to a section referred to in paragraph 1 above) in accordance with the following scale:—

Money value not exceeding	£5,000	.. ..	Nil
,, ,, ,, ,,	£20,000	.. ..	£10
,, ,, ,, ,,	£50,000	.. ..	£20
,, ,, ,, ,,	£100,000	.. ..	£50

3. A charge will be made for securities to be admitted to the Official List other than those referred to in paragraph 1 above involving a money value in excess of £100,000:—

(a) Category I.

In the case of securities issued as a result of prospectuses, offers for sale, placings, introductions, rights, open offers, reconstructions and vendor consideration, a charge will be made on admission to the official list in accordance with the following scale:—

Money value not exceeding	£200,000	..	£100
,, ,, ,, ,,	£400,000	..	£250
,, ,, ,, ,,	£600,000	..	£350
,, ,, ,, ,,	£800,000	..	£450
,, ,, ,, ,,	£1,000,000	..	£600
,, ,, ,, ,,	£2,500,000	..	£1,000
,, ,, ,, ,,	£5,000,000	..	£1,500
,, ,, ,, ,,	£10,000,000	..	£2,000
,, ,, ,, ,,	£20,000,000	..	£2,750
,, ,, ,, ,,	£30,000,000	..	£3,500
,, ,, ,, ,,	£50,000,000	..	£4,500
,, ,, ,, ,,	£75,000,000	..	£5,750
,, ,, ,, ,,	£100,000,000	..	£7,000
,, ,, exceeding	£100,000,000	..	£8,500

(b) Category II.

In the case of securities issued as a result of capitalisations, conversions and further issues of identical securities not included in Category I. Listing charges will be one-half of the scale for Category I.

In the case of issues of debt securities denominated in a foreign currency by all companies or organisations wherever domiciled, the Council are prepared to consider applications for a reduction in the prescribed charges for listing of one-half of those included in paragraph (a) above.

Annual Charges

Except in the case of a security listed in the sections of the Official List referred to in paragraph 1, an annual charge will be made for each company, corporation or authority in accordance with the following scale:—

Nominal value of listed equity not exceeding	£1,000,000	..	£250
,, ,, ,, ,, ,, ,, ,,	£2,000,000	..	£350
,, ,, ,, ,, ,, ,, ,,	£3,000,000	..	£450
,, ,, ,, ,, ,, ,, ,,	£4,000,000	..	£550
,, ,, ,, ,, ,, ,, ,,	£5,000,000	..	£650
,, ,, ,, ,, ,, ,, ,,	£7,500,000	..	£800
,, ,, ,, ,, ,, ,, ,,	£10,000,000	..	£1,000
,, ,, ,, ,, ,, exceeding	£10,000,000	..	£1,500
Where fixed income securities only are listed	.. .. ..	..	£250

In the case of foreign companies or organisations the charge will be one-half of the scale.

NOTE:—Where the money value of an issue is in doubt it will be fixed by the Committee for the purposes of this Table.

Appendix 5
Contents of a Prospectus

SUMMARY OF INFORMATION—OFFER FOR SALE OF SHARE CAPITAL

	Reference Companies Acts, 1948 and 1967	*Reference Appendix 34**
1. Statement that the document gives details of the Company in compliance with the Regulations of The Stock Exchange and that the directors collectively and individually accept responsibility for statements made.		16
2. Statement that a copy of prospectus and supporting documents has been sent to Registrar of Companies.	S 41	
3. Statement that application has been made to The Stock Exchange for permission to deal in and for quotation for issue.		7
4. Date and time of opening of application lists.	Fourth Sch. 5	
5. Company's full name, date and country of incorporation, registered number and authority under which it was incorporated.		15, 24 & 26
6. Authorised and issued or agreed to be issued share capital, amount paid up, description and nominal value of shares. Where 10% or more of capital is unissued a statement that no issue		18

* Rules and Regulations of The Stock Exchange.

	Reference Companies Acts, 1948 and 1967	*Reference Appendix 34*
altering the control of the company will be made without shareholders' approval.		
7. Loan capital and outstanding indebtedness of company and subsidiaries, including bank overdrafts, guarantees, mortgages, liabilities under acceptances or acceptance credits, charges, hire purchase commitments and any material contingent liabilities.		19
8. Voting rights of single-class capital, and, in cases where there is more than one class of share, voting rights of shareholders and rights to dividend, capital, redemption and issue of further shares, with consents to variation of rights.	Fourth Sch. 17	25
9. Terms of offer for sale, followed by instructions for application and conditions of allotment.	Fourth Sch. 6	
10. Full name, address and description of all directors.	Fourth Sch. 3	20
11. Name, and address of auditors (and reporting accountants).	Fourth Sch. 15	23
12. Name and address of bankers, solicitors, brokers, registrars and trustees (if any).		22
13. Full name and qualification of secretary, and address of registered office and transfer office.		21
14. *History and Business*		
The general nature of the business, including the date business commenced, the relative importance of different activities (if applicable) and details of existing and projected subsidiaries.	Fourth Sch. 18	28, 30 & 32
A statement showing the sales turnover figures for the past five		

	Reference Companies Acts, 1948 and 1967	*Reference Appendix 34*
years, containing a reasonable breakdown between the more important activities.		
15. *Management and Labour*		
Statement usually including age and length of service of directors, service contracts, number of employees and other details covering continuity of management and labour relations, including pension arrangements.		42
16. *Plant and Premises*		
Situation, area of factories and other main buildings, with details of tenure, freeholds, leaseholds, etc. (in the case of property companies a special layout is required.)		29
17. *Working Capital*		
A statement that, in the opinion of the directors, working capital is sufficient, and if not, proposals to provide for same. Where new money is being raised by this issue of ordinary shares, or has been so raised during the past two years, an estimate of the proceeds of the issue and an indication of their application.	Fourth Sch. 4 & S. 45	32 & 33
18. *Accountants' Report*		
A report signed by the auditors, including:		
(*a*) *Profits*. Five-year profits record (or less if incorporated more recently), both for parent company and (if applicable) group; notes to this paragraph usually include: (i) the aggregate directors' emoluments during the last year and the amount payable under the arrangements in force	Fourth Sch. 19	34

	Reference Companies Acts, 1948 and 1967	*Reference Appendix 34*
at the date of the prospectus; (ii) details of overseas interests (where material) with the basis on which foreign currencies and taxation have been dealt with, and any restrictions on remittance of funds.		
(*b*) *Assets and Liabilities.* Figures at the date of last balance-sheet for both parent company and group, including an explanation of the bases used for the valuations of fixed assets and a reasonably detailed indication of the nature of the tangible assets.	Fourth Sch. 19	34
(*c*) *Intended Purchase.* If proceeds of issue to be used in purchase of business or shares in a company, a separate report on the profits of the business or company for the last five years, and of its assets and liabilities.	Fourth Sch. 20–21	35
(*d*) *Dividends.* Dividend record on each class of share for five years (or less as in (a) above).	Fourth Sch. 19	34
(*e*) *Accounts.* If date of last accounts earlier than three months before the date of the prospectus, a statement that no subsequent accounts have been made up.		
19. *Profits, Prospects and Dividends* A statement of current trading with an indication, in the absence of unforeseen circumstances, of the outlook for profits and dividends. Where a profit forecast is made, this must be supported by reporting accountants	Fourth Sch. 19	31

	Reference Companies Acts, 1948 and 1967	*Reference Appendix 34*
and the issuing house or sponsoring broker.		
20. *Capital Issues*		
Particulars of any capital of the Company or any of its subsidiaries issued during the past two years for a consideration other than cash.	Fourth Sch. 8	36
Particulars of any capital of the Company or any of its subsidiaries issued during the past two years on a deferred or partly-paid basis.	Fourth Sch. 8	37
21. *General Information*		
(*a*) Particulars of any issue or change of capital of the company or its subsidiaries within past two years.	Fourth Sch.	30 & 40
(*b*) Particulars of acquisitions within past two years by means of issuance of shares or for cash, with details of directors' interest and goodwill element.	10	
(*c*) Names and shareholdings of substantial or controlling shareholders, or a negative statement. Details of holdings of directors and their families distinguishing between beneficial and other interests.	1	41
(*d*) Particulars of present promotion, with consideration of any benefit paid to promoter currently and within past two years.	13	43
(*e*) Particulars of preliminary expenses and expenses of issue.	12	39
(*f*) Statement that no part of proceeds of issue is payable to company, if applicable.		
(*g*) Particulars of capital under op-	7	38

	Reference Companies Acts, 1948 and 1967	*Reference Appendix 34*
tion and any commissions, discounts, brokerages or other special terms granted.		
(*h*) Statement of surtax clearance and indemnity as to surtax and estate duties, where applicable.		47 & 48
(*i*) *Articles of Association* Details of relevant provisions including those governing:		26
(i) Power of directors to vote remuneration to themselves, or proposals, arrangements or contracts in which they are materially interested.		
(ii) Retirement of directors under an age-limit.	Fourth Sch. 2	
(iii) Borrowing powers.		
(iv) Directors' qualifying share-holdings.		
(*j*) *Contracts* (not being contracts entered into in the ordinary course of business). All material contracts entered into during the past two years, by company and subsidiaries. Particulars of any consideration (concerning these contracts) passing to and from the company.	Fourth Sch. 14	49
(*k*) Statement that a Certificate of Exemption has been given by Stock Exchange, where applicable. (This allows certain variations from the full provisions of the Fourth Schedule of the Act where it may prove unduly burdensome owing to the size of the issue, number of possible applicants, etc.)	S. 39	
(*l*) Details of any claim or litigation		44

	Reference Companies Acts, 1948 and 1967	*Reference Appendix 34*
pending, or a statement that there is none.		
(*m*) Statement that no long-service agreements will prevent disposal of management.		
(*n*) Declaration that no other capital issues have been made; options granted; commissions, brokerages, or other special terms granted within past two years.	11	38 & 40
(*o*) Statement that any experts contributing to the prospectus (normally accountants and surveyors) have given and have not withdrawn their consent to the issue of the prospectus and to the inclusion of their report.	S. 40	46
(*p*) A statement that copies of all relevant documents supporting the prospectus may be examined for a period of not less than fourteen days at a place within the City of London.		50
(*q*) The address(es) at which copies of the prospectus may be obtained.		
22. The date.		

ADVERTISEMENT—PLACING OR INTRODUCTION

The principal difference from the prospectus issued with an offer for sale is that, in place of Paragraph 3 of the prospectus mentioned above, a statement is made that the advertisement is issued in compliance with the regulations of The Stock Exchange, and that the directors accept full responsibility for the accuracy of the information given and also confirm that nothing relevant has been omitted (App. 34 (18)).

PROSPECTUS—ISSUE OF LOAN CAPITAL

In addition to the details included where applicable in the issue of ordinary shares, a prospectus covering the issue of loan capital will normally include, prior to the paragraph dealing with Future Prospects in the main body of the prospectus, paragraphs describing the use to which the proceeds of the issue will be placed; the asset cover; and the interest cover of the stock.

A complete section will also be devoted to particulars of the stock, quoting the provisions of the trust deed and giving the date of the resolution by which the directors created the stock (App. 34 (27)).

The main provisions which are quoted will normally include the following:

1. *Definitions*
   Definitions of the principal terms in the deed, of which the 'Adjusted Total of Capital and Reserves' and the 'Borrowings' may be the two most important.

2. *Security*
   A description of the charge on the assets (floating or specific).

3. *Redemption*
   The terms of redemption with details of sinking fund, if any.

4. *Security for Temporary Borrowings*
   Details of floating charges which the company may create on their undertakings for securing temporary borrowings (normally bank overdrafts).

5. *Further Issues of Stock*
   Details of the provisions under which the company may issue stock ranking *pari passu* in point of security.

6. *Undertakings by the Company*
   Details of action which cannot be taken by the company without the sanction either of the trustees or of an extraordinary resolution, usually a series of negative pledges by the company in respect of the size of aggregate borrowings, and prior or *pari passu* borrowings, the disposal of all or a substantial part of the undertaking, and the borrowing and issuance of shares by the subsidiaries.

Appendix 6
Listing Agreements—Companies

. . . . (name of company) The following is an extract from the minutes of a meeting of the board of directors held the . . . . day of . . . .
19 . . . . . .

In compliance with the requirements of the Council of The Stock Exchange, it was resolved that the company agrees (all such agreements to be read and construed in accordance with and subject to the notes to the Listing Agreement currently appearing in Chapter 2 of the document 'Admission of Securities to Listing' published by The Stock Exchange) as follows:—

1. To notify the Department in advance of the date fixed for any board meeting at which the declaration or recommendation or payment of a dividend is expected to be determined upon, or at which any announcement of the profits or losses in respect of any financial period or part thereof is to be approved for publication.
2. To notify the Department immediately after the relevant board meeting has been held of:—
   (a) any preliminary profits announcements for any year, half-year or other period;
   (b) all dividends and other distributions to members recommended or declared or resolved to be paid and of any decision to pass any dividend or interest payment;
   (c) short particulars of any proposed change in the capital structure, or redemption of securities.
3. To notify to the Press the basis of allotment of securities in prospectus and other offers and, if applicable, in respect of excess applications, such notice to appear not later than the morning of the business day next after the allotment letters or other relevant documents of title are posted.
4. To notify the Department without delay of:—
   (a) particulars of any material acquisitions or realisations of assets comprised in the definition set out in the Chapter on Acquisitions

and Realisations contained in 'Admission of Securities to Listing';

(b) any information required to be disclosed to The Stock Exchange under the provisions of The City Code on Take-overs and Mergers;

(c) any changes in the directorate;

(d) any proposed change in the general character or nature of the business of the company or of the group;

(e) any information required to be notified to the company under Section 33 of the Companies Act 1967 (or which would be so required if the company were subject to the provisions of that Act);

(f) any change in the status of the company under the close company provisions of the Income and Corporation Taxes Act 1970 (and of any amendments thereto);

(g) any other information necessary to enable the shareholders and the public to appraise the position of the company and to avoid the establishment of a false market in its securities.

5. To send with the notice convening a meeting of holders of securities to all persons entitled to vote thereat proxy forms with provision for two-way voting on all resolutions intended to be proposed.

6. To forward to the Department copies of:—

(a) proofs for approval (through the company's brokers), of all circulars to holders of securities, notices of meetings, forms of proxy and notices by advertisement to holders of bearer securities;

(b) all circulars, notices, reports, announcements or other documents at the same time as they are issued;

(c) all resolutions passed by the company other than resolutions concerning routine business at an annual general meeting.

7. To notify the Department of an explanation for the delay in any case where no annual report and accounts have been issued by the company within the six months following the date of the end of the financial period to which they relate, at the same time indicating when it is expected that such report and accounts will be published.

8. To prepare a half-yearly or interim report which must be sent to the holders of securities or inserted as paid advertisements in two leading daily newspapers not later than six months from the date of the notice convening the annual general meeting of the company.

9. To circulate with the annual report of the directors.:—

(a) a statement by the directors as to the reasons for adopting an alterative basis of accounting in any case where the auditors have stated that the accounts are not drawn up in accordance with the standard accounting practices approved by the accountancy bodies;

(b) a geographical analysis of turnover and of contribution to trading results of those trading operations carried on by the company (or group) outside the United Kingdom;

(c) the name of the principal country in which each subsidiary operates;

(d) the following particulars regarding each company in which the group interest in the equity capital amounts to 20% or more:—

 (i) the principal country of operation;

 (ii) particulars of its issued share and loan capital and, except where the group's interest therein is dealt with in the consolidated balance sheet as an associated company, the total amount of its reserves;

 (iii) the percentage of each class of loan capital attributable to the company's interest (direct or indirect);

(e) a statement as at the end of the financial year showing the interests of each director in the share capital of the company appearing in the register maintained under the provisions of the Companies Act 1967 (or which would be required so to appear if the company were subject to the provisions of that Act), distinguishing between beneficial and non-beneficial interests; such statement should include by way of note any change in those interests occurring between the end of the financial year and a date not more than one month prior to the date of the notice of meeting or, if there has been no such change, disclosure of that fact;

(f) a statement showing particulars as at a date not more than one month prior to the date of the notice of meeting of an interest of any person, other than a director, in any substantial part of the share capital of the company and the amount of the interest in question or, where appropriate, a negative statement;

(g) (i) a statement showing whether or not, so far as the directors are aware, the close company provisions of the Income and Corporation Taxes Act 1970 (and of any amendments thereto) apply to the company and whether there has been any change in that respect since the end of the financial year;

 (ii) in the case of an investment trust a statement showing the status of the company under the provisions of the Income and Corporation Taxes Act 1970 (and of any amendments thereto) and of any change in that status since the end of the financial year;

(h) particulars of any contract subsisting during or at the end of the financial year in which a director of the company is or was materially interested and which is or was significant in relation to the company's business;

(i) particulars of any arrangement under which a director has waived or agreed to waive any emoluments;

(j) particulars of any arrangement under which a share-holder has waived or agreed to waive any dividends.

10. (a) To procure that any service contract granted by the company, or any subsidiary of the company, to any director or proposed director of the company not expiring or determinable within ten years by the employing company without payment of compensation (other than statutory compensation) must be made subject to the approval of the company in general meeting.

(b) To make available for inspection at the registered office or transfer office during usual business hours on any weekday (Saturdays and public holidays excluded) from the date of the notice convening the annual general meeting until the date of the meeting and to make available for inspection at the place of meeting for at least 15 minutes prior to the meeting and at the meeting copies of all service contracts, unless expiring or determinable within one year by the employing company without payment of compensation, of any director of the company with the company or any of its subsidiaries and, where any such contract is not reduced to writing, a memorandum of the terms thereof;

(c) To state in a note to the notice convening the annual general meeting that copies or, as the case may be, memoranda of all such service contracts will be available for inspection or, if there are no such contracts, to state that fact.

11. To certify transfers against certificates or temporary documents and to return them on the day of receipt or, should that not be a business day, on the first business day following their receipt and to split and return renounceable documents within the same period.

12. To register transfers and other documents without payment of any fee.

13. To issue, without charge, certificates within:—

(a) one month of the date of expiration of any right of renunciation;

(b) 14 days of the lodgment of transfers.

14. To arrange for designated accounts if requested by holders of securities.

15. Where warrants to bearer have been issued or are available for issue; (i) to issue certificates in exchange for warrants (and vice versa, if permitted) within 14 days of the deposit of the warrants (or certificates); and (ii) to certify transfers against the deposit of warrants.

16. In the absence of circumstances which have been agreed by the Council to be exceptional to obtain the consent of the company in general meeting prior to issuing for cash:—

(a) equity capital or capital having an equity element.

(b) securities convertible into equity capital, or

(c) warrants or options to subscribe for equity capital;
otherwise than to the equity shareholders of the company and, where appropriate, holders of other equity securities of the company entitled thereto.

17. In the event of a circular being issued to the holders of any particular class of security, to issue a copy or summary of such circular to the holders of all other listed securities unless the contents of such circular are irrelevant to such other holders.

I hereby certify that the above is a true and correct extract from the minutes of the board.

Secretary

Appendix 7
Dealing in Australia

STOCK EXCHANGES

Australian Associated Stock Exchanges
Adelaide; Brisbane; Hobart; Melbourne; Perth; Sydney.

RECOGNISED STOCK EXCHANGES

Ballarat, Vic.; Bendigo, Vic.; Newcastle, N.S.W.

PRINCIPAL STOCK EXCHANGES

The Stock Exchange of Melbourne; The Sydney Stock Exchange Ltd.

SECURITIES LISTED

A.A.S.E. at 30 June 1976.

	No. of issues	*Nominal value ($A million)*	*Market value ($A million)*
Commonwealth Government securities	88	14,500	12,400
Semi-Government and public authorities	1,329	1,157	1,025
Fixed-interest securities	936	2,808	2,537
Common and other stock issues	2,242	7,614	19,609
	4, 595	26,079	35,571

SYSTEM

Trading-post.

HOURS OF TRADING

10.00 a.m. – 12 noon
2.00 p.m. – 3.00 p.m.

TRANSACTIONS

Marketable parcels are designated by the Australian Associated Stock Exchanges as follows:

1. Shares, Share Options or Convertible Loan Securities-
   1,000 where the price does not exceed 25 cents

500	where the price exceeds	25¢ but does not exceed	50¢
100	" " " "	50¢ " " " "	$ 5
50	" " " "	$ 5 " " " "	$ 10
20	" " " "	$ 10 " " " "	$ 25
10	" " " "	$ 25 " " " "	$ 50
5	" " " "	$ 50 " " " "	$100
2	" " " "	$100 " " " "	$250
1	" " " "	$250	

2. Rights to a New Issue –

100	where the price does not exceed	$ 5	
50	where the price exceeds	$ 5 but does not exceed	$ 10
20	" " " "	$ 10 " " " "	$ 25
10	" " " "	$ 25 " " " "	$ 50
5	" " " "	$ 50	

3. Company Loan Securities (non-convertible). Commonwealth Loans & Public Securities – $ 100.

Odd lots are traded through the odd-lot specialist.

EXPENSES

(a) Stamp Duties on Market Transactions

The following rates apply to transactions in listed marketable securities by members of the Australian Associated Stock Exchanges. These rates are payable by both buyers and sellers. The appropriate legislation in each State should be consulted for full particulars of all exemptions from duty.

(1) Where the consideration exceeds $ 100 – for every $ 100 or part of $ 100 30¢

(2) Where the consideration is less than $ 100 – for every $ 25 or part of $ 25 7¢

* In Western Australia the transaction duty is slightly different where the consideration is less than $ 100. Where the consideration –

Does not exceed $ 25	8¢
Exceeds $ 25, but does not exceed $ 50	15¢
Exceeds $ 50, but does not exceed $ 75	23¢
Exceeds $ 75, but is less than $ 100	30¢

NOTE: In P. N. G. transaction duty is as follows:

Where the consideration exceeds $ 100 – For every $ 100 or part of $ 100 50¢

Where the consideration is less than $ 100 – For every $ 10 or part of $10 5¢

Details of stamp duties on transfers for transactions through persons other than A. A. S. E. Member Firms and/or non-market transactions together with A. A. S. E. rates of brokerage are available in the Location of Share Registers published by The Sydney Stock Exchange Limited Research and Statistics Department.

(b) A. A. S. E. Rates of Brokerage

Listed Companies

Rates of brokerage on shares, capital stock, rights to new issues, share options or convertible loan securities in companies listed on a Recognised Stock Exchange (except as hereinafter provided) shall be

(a) On each order given at the one time to buy or sell on behalf of the one beneficial interest, securities in the one company of the same class and paid up value–

(1) $5.00 and

(2) (a) on the first $5,000 of consideration — 2.5%
(b) on the next $10,000 of consideration — 2.0%
(c) on the next $35,000 of consideration — 1.5%
(d) on that amount by which the consideration exceeds $50,000 — 1.0%

In the case of an order to purchase rights to a new issue consideration means the sum of the purchase price of the rights and the minimum application money payable PROVIDED that the concessional rates in clause (2) (b), (c) and (d) above shall apply only–

(i) on that part of the order completed within one calendar month from the date of the first transaction carried out against the order. The balance of the uncompleted order shall after one calendar month from the date of the first transaction be deemed to be a new order, and

(ii) in the case of an order to buy comprising both shares and rights to a new issue provided that the money payable on application for the new issue would make the shares arising from the issue of the same paid up value as the quoted shares.

PROVIDED FURTHER that in the case of a selling order when the consideration is less than $25 total brokerage shall be $2.00.

(b) When a client gives an order at the one time to re-sell or re-purchase securities which is completed within one calendar month of the date on which the purchase or sale of those securities was made, the following rates shall apply to the re-sale or re-purchase as the case may be–

(i) $ 5.00 and
(ii) (a) on the first $ 5,000 of consideration 1.25%
(b) on the next $ 10,000 of consideration 1.0%
(c) on the next $ 35,000 of consideration 0.75%
(d) on that amount by which the consideration exceeds $50,000 0.5%

PROVIDED THAT for any balance of an order to re-sell or re-purchase uncompleted within one calendar month, brokerage shall be charged at the rate set out in clause (a) and the order shall have the benefit of concessional rates provided in that clause if applicable.

PROVIDED FURTHER that the concessional rates in clause (b) above shall only apply when the client, unless otherwise arranged has within five business days of the date of the original transaction made payment in full of the purchase price and other charges for the securities or settlement of the sale has been effected.

Unlisted Companies

Rates of brokerage on shares, capital stock, rights to new issues, share options or convertible loan securities in companies not listed on a Recognised Stock Exchange (except as hereinafter provided) shall be –
(a) $ 5.00 and
(b) double the rates applicable under sub-clause (a) (ii)
PROVIDED that when the consideration involved in a transaction is $ 20,000 or more and the beneficial ownership is vested in the one person then the ordinary rates shall apply.

Company Loan Securities (Non-Convertible)

Rates of brokerage in respect of company loan securities (non-convertible) on the paid up value of the securities shall be –

(a) *Short Term*
When the date of sale or purchase is within one year immediately preceding the maturity date 0.25%

(b) *Long Term*
When the date of the sale or purchase is not within one year immediately preceding the maturity date –
(i) on the first $ 10,000 paid up value 1.0%
(ii) on that amount by which the paid up value exceeds $ 10,000 0.5%

Commonwealth Loans

Rates of brokerage in respect of securities issued by the Commonwealth of Australia on the face value of the security shall be –

(a) *Short Term*
When the date of the sale or purchase is within five years immediately preceding the maturity date of the security –

(i)	on the first $ 10,000 – face value	0.25%
(ii)	on the amount by which the face value exceeds $ 10,000	0.125%

PROVIDED THAT on any one order with any client which is not less than $25,000 in face value and of the same series, no fixed rates of brokerage shall apply.

(b) *Long Term*
When the date of the sale or purchase is not within five years immediately preceding the maturity date of the security

(i)	on the first $ 50,000 – face value	0.25%
(ii)	on the next $ 50,000 – face value	0.125%
(iii)	on the next $ 100,000 – face value	0.05%
(iv)	on the amount by which the face value exceeds $ 200,000	0.025%

PROVIDED THAT the concessional rates in clause (a) sub-clause (ii) and clause (b) sub-clause (ii), (iii) and (iv) above shall apply only in respect of any sale or sales purchase or purchases (as the case may be) when there is an order given at the one time on behalf of the one beneficial interest –

(i) when the date of the sale or purchase is within ten business days after the date on which the first transaction was carried out against the order, and

(ii) provided that short term securities under clause (a) and long term securities under clause (b) above shall be aggregated separately.

(c) When the value of the securities of any one issue in either clause (a) or (b) above is not more than $ 80, 10¢ for each $ 20.

(d) When a member initiates a transaction with the Reserve Bank of Australia, no brokerage shall be charged against the Bank.

(e) When a member executes an order on behalf of the Commonwealth Treasury other Commonwealth Departments or the Reserve Bank of Australia –

(i) *Short Term*
When the date of sale or purchase is within five years immediately preceding the maturity date of the security –

on the first $ 10,000 face value	0.25%

on the next $ 40,000 face value 0.125%
on the next $ 50,000 face value 0.0625%
on the next $ 100,000 face value 0.025%
on the amount by which the face value exceeds
$ 200,000 0.0125%

(ii) *Long Term*
When the date of the sale or purchase is not within five years immediately preceding the maturity date of the security –
on the first $ 50,000 face value 0.25%
on the next $ 50,000 face value 0.125%
on the next $ 100,000 face value 0.05%
on the amount by which the face value exceeds
$ 200,000 0.025%

(iii) The concessional rates in clause (e) sub-clauses (i) and (ii) above are subject to the same proviso as sub-clauses (a) and (b) hereof.

Public Securities

Rates of brokerage in respect of securities classified as 'public securities' within the meaning of the Income Tax Assessment Act (other than securities issued by the Commonwealth of Australia) on the paid up value of the security shall be –

(a) *Short Term*
When the date of the sale or purchase is within one year immediately preceding the maturity date –
(i) on the first $ 10,000 . . 0.25%
(ii) on that amount by which the paid up value exceeds $ 10,000 . . 0.125%

(b) *Long Term*
When the date of the sale or purchase is not within one year immediately preceding the maturity date . . 0.25%

(c) On any one transaction with any client which includes a sale or purchase of Semi-Government securities which are approved investments by the Reserve Bank for Authorised Short Term Money Market Dealers with a maturity not exceeding five years and which is not less than $ 25,000 in face value and of the same series no fixed rates of brokerage shall apply.

Put And Call Options

On options for the sale or purchase of issued shares or stock in companies listed on a Recognised Stock Exchange brokerage shall be due and payable –

(1) by the writer of an option . . if and when the option is exercised and
(2) by the purchases of an option . . one half on the granting of the option

and the balance if and when the option is exercised.
at the following rates on each order given at the one time to write or purchase an option for the sale or purchase of issued shares or stock of the one class and paid up value –

(a) $ 5.00 and
(b) (i) on the first $ 5,000 consideration based on the exercise price 2.5%
(ii) on the next $ 10,000 consideration based on the exercise price 2.0%
(iii) on the next $ 35,000 consideration based on the exercise price 1.5%
(iv) on that amount by which consideration based on the exercise price exceeds $ 50,000 1.0%

Exchange Traded Call Options

On contracts traded on the Australian Options Market of the exchange on both opening and closing, buying and selling transactions in option contracts in the one class for the one beneficial interest.
A on the first $ 5,000 of premium 2.5%
B on the next $ 10,000 of premium 2.0%
C on the next $ 35,000 of premium 1.5%
D on that amount by which the premium exceeds $ 50,000 – 1.0%

PROVIDED THAT on each transaction a minimum commission of $ 20.00 shall be charged.

SETTLEMENT

Transactions for cash, bank cheque or through a bank. For foreign clients, however, 'overseas delivery' can be specified giving up to six weeks' delay in delivery.

DELIVERY

With the exception of Government and semi-Government bonds, all securities are registered. There are advantages in utilising an Australian nominee company, since rights issues are frequent and often made at par.

SAFE KEEPING

Safe-deposit boxes available at city branches and large suburban branches of all banks. Annual rental up to $A 20.
Safe custody of sealed envelopes and small packages available to customers only – no fee.

Appendix 8
Dealing in Austria

STOCK EXCHANGE
Vienna

SECURITIES LISTED AT 31 DECEMBER 1976

	No. of issues	*Nominal value*	*Market value*
		(million schillings)	
Government securities	140		
Municipal and public boards	50	207,607	207,000
Bond issues	920		
Common and other stock issues	87	8,400	23,300
Foreign issues	30	n.a.	n.a.

SYSTEM
Transactions are arranged by 'Sensale' as intermediaries.

HOURS OF BUSINESS
11.30 a.m.–1 p.m., Monday to Friday.

EXPENSES

	National and foreign	
	Non-banker %	*Banker* %
(*a*) *Bonds*		
Sensal's commission	0.1	0.1
Banker's commission	0.5	0.25
	0.6	0.35
(*b*) *Shares*		
Sensal's commission	0.175	0.175
Banker's commission	0.775	0.375
	0.95	0.55

(*c*) *Unit Trust Certificates* issued by Osterreichische Investmentgesellschaft m.b.H., if listed.

Sensal's commission	0.175	0.175
Banker's commission	0.425	0.125
	0.6	0.3

	(Schillings)	
(a)–(c) Minimum commission for small orders	7.00	5.00
(However, the commission may not amount to more than 5% of the total amount)		

(*d*) *Stock Exchange Turnover Tax*

	Dealer's transactions %	*Other than dealer's transactions* %
National Government, county and municipality bonds	0.02	0.04
Bank and railway bonds	0.03	0.06
Other bonds	0.05	0.1
Unit-trust certificates	0.06	0.12
Shares	0.075	0.15

SETTLEMENT

Settlement by means of a special stock-clearing office (Arrangementbüro).

TRANSFER

All bonds and nearly all stocks are bearer securities.

Appendix 9
Dealing in Belgium

STOCK EXCHANGES

Brussels; Antwerp; Ghent; Liège.

PRINCIPAL STOCK EXCHANGE

Brussels.

SECURITIES LISTED AT 31 DECEMBER 1976

	No. of issues	*Nominal value*	*Market value*
		(milliard francs)	
Government securities	147	n.a.	1,100.6
Municipal and public boards	165	—	—
Bond issues	46	—	—
Common and other stock issues	249	—	335·7
Foreign issues	150	—	n.a.

SYSTEM

Call-over.

HOURS OF BUSINESS

11.30 a.m.–2.30 p.m.

TRANSACTIONS

For future delivery contracts the Stock Exchange Committee fixes the minimum amounts to be traded for each security; these vary from 10 to 1000 securities according to their market value. There are no minimum amounts for cash transactions.

EXPENSES

(*a*) *Commission*

(i) *Cash Settlement*

Government securities	0.45% with degrees scale on market value including accrued interest
Securities redeemable by drawings	0.8% with degrees scale on market value
Belgian Railways preferred stocks	0.8% with degrees scale on market value.
All other listed stocks	1% with degrees scale on market value.
Minimum commission	40 francs.

(ii) *Account Settlement*

All shares quoted for the account	0.8% with degrees scale
Minimum commission	40 francs
Carry-overs for the following account	0.4%

(iii) *Weekly Public Sales*

Unlisted shares	0.75% on market value

Moreover a fixed commission of 100 F. in all bargains.

(*b*) *Listing Fee paid by the client*

(i) *Cash Settlement*

Government Stock	0.01%
Industrial bonds	0.025%
Shares	0.025%

(ii) *Account Settlement*

On all shares	0.025%

The listing fees are payable by both buyers and sellers, but only half the fee for both bonds and shares is payable by the client, the other half being paid by the broker.

(*c*) *Contract stamps*

Contract stamps are payable both on sale and purchase of securities, and on subscription for new issues, at the following rates:

(i) *Cash Settlement*

Government securities	0.07% of total cost or proceeds including other expenses
All other bonds	0.14% ,, ,,
Shares	0.35% ,, ,,

(ii) *Account Settlement*

Shares	0.17%
Carry overs for the following account	0.085%

SETTLEMENT

(*a*) *Cash Settlement*

Dealing in all bonds and listed stocks can be for cash settlement. Fluctuations in prices of securities for cash dealings are restricted from one day to the next, the maximum being 2% for fixed-interest stocks, 5% for stocks listed on the 'parquet market' (shares with a small market and with only one daily price) and 10% for stocks listed on the 'corbeille market' (shares with a very wide market having several prices during the market session), with exceptions for the 88 shares listed at the Account Settlement for which the fluctuations in prices are free.

(*b*) *Account Settlement*

Dealings for settlement in fortnightly accounting periods is permitted for 88 shares, generally those of the largest companies quoted. The fluctuations in prices are free.

(*c*) *Unlisted Shares*

Auctions in unlisted securities take place at intervals through public sales, organised by the Committee of the Stock Exchange. Alternatively these securities may be traded over the counter. Public sales provide for certain delays in delivery and settlement, but over-the-counter transactions must be settled for cash on the following day.

TRANSFER

Most securities quoted on Belgian stock exchanges are bearer.

SAFE KEEPING

Belgian banks charge a fee of 0.15% on the nominal value for Government securities and on the market value for other issues.

Appendix 10
Dealing in Brazil

STOCK EXCHANGES
Alagoas; Bahia; Ceará; Santa Catarina; Minas-Espírito Santo-Brasília; Paraná; Recife; Rio Grande do Norte; Rio Grande do Sol; Rio de Janeiro; São Paolo; Santos.

PRINCIPAL STOCK EXCHANGES.
Rio de Janeiro; São Paulo.

SECURITIES LISTED AT 31 DECEMBER 1976.

		No. of Companies	*Nominal Value (Cr$ millions)*
Rio de Janeiro	Shares	199	151,723
São Paulo	,,	307	71,920

SYSTEM
Trading-post

HOURS OF BUSINESS
10 a.m. – 1 p.m. Monday to Friday.

TRANSACTIONS
Round lots of 1000 shares are traded on the main market. Odd lots of less than 1000 shares are traded on the fractions market.

EXPENSES
There are no expenses other than commissions.
Commission Fees (based on the total value of operations carried out on any one day for the same client)

Up to Cr$ 20,000	1.5%
Over Cr$ 20,000 up to Cr$ 110,000	1.0%
Over Cr$ 110,000	0.5%

Minimum charge is Cr$30.

SETTLEMENT

Cash settlement from 2–4 days after dealing with fines for late payment or delivery. If delivery is not complete within four days the Exchange may buy back the shares.

TRANSFER

The majority of shares are bearer. Nominative and endorsable nominative shares with blank endorsement are also traded.

Appendix 11
Dealing in Canada

STOCK EXCHANGES

Alberta; Montreal; Toronto; Vancouver; Winnipeg.

PRINCIPAL STOCK EXCHANGE

Toronto.

SECURITIES LISTED AT 31 DECEMBER 1975

	No. of Issues	*Market value ($ billion)*
Common and other stock issues (including foreign issues)	1,279	$194.9

SYSTEM

Trading-post.

HOURS OF BUSINESS

10. a.m.–4. p.m.

TRANSACTIONS

Normal units (board lots) are as follows:

Share Price		*Unit*
On securities selling under	$ 0.10	1000 shares
On securities selling at and under	$ 0.10 $ 1.00	500 shares
On securities selling at and under	$ 1.00 $100.00	100 shares
On securities selling at and over	$100.00	10 shares

MARGIN TRADING

On securities selling:

At $ 2.00 and over	50%
At $ 1.75 to $ 1.99	60%
At $ 1.50 to $ 1.74	80%

Securities selling under $ 1.50 may not be carried on margin.

EXPENSES

Commission rates (paid by both seller and buyer)
Bonds: Bonds, treasury bills and debentures are not traded on the floor of Canadian Stock Exchanges. For trades which take place off-the-floor, the trades are made on a net basis, i.e. without commission.

SHARES

Price Level		*% Of Order Value*
a) On shares selling under	$14.00	2.50%
b) On shares selling over	$30.00	1.64%
c) On shares selling at	$14.00	
up to and including	$30.00	0.8875% of the value plus $0.22575 per share

TAPERING LARGE VALUE ORDERS

The above charges may be reduced for orders with values over $20,000 as follows:

On the first $20,000	No reduction
On the next $20,000	70% of the base rate
On the next $20,000	50% of the base rate
On the remainder	30% of the base rate

MINIMUM

Total considerations less than $10, commission at discretion.
Total considerations $10 but less than $50, minimum commission $2.
Total consideration $50 or more, minimum commission $5.
Rights, warrants and fractional shares under different basis with minimum commission $1 even on considerations of over $50.

SETTLEMENT

Settlement date five days after transaction.

TRANSFER

Most bonds are in bearer form.

Most shares are registered, but transferred by means of transferable certificates. Foreign holders should register these in good marking names to avoid probate problems.

SAFE CUSTODY

Securities may be kept either in Canadian banks (subject to safe-custody charges and charges for receipt and delivery) or in U.K. authorised depositaries (subject to insurance charges on transport to and from Canada).

Appendix 12
Dealing in Denmark

STOCK EXCHANGE
Copenhagen.

SECURITIES LISTED AT 31 DECEMBER 1976

	No. of issues	*Nominal value (million Danish kroner)*	
Bonds	1504	228,592,778	in the Official List
Shares	321	10,669,450	

SYSTEM
Auction on the Main Exchange. Free dealings between members on the after Exchange.

HOURS OF BUSINESS
10.30 a.m.–approx. 2.00 p.m.

TRANSACTIONS
Normal units are as follows:

Bonds 20,000 kr. nominal value
Shares 4,000 kr. nominal value

EXPENSES
(*a*) *Stock Exchange Turnover Tax*
Shares ½% of market value (¼% paid by buyer and seller)
Bonds Nil

(*b*) *Commission*

	On consideration	*Minimum*
(i) *Bonds*		
Quoted on the Main Exchange	0.15%	D. kr. 10

	On Consideration	*Minimum*
(ii) Shares		
Quoted on the Main Exchange	0.5%	D. kr. 10
Quoted on the after Exchange	1.0%	D. kr. 10

Reduced commission may be given to other firms of stock-brokers, not members of the Copenhagen Exchange, and to banks.

SETTLEMENT

Settlement date three days after transaction.

TRANSFER

Bonds and the great majority of shares are in bearer form.

Appendix 13
Dealing in France

STOCK EXCHANGES

Bordeaux; Lille; Lyons; Marseilles; Nancy; Nantes; Paris.

PRINCIPAL STOCK EXCHANGE

Paris.

SECURITIES LISTED AT 31 DECEMBER 1976

	No. of issues	*Nominal value*	*Market value*
		(thousand francs)	
Government securities	17	15,511,280	34,275,723
Municipal and public boards	450	176,169,655	179,569,766
Bond issues	694	72,661,658	71,009,919
Common and stock issues	665	66,583,736	133,994,957
Foreign bond issues	108	—	—
Foreign stock issues	160	—	—

SYSTEM

Combination of call-over on the 'open market' and a form of specialist on the 'closed market'.

The 56 foreign securities which are dealt in for account settlement during the session are quoted again during an additional session held in the afternoon, the prices reflecting the first hour of business on the New York Stock Exchange.

HOURS OF BUSINESS

11.30 a.m.–12.30 p.m. for bonds enjoying a small market.

12.30 p.m.–2.30 p.m. for all other securities.

TRANSACTIONS

230 stocks, the largest and most representative foreign and domestic securities, are dealt in for both cash and account settlement. All other issues are dealt in for cash settlement.

EXPENSES

(*a*) *Cash Transactions*

(i) *Brokerage*	
Government stocks	0·3%
Commercial bonds	0·5%
Shares	0·7%
(ii) *Tax*	
Commercial bonds	0·3%
Shares	0·3%
(iii) *Tax on financial activities:*	
all securities of the brokerage.	17.6%

(*b*) *Account Transactions*

(i) *Brokerage*	
Government stocks	0.2%
Commercial bonds	0·4%
Shares	0·5%
(ii) *Tax*	
Commercial bonds	0·3%
Shares	0·3%
(iii) *Tax on financial activities:*	
all securities of the brokerage.	17.6%

SETTLEMENT

Transactions can be carried out for cash settlement or account settlement. The account is settled at the end of each month and the market in shares for this settlement is both larger and the expenses lower than for cash settlement.

TRANSFER

Shares can be issued in bearer or registered form, at the option of the shareholder. Partly-paid shares must be in registered form.

Unless otherwise instructed, shares purchased will be deposited with the central clearing agency, Sicovam.

Appendix 14
Dealing in Italy

STOCK EXCHANGES

Bologna; Florence; Genoa; Milan; Naples; Parma; Turin; Trieste; Venice.

PRINCIPAL STOCK EXCHANGE

Milan.

SECURITIES LISTED AT 31 DECEMBER 1976.

	No of issues	*Nominal value*	*Market value*
		(million lire)	
Government Securities	28	7,738,261	n.a.
Municipal and public boards			
Bond Issues	648	44,942,354	n.a.
Convertible bond issues	15	243,856	n.a.
Common and other stock issues	172	4,559,035	6,994.031
Foreign bond issues	1	7,673	n.a.
Foreign share issues	1	51.7a	79.9a

SYSTEM

Call-over.

HOURS OF BUSINESS

10 a.m. – 1 p.m.

EXPENSES

(*a*) *Contract tax* (through stockbrokers).

Cash contracts per 100,000 lire or fraction

Government stock	2.50 lire
Mortgages and bonds	5.00 lire
Shares	12.50 lire

(*b*) *Commission*

Official Commission Rates

Category A – banks, commission agencies and nominee companies.
Category B – mutual funds and financial companies.
Category C – private clients or other groups not included in A or B.

		of nominal value
(i) Government Securities	Category A	0.05%
	Category B	0.10%
	Category C	0.15%
(ii) Commercial Bonds	Category A	0.10%
	Category B	0.20%
	Category C	0.30%
(iii) Shares	Category A	0.3%
	Category B	0.4%
	Category C	0.6%

(iv) *Minimum Commissions*

Bonds	2,000
Shares	1,000

SETTLEMENT

Monthly accounting periods.

TRANSFER

The great majority of bonds are bearer.
Listed shares issued before 1977 are registered.
Non-voting savings shares introduced by Law No. 216, passed in 1974 and due for issue in 1977, may be bearer.

Appendix 15
Dealing in Japan

STOCK EXCHANGE

Fukuoka; Hiroshima; Kyoto; Nagoya; Niigata; Osaka; Sapporo; Tokyo.

PRINCIPAL STOCK EXCHANGE

Tokyo.

SECURITIES LISTED AT 31 DECEMBER 1976

	No. of issues	*Nominal value*	*Market value*
		(*million yen*)	
Government securities	27	12,930,558	12,231,041
Municipal and public boards	62	3,289,140	30,000,413
Bond issues	28	395,068	394,963
Common and other stock issues	1,433	10,292,960	52,993,930
Foreign issues	0	—	—
–bonds	17	210,336	197,342
–shares	17	2,346,624	30,049,848

SYSTEM

Trading-post.

HOURS OF BUSINESS

9 a.m.–11 a.m., 1 p.m. to 3 p.m.

For special designated stocks closing trading begins after the official hour for each session.

MARKETS

(*a*) *Listed Stocks*

(i) *First Section*

Domestic listed stocks satisfying certain requirements, including: paid-up capital of at least 1,000 million yen; minimum of 3,000 'floating' shareholders with 500 to 50,000 shares; 'floating' shareholders must own at least 3 million shares plus 25% of issued shares in companies with less than 60 million share capital, or 12 million shares and 10% of issued shares in companies with more than 60 million share capital.

(ii) *Second Section*

Listed stocks in smaller domestic companies satisfying certain conditions, including: paid-up capital of at least 500 million yen; minimum of 2,000 shareholders. All domestic companies are first listed for one year on the second section.

(iii) *Foreign Section*

All foreign securities.

(*b*) *Special Designated Stocks*

Eight leading stocks, while traded normally during the sessions, have their opening and closing prices determined on a special auction system. A stock is replaced by another if a more eligible security is selected.

(*c*) *Margin Stocks*

Only certain stocks in the first section (430 of the 917 stocks in 1976) and none in the second section, are eligible for margin trading. Margin trading is not authorised for foreign investors, but represents between 25% to 35% of domestic turnover.

TRANSACTIONS.

The unit of transaction of the First and Second Section is 1000 shares, except for the following cases, were the unit is 100 shares:

(*a*) Where the nominal value of the share is 500 yen or more.

(*b*) Where the nominal value is less than 500 yen, but the average market price for the latest six months is more than 3,000 yen.

EXPENSES

(*a*) *Commission rates*

(i) *Shares and Subscription amount*

Consideration (yen)	*rate (to consideration) %*	*additional fixed fee (yen)*
under 0.2 mils	nil	2,500
1 mils or less	1.25	nil
3 mils or less	1.05	2,000
5 mils or less	0.95	5,000
10 mils or less	0.85	10,000
30 mils or less	0.75	20,000
50 mils or less	0.65	50,000
100 mils or less	0.60	75,000
over 100 mils	0.55	125,000

(ii) *Bonds* (per 100 yen Par Value in case of straight bonds and a percentage of contract value in case of convertible bonds)

Contract Value (Par Value) (yen)	*Government*	*Government-guaranteed*	*Foreign (on yen basis)*	*Municipal and Bank Debenture Interest-bearing)*	*Corporate and Others*	*Con-vertible*
under y0.5 mils	0.20	0.30	0.40	0.40	0.50	1.0
y0.5 mils under y1 mils.						0.9
y1 mils under y3 mils			0.30			0.8
y3 mils under y5 mils						0.7
y5 mils under y10 mils	0.15	0.20	0.20	0.30	0.40	0.6
y10 mils. under y100 mils	0.10	0.15	0.15	0.20	0.30	0.5
y100 mils or more	0.05	0.10	0.10	0.15	0.20	

(*b*) *Other Charges*

The securities transaction tax is levied on all sales at a rate of 0.30 yen per 100 yen of market value of securities sold.

SETTLEMENT

Settlement on the third business day following the date of the transaction. Penalties paid for late delivery.

DELIVERY

Renounceable stock certificates normally in amounts of 1,000 shares. Power of attorney in favour of a Japanese bank or securities house should be given to protect shareholders' interests in the case of rights, etc., and securities should be held in Japan to effect sales easily.

SAFE KEEPING

Service fee is chargeable by securities companies on foreigners' account for safe keeping of securities and other services. Annual fee is at least 20,000 yen but not over 400,000 yen.

Appendix 16
Dealing in The Netherlands

STOCK EXCHANGE
Amsterdam.

SECURITIES LISTED AT 30 DECEMBER 1976
(*a*) *Dutch Common and Preferred Shares*

	Nominal value	*Market value*
	(million guilders)	
1. International concerns[1]	5,852	26,530
2. Trade, industry	2,717	7,509
3. Bank and insurance	1,338	5,523
4. Investment companies	2,700	8,214
5. Transport	689	1,006
6. Miscellaneous	127	815
	13,423	49,597

[1] i.e. AK 20, Hoogovens, Royal Dutch, Philips, Unilever N.V.

(*b*) *Dutch Bonds*

Government	17.1	n.a.
Local government	13.0	n.a.
Private sector	18.9	n.a.
	49.0	

(*c*) *Number of Securities Listed*

		Domestic	*Foreign*
Shares	616	288	328
Bonds	1,484	1,334	150
Total	2,239	1,622	478

SYSTEM

Auction market with specialised dealers (*hoekman*).

HOURS OF BUSINESS

11.30 a.m.–1.15 p.m. Monday to Friday.

EXPENSES

Commissions charged to the public for both shares and bonds are calculated on consideration as follows:

(*a*) up to D. fl 20,000 . . . . 1.0%

(*b*) over D. fl 20,000 and up to D. fl 200,000 . . . 0.78%

(*c*) over D. fl 200,000 . . . 0.7%

A fee of D. fl 3 is also charged for each settlement of each separate security.

SETTLEMENT

Cash settlement (four days' delivery).

TRANSFER

The great majority of stocks are in bearer form.

SAFE KEEPING

Brokers and banks are free to charge for safe custody. Charge of an average portfolio is 0.05–0.1% of the real value.

Appendix 17
Dealing in Norway

STOCK EXCHANGES
Oslo; Bergen; Trondheim.

PRINCIPAL STOCK EXCHANGE
Oslo.

SECURITIES LISTED AT 31 DECEMBER 1976

	No. of issues	*Nominal value*	*Market value*
		(*million Norw. kroner*)	
Government securities	28	2,314	—
Municipal and Public Boards	68	3,231	—
Bond issues	204	8,680	—
Common and other stock issues	169	4,997	9,606

SYSTEM
Call-over.

HOURS OF BUSINESS
Official quotation takes place Monday to Friday at 10.30 a.m.

EXPENSES
(*a*) *Treasury Stamp Duty*
Shares
For every 100 kr. or part thereof of the amount on the contract note 1 kr.
(*b*) *Commissions*
Norwegian Government and other bonds exempt from stamp duty 0.15%
Foreign bonds and other domestic bonds 0.25%
Convertible bonds 0.5%
All shares and investment company units 0.75%

All other bonds, debentures and shares guaranteed by the Government $\frac{1}{4}\%$

All other shares $\frac{1}{2}\%$

Commission is charged to both buyer and seller.

Minimum commission on any transaction shall not be less than 3 kr. and not less than 0.30 kr. per share.

TRANSFER

Shares are issued in registered form only.

OVERSEAS HOLDERS

Investment in Norwegian shares by non-residents, and also the repatriation of proceeds from sales, is subject to licence from the Bank of Norway.

The Norwegian Companies Act limits non-resident participation to 10% of paid-up capital of banks and insurance companies, 40% of paid-up capital of shipping and whaling companies. The majority of other Norwegian companies, either because of concession laws or Articles of Association, may bar non-residents from being accepted as shareholders.

Appendix 18
Dealing in South Africa

STOCK EXCHANGE
Johannesburg.

SECURITIES LISTED AT 31 DECEMBER 1976

	No. of issues	*Nominal value*	*Market value*
		(thousand rands)	
Government stocks	72	7,765,921	7,016,826
Municipal stocks	312	1,329,618	1,113,459
Statutory corporation loans	182	2,644,365	2,393,491
Debentures and notes	87	436,062	348,793
Preference shares	211	179,195	117,548
Ordinary shares	608	3,871,786	18,722,516

SYSTEM
Two-way open auction.

HOURS OF BUSINESS
9.30 a.m.–4.00 p.m.

TRANSACTIONS
100 shares. Odd-lot dealing in lesser amounts is permitted.

EXPENSES
(*a*) *Marketable Securities Tax*
Applied on purchases and sales of all shares, options and debentures at rate of 1%. Where transactions are exempt from M.S.T. contracts bear stamps of 25c per R 100 or part.
(*b*) *Transfer Stamp Duty*

Government securities, local authorities and public boards	nil

All South African and South West African registered companies lodged for transfer in South Africa or South West Africa[a]	10c per R10 of consideration if registered within six months, 30c thereafter.

Note

[a] If M.S.T. has been paid, transfer is exempt from stamp duty.

(*c*) *Commission*

(i) *Government and Municipal Stocks*

On the first R20,000 of the consideration	0.25%
On the excess of R20,000 up to R100,000	0.125%
On any excess above R100,000	0.0625%

(ii) When dealing with a specified list of banks and Government agencies, the above commissions are reduced by half.

(iii) *Debentures and loans*
Basic charge 0.25% of nominal value, plus brokerage

Fixed interest stocks	0.6% of nominal value
Convertibles	0.85% of nominal value

(iv) *On shares* (including options):

Basic charge	0.5 cts per share (maximum R25).
Brokerage	0.85% on consideration.

SETTLEMENT

Cash settlement within seven business days.

TRANSFER

All securities are registered.

SAFE KEEPING

Charges depend on the size of the account and are at the discretion of the banks.

Appendix 19
Dealing in Spain

STOCK EXCHANGES
Barcelona, Bilbao, Madrid.

PRINCIPAL STOCK EXCHANGE
During 1976: Madrid 72%; Barcelona 20% and Bilbao 8% Provincial Brokers volume represents about 20% of National market dealing.

SECURITIES LISTED AT 31 DECEMBER 1976

	No. of issues	*Nominal value*	*Market value*
		(million pesetas)	
Government Securities, Municipal and Public Boards	368	383.967	296.992
Bond issues	1.037	676.671	475.465
Common and other stock issues	871	857.164	1.642.362
Foreign issues (dealings not yet allowed)	—	—	—

SYSTEM
Auction market.

HOURS OF BUSINESS
10 a.m. to 11.15 a.m.

EXPENSES

(*a*) *Contract Stamp Tax*

On the following scale:

to 5000 pesetas	10 pesetas
over 5,000 to 30,000	30 ,,
over 30,000 to 150,000	140 ,,
over 150,000 to 250,000	275 ,,
over 250,000 to 500,000	550 ,,
over 500,000 to 1,000,000	1,100 ,,

(*b*) *Commission*

Government Securities 1.5%	minimum	7.50 Ptas.
Municipal and public Boards, 1.75%	,,	10.00
Common and other stock issues 2.5%	,,	15.00

SETTLEMENT

Daily – cash dealings only

TRANSFER

Except for some forms of Government Securities, all other Government Public Debt and Bonds are bearer.

Bank, shipping and insurance shares are registered. The great majority of the remaining shares are in bearer form.

Appendix 20
Dealing in Sweden

STOCK EXCHANGE
Stockholm.

SECURITIES LISTED AT 31 DECEMBER 1976

	No. of issues	*Nominal value*	*Market value*
		(million Swedish kronor)	
Government securities	84	58,928	57,513
Municipal loans	195	6,497	5,043
Bond issues	1112	110,056	90,562
Common and other stock issues	98	18,717	43,831
Foreign issues (only bonds)	13	380	329

SYSTEM
Call-over and afterwards free negotiations.

HOURS OF BUSINESS
9.30 a.m.–2.30 p.m. (shares 10.45 a.m.–2.30 p.m.).

TRANSACTIONS
Both 'round lots' and 'odd lots' are dealt in the market-place, but only 'round lots' are published in the official lists.

EXPENSES
(*a*) *Federal Tax*

- (i) Domestic and foreign shares: 0.15% payable on all transactions, normally changed between seller and buyer.
- (ii) Government and public bonds: tax-free.
- (iii) Other bonds: 0.05% on all transactions, normally charged between seller and buyer.

(*b*) *Commissions* (paid by both seller and buyer)

Securities listed	% on consideration	*Kronor per unit*
Swedish shares	0.45	—
Swedish bonds with fixed interest	0.10	—
Foreign bonds	0.25	—
Swedish premium bonds	0.20	0.20–0.20

Minimum commission at least 15 kr. when consideration does not amount to 500 kr., otherwise 30 kr.

Unlisted series	% on consideration
Shares	0.70
Swedish bonds	0.20
Swedish unsecured debentures	0.25
Foreign bonds and unsecured debentures	0.375

Minimum commissions as for listed securities.

SETTLEMENT

For shares four days after the date of the transaction.
For bonds two days after the date of transaction.

TRANSFER

Virtually all bonds in bearer form. Shares dealt in are generally endorsed in blank by the registered owner. Bearer shares can be issued only after exemption given by the Government.

SAFE KEEPING

From 1976 banks charge their customers 3.75 kr. per 1,000 kr. of the market value at the end of the year.

Appendix 21
Dealing in Switzerland

STOCK EXCHANGES

Basle; Geneva; Lausanne; Neuchatel; St. Gall; Zurich.

PRINCIPAL STOCK EXCHANGE

Zurich.

SECURITIES LISTED AT 31 DECEMBER 1976

	No. of issues	*Nominal value*	*Market value*
		(million francs)	
Federal securities	39	–	10,529
Municipal and Cantonal	451	–	13,597
Bond issues	1,049	–	37,942
Common and other stock issues	156	–	49,373
Foreign bond issues	1,917	–	86,228
Foreign stock issues	294	–	–

SYSTEM

Call-over.

HOURS OF BUSINESS

Opening hours, Monday to Friday

- 09.30 Unofficial trading in unlisted securities.
- 10.00 Swiss Bonds.
- 10.15 Swiss stocks and foreign bonds.
- 11.00 Foreign stocks.

There is no official closing time.

EXPENSES

(a) *Federal Stamp Tax*

0.05% on Swiss securities,
0.1% on foreign securities.

(b) *Canton Tax*

S. fr. 0.10 for each S. fr. 1,000 transacted.

(c) *Stock Exchange fee*

S. fr. 0.05 for each S. fr. 1,000 transacted.

(d) *Commissions*

Swiss Bonds	0.375%
Foreign Bonds	0.50%
Shares – market price over S. fr. 150.	0.625%
market price under S. fr. 150.	1.0%
Minimum commission	S. fr. 10.0

SETTLEMENT

Spot transactions are settled within 2–5 days of dealing. Forward deals may be closed on any day, but settlement is not effected until the end of the current, second or third month.

TRANSFER

Virtually all bonds are in bearer form.

Approximately two-thirds of share issues are in bearer form, others registered. Some company articles forbid foreign holders, except through the medium of a Swiss-domiciled bank, in which case voting rights are forfeited.

SAFE KEEPING

(*a*) *Bonds*

A fee of 1 fr. per 1,000 fr. face value per year.

(*b*) *Shares*

A fee of 1 fr. per 1,000 fr. market value per year.
Minimum fee per account usually 5 fr.

Banks operate a centralised security deposit system (SEGA) for collective safe keeping and simplicity of transfer.

Appendix 22 Dealing in the United States

STOCK EXCHANGES

New York Stock Exchange; American Stock Exchange, New York.

Regional exchanges at Boston; Chicago Board of Option Exchange; Cincinnati; Midwest at Chicago; Pacific Stock Exchange; Philadelphia–Baltimore–Washington; Spokane; Intermountain Stock Exchange; Exempted Stock Exchange in Honolulu.

PRINCIPAL STOCK EXCHANGE

New York Stock Exchange.

SECURITIES LISTED AT 31 DECEMBER 1976

	No. of issues	*Nominal value* (*$ million*)	*Market value* (*$ million*)
Government securities and N. Y. City Bonds	83	186,532	183,102
Foreign Government	127	2,926	2,545
Other bond issues	2,474	153,775	129,758
Common and other stock issues	2,077	—	670,930
Foreign company stock issues	24	—	14,180

SYSTEM

Trading-post.

HOURS OF BUSINESS

10 a.m.–4 p.m.

TRANSACTIONS

Normally in lots of 100 (round lots). Amounts less than 100 (odd lots) command wider prices.

(*a*) *New York State Transfer Tax* (paid by the seller with 50% reduction to individual non-residents)

Price Range	*Normal Rate*	*Rate including 1975 Temporary Surcharge (cents per share)*
$ 0–4·99	1.25	1.56
5–9·99	2.50	3·13
10–19·99	3·75	4·69
20 & over	5·00	6.25

(*b*) *Commission Rates*

All commissions negotiable since 1 May 1975.

SETTLEMENT

Most bonds are in bearer form.

Most stock is registered, but transferred by means of renounceable certificates. Foreign holders should register in 'good marking names' to avoid probate problems.

SAFE KEEPING

Securities may be kept either in an American bank (subject to charges for safe custody and for receipt and delivery) or in a U.K. authorised depositary (subject to insurance charges on transport to and from America).

Appendix 23
Dealing in West Germany

STOCK EXCHANGES

West Berlin; Bremen; Düsseldorf; Frankfurt am Main; Hamburg; Hanover; Munich; Stuttgart.

PRINCIPAL STOCK EXCHANGES

Düsseldorf; Frankfurt am Main.

SECURITIES LISTED AT 31 DECEMBER 1976

	No. of issues	*Nominal value*	*Market value*
		(million DM)	
Düsseldorf			
Domestic			
Stocks, Bonds	185	33,273	n.a.
Foreign			
Stocks	65	39,879	n.a.
Bonds	240	26,026	n.a.
Frankfurt am Main			
Domestic			
Stocks	235	32,500	109,000
Bonds	3,777	214,500	n.a.
Foreign			
Stocks	150	58,300	n.a.
Bonds	374	30,900	n.a.

SYSTEM

Trading-post.

HOURS OF BUSINESS

11.30 a.m. – 1.30 p.m.

TRANSACTIONS

Minimum of 50 shares for securities admitted to a consecutive quotation.

MARKETS

(*a*) *Official Market.* Bonds and shares officially listed. Quote must be fixed by an official quotation-broker.

(*b*) *Semi-official Market.* A free market in all securities, including those officially listed, not confined to a certain place or time. The *Over-the-Counter Market* is executed mainly during trading sessions in the Stock Exchange in securities introduced by a special committee. In telephone trading all securities may be handled, including over-the-counter and unlisted stocks.

EXPENSES

(*a*) *Securities Turnover Tax*

Public loans	1%
Bonds	2%
Share or promissory notes	2.5%

(*b*) *Specialist Fees*

Bonds	
Amounts up to DM 50,000	0.75% of nominal value
Over DM 50,000 and up to DM 100,000	0.05% ,, ,,
Over DM 100,000	0.0375% ,, ,,
Minimum charge	DM 37.50
Shares	0.1% on consideration
Over DM 100,000	0.0375% of nominal value
Over DM 500,000	0.025% ,, ,,
Over DM 1,500,000	0.015% ,, ,,
Over DM 5,000,000	0.010% ,, ,,
Minimum charge	DM 50.00

(*c*) *Commission* (based on normal charges made by banks, but special terms are often made)

(i) *Foreign Individuals*

Government stocks	0.4%[1]
Bonds	0.4%[1]
Shares	0.8% of consideration

(ii) *Foreign Authorised Dealers*

Government Stocks	0.2%[1]
Bonds	0.2%[1]
Shares	0.4% of consideration

[1] Commission based on percentage of bond price or nominal value, whichever is larger.

SETTLEMENT

Settlement is for cash and must be completed on the second trading day after dealing. Dealings and quotation are by number or units of shares. Fixed interest securities are traded and listed in percentage of their nominal value.

TRANSFER

The majority of shares, with the exception of those of a few large companies, mostly insurance firms, are bearer. A centralised clearing system, Girosammelverwahrung, is employed, and where shares are held in safe keeping in the centralised clearing system a warrant will be issued as a note of title.

Glossary

ABOVE THE MARKET At a price in excess of the normal market quotation.

ACCOUNT (i) The Stock Exchange year is divided into periods, normally of two weeks' duration but over Bank holidays of three weeks, and these are termed accounts. Purchases and sales made during one of these periods are settled on Account Day.

(ii) The ledger entries of a client, jobber, etc.

(iii) The term can be used in reference to clients—'He introduced several new accounts'.

(iv) Dealing for the new account ('new time') refers to transactions carried out for settlement on the next Account Day but one. Such transactions are permitted in the last two days of the existing account.

ACCRUED INTEREST The amount of interest which would be due to the holder of the security if interest were paid on a day-to-day basis. In the case of short-dated Government securities, the accrued interest on a daily basis is paid to the seller by the buyer. When yields are calculated on other fixed-interest securities, it is normal to make an allowance for the accrued interest in these calculations.

ACTIVE, ACTIVITY Used to describe securities in which a comparatively large number of bargains have been transacted.

AD VALOREM *Ad valorem* is Latin for 'according to value'. The Stamp Act requires that a buyer of most registered securities shall pay a duty based on the value of the purchase.

AGENT A Register of Agents is maintained by The Stock Exchange. They include chartered accountants, solicitors and others professionally engaged in investment to whom a return of commission may be granted.

ALLOTMENT (i) The amount of stock or shares allocated to an applicant at the time of an issue.

(ii) 'Allotment letter' is the document of title representing an allotment.

ANOMALY SWITCH Normally used in reference to the gilt-edged market, an anomaly indicates that the prices of two stocks have moved out of their normal relationship. An 'anomaly switch' is often carried out when this situation occurs, selling one stock and buying the other, with the object of reversing the process when the price relationship returns to normal.

APPRECIATION Improvement in capital value.

ARBITRAGE Transactions in securities quoted in two centres, buying in one and selling in the other.

ASSET COVER Normally used in reference to fixed-interest capital, particularly loan capital, asset cover is the multiple by which the net tangible assets of the company cover the total amount of loan capital in question, i.e. 'asset cover five times'.

ASSET VALUE (per share) The balance-sheet figure for the net assets available for each ordinary share, calculated by ascertaining the net assets available for the ordinary and dividing it by the number of ordinary shares in issue.

ASSOCIATE MEMBER A member of The Stock Exchange who is not a partner in his firm.

AUTHORISED CAPITAL The nominal capital of a company which is authorised by the Memorandum of Association.

AUTHORISED CLERK An employee of a member firm who is permitted to deal in securities on the floor of The Stock Exchange.

BALANCE (i) When referring to an uncompleted transaction, the amount still to be bought or sold.

(ii) When referring to a certificate, the amount due to a seller who has disposed of only part of his holding.

(iii) When referring to accounts, the process of ensuring that all entries have been properly completed in the books of account is known as 'finding the balance'.

BARGAIN Any deal on The Stock Exchange.

BEAR (i) Anyone who anticipates a fall in prices.

(ii) An individual who, in this anticipation, has sold securities in the hope of repurchasing them at lower levels.

BEARER Securities that are transferable without the need for registration.

BELOW THE MARKET At a price beneath the normal market quotation.

BEST At the most advantageous price obtainable at the time of dealing.

BETTER In reference to share prices, at an improved level.

BID (i) Price at which a jobber will agree to buy stock or shares in the market.

(ii) Also short for 'take-over bid', when one company offers to purchase a controlling interest or the whole of another company's shares.

BLUE BUTTON An unauthorised clerk, so called because of the circular blue badge which used to be worn in the buttonhole and which has now been replaced by a blue badge showing the name of the firm.

BOND (i) A term used widely in America and elsewhere to denote a fixed-interest security, such as a debenture.

(ii) In connection with local authority issues, short-dated securities, issued normally in units of £1,000.

BONUS (i) A capitalisation issue.
(ii) An increment to the salaries of stock-exchange employees, normally based on the profits of the firm.

BOOK The operation of a jobber dealing in a specific security is termed 'making a book'.

BOX (i) A small room adjacent to the floor of The Stock Exchange, used by the dealing staff of broker firms.
(ii) A container in the Settlement Room where tickets may be placed for collection.
(iii) A compartment in the security vaults beneath The Stock Exchange building.

BULL (i) Anyone who anticipates a rise in prices.
(ii) Anyone who, in anticipation of this, purchases securities in the hope of selling them at a higher level.

BUYING IN Procedure used in order to obtain the delivery of securities which have not been forthcoming after a reasonable time.

CALL (i) The right to demand payment of additional money due on 'partly paid' securiies.
(ii) The option to buy a security at an agreed price at a future date.

CALL-OVER The procedure of fixing opening and closing prices in stock exchanges where auction markets are operated.

CAPITALISATION ISSUE An issue of shares to existing shareholders, without payment, normally created by the capitalisation of reserves (also known as a bonus issue).

CARRY-OVER See Contango.

CASH (i) With reference to company accounts, the item indicating the total credits at the bank.
(ii) 'Cash bargains' or 'dealing for cash' refers to transactions in securities where the settlement is normally on the first business day after the transaction is done, i.e. gilt-edged securities, new issues transferable on allotment letters, etc.

CASH FLOW The amount of money generated by a company each year from its own trading operations.

CENTRE The office of The Stock Exchange responsible for operations under the CHARM and TALISMAN settlement systems.

CERTIFICATE The document of title to a holding of stocks or shares.

CERTIFIED, CERTIFICATION Transfers so stamped, either at the office of the company's registrar or at The Stock Exchange, indicate that the certificate representing the shares transferred has been duly exhibited.

CHARM (CHecking Accounting and Reporting for Member Firms) The intermediate settlement system leading to the pooling system TALISMAN.

CHARTIST An individual who studies the movement of share prices or indices over periods of time, usually by means of graphs.

CHECKING (i) The overnight matching of bargains reported by brokers and jobbers to the central computer system and confirmed by The Centre on the morning following a deal.

(ii) 'Checking the market' is enquiring of more than one jobber the price and amount of shares in a given security.

CHOICE When it is possible to sell or to buy shares at the same price with different jobbers, this is called 'having the choice'.

CLEAN The price of a security (normally fixed-interest) after the deduction of any accrued interest.

CLOSE (i) To reverse an open position by either buying a security which has been sold or selling one which has been previously purchased.

(ii) A small fraction (usually £$\frac{1}{64}$) used in quoting securities, i.e. '96 close to close' means $95\frac{63}{64}-96\frac{1}{64}$.

(iii) Close company status was introduced in the Finance Act, 1965, to define certain companies. The principal criterion is that the company should be controlled by five or fewer persons.

CLOSED END In America and other overseas areas, a 'closed-end trust' indicates an investment trust with a fixed capital, as opposed to an 'open-end trust', indicating a unit trust whose issue of units can expand or contract.

CLOSER When a broker asks a jobber, ' Have you anything closer?', he is enquiring whether the jobber will narrow the margin between the buying and selling prices.

CLOSING THE BOOKS The procedure carried out by the registrar of a company at the time of a dividend or other distribution. Only shareholders on the register at the date of closing the books will receive a distribution.

COMMISSION The brokerage fee charged by member firms, normally based on the minimum scale shown in Appendix 2.

COMMON STOCK The term used in America and other countries to denote equity capital.

CONCESSION Normally used in reference to the minimum scales of commissions where certain bargains attract a reduced scale.

CONSIDERATION The cost of a purchase before adding expenses, calculated by multiplying the amount of stock or number of shares by the price per unit.

CONSOLIDATED ACCOUNTS Accounts which include not only those of the parent company but also the subsidiaries.

CONTANGO Continuation of an open position for a consideration. Securities which have been bought or sold for settlement during one account can be 'carried over' to another account so that settlement is deferred.

CONTINGENT An order which depends upon another order, normally in the opposite direction, being executed at the same time.

CONTINUATION Normally used to explain the commission charge on a bargain where part of the initial order has already been transacted previously.

CONTRACT The invoice signed by the firm of stockbrokers confirming a sale or a purchase.

CONTRACT STAMP The Government stamp affixed to the contract note and paid at the scale shown in Table 4 (p. 59).

CONVERTIBLE Used to describe a security which, normally at the option of the holder, can be converted into another class of security. In particular this refers to loan stocks which may be converted into ordinary shares.

CORPORATE MEMBER A Member firm which is constituted as a company, rather than as a partnership.

COUPON (i) The rate of interest payable on a fixed-interest security, i.e. 'a 5% coupon'.

(ii) On a bearer document, a warrant which is detachable from the certificate and which entitles the owner to some distribution, normally a dividend.

COVER See Asset Cover and Dividend Cover.

CROSS Purchase and sale transactions in the same amount of the same security which are matched within the broker's office, for which delivery can be simplified.

CUM This phrase is used in connection with dividends, rights, etc., and indicates that shares are entitled to the distribution concerned. It is the Latin for 'with'.

CUMULATIVE Normally descriptive of preference shares to indicate that, if the dividend is not paid out of current earnings, it ranks for payment out of future earnings.

DEAL A bargain or transaction.

DEALER One who carries out a bargain. Members of either broking or jobbing firms whose occupation is to buy and sell shares in The Stock Exchange are normally entitled 'dealers'. The term can also apply to institutional employees who are responsible for giving orders to brokers.

DEBENTURE A stock issued by a company, in exchange for the loan of money, normally secured by the pledging of certain assets.

DEED (i) The form of document by means of which securities are transferred from seller to buyer.

(ii) The trust deed securing the issue of loan capital.

DELIVERY The transfer of securities between seller and buyer, or the documents concerned in the transfer. 'Good delivery' indicates that the documents are in order; 'bad delivery' indicates that the documents do not conform with the regulations.

DIFFERENCES The balances due to clients and other member firms at the end of each account.

DISCOUNT (i) The margin by which a stock or share stands below either its issue price or parity value.

(ii) Make allowance for future developments, i.e. 'the price fully discounts an increase in dividend'.

(iii) To quantify the present value of a sum of money at the end of a certain number of years at a given rate of interest.

DISCRETION Orders 'at discretion' are those where the broker is required to use his own judgement in the execution of a transaction. 'Discretionary accounts' are operated for clients to whom reference need not be made in the management of their investments.

DIVIDEND COVER The ratio of the available earnings to the dividend distribution, which can be quoted either as a multiple, i.e. 'dividend cover five times', or as a priority percentage, i.e. 'dividend cover 0–20%'.

DRAWINGS Selection of securities for redemption, usually by means of a ballot.

EASIER Descriptive of the market where share prices are lower.

EQUITY Ordinary shares. These are the shares which have the right to participate in all the profits and assets of a company after the rights of the prior fixed charges have been satisfied.

EX The opposite of 'cum': shares quoted 'ex dividend' or 'ex rights' are not entitled to participate in the forthcoming distribution. The word is the Latin prefix meaning 'without'.

EXCESS SHARES At the time of a rights issue, shareholders are entitled to apply for their proportion of the issue. Any shares for which application has not been received, or which are available through fractions of a share which cannot be allocated, are sometimes made available to shareholders as 'excess shares' and rationed between those who apply for them.

EXECUTE To carry out an order.

FEE The charge payable for the performance of a service.

FIRM (i) Descriptive of the market where prices are steady.

(ii) A 'firm' offer or bid is one which is not conditional, as opposed to 'subject' offers and bids (i.e. subject to their being available).

(iii) 'In firm hands' is descriptive of holders of securities who are not short-term operators.

FIXED ASSETS The assets which are continually employed in a business and which are not intended for conversion into cash in the course of normal trading, e.g. buildings, plant and machinery.

FIXED-INTEREST Where the interest or dividend payable per annum is not variable.

FLOATING CHARGE A charge on assets not specifically secured on such assets.

FLOATING RATE Rate of interest which is varied at intervals to follow the interest rates ruling at the time (i.e. linked to inter-bank rates or Minimum Lending Rate)

FLOOR The trading area of The Stock Exchange.

FRACTIONS (i) In Stock Exchange quotations, particularly those securities quoted per cent, fractions of a £ are used down to $\frac{1}{64}$ (=1.5625p).

(ii) In rights or capitalisation issues, the amount issued may not exactly divide proportionately among shareholders. Since only whole numbers of shares can be issued, the 'fractions' will be sold in the market and the proceeds either distributed in cash to the shareholders or retained by the company.

FRANKED INCOME Income which has already suffered corporation tax. When received by another corporation, this income does not attract a further liability to corporation tax.

FREE (i) Referring to securities, particularly new issues, where a purchase does not attract *ad valorem* stamp duty.

(ii) Sales of very small amounts of securities are uneconomical to jobbers owing to the high cost of paperwork involved. They may therefore require the seller to pay the normal *ad valorem* stamp duty and company's fee in order to compensate for these costs. Such sales would be done at the normal bid price in the market, but 'free'.

FREE MARKET A market where it is possible to deal in reasonably large amounts at all times.

FREE OF TAX Usually descriptive of dividend or interest payments where income tax is not payable by the recipient, e.g. building society interest.

FUNDING Raising long-term or permanent capital to repay a debt.

FUNDS (i) Cash.
(ii) A common term for Government securities.
(iii) Investment portfolios.

GEARING The relationship between fixed-interest capital and equity. An ordinary share which is 'highly geared' is one where the fixed-interest capital is high compared with the equity capital. The opposite is one which is 'low geared'.

GILT-EDGED A term generally applied to issues of British Government, Dominion and colonial Government, U.K. corporation and certain public authority stocks, originally indicating a first-class security.

GIVER (i) Someone who has purchased shares and wishes to delay delivery until the following account, effecting a contango. The giver normally has to pay a rate of interest to the deliverer of the security to compensate for the delay in payment.

(ii) In an options transaction one who acquires an option to sell.

GOVERNMENT BROKER The individual member of The Stock Exchange who acts on behalf of the Bank of England and the Government.

GROSS In connection with yields, the return on an investment before the deduction of tax.

HALF COMMISSION The Stock Exchange rules permit the return of commission to employees in member firms. The maximum which has traditionally been allowed to Stock Exchange members employed by firms is 50 per cent.

HAMMERED When a member or member firm is unable to comply with his liabilities, he is declared a defaulter. The term is derived from the use of a wooden mallet which used to be struck to command the attention of members to the announcement in The Stock Exchange.

HOUSE The colloquial expression for either the premises of The Stock Exchange or the trading floor.

INDEX, INDICES Indicators, often constructed from a series of share prices, which are used to illustrate market movement.

INSTITUTION A term used to indicate a class of corporate investors, particularly the insurance companies, investment trusts, unit trusts, merchant banks and pension funds.

INTEREST COVER See Dividend Cover.

INTRODUCTION Securities which do not enjoy a listing on The Stock Exchange may obtain this by means of an 'introduction' under certain circumstances, provided that the capital is already widely held and that no part of it requires to be sold immediately.

INVESTMENT COUNSELLOR An individual who specialises in investment advice and the management of portfolios.

INVESTMENT TRUST A limited company whose assets are wholly or largely investments and whose operations are primarily the management of those investments. The Finance Act, 1965, lays down certain criteria for these companies as far as taxation is concerned.

IRREDEEMABLE Having no final date of redemption.

ISSUE Although to be exact this term should refer to the creation of additional stock or shares, it is generally used to indicate any listing of a previously unlisted security.

ISSUING HOUSE An organisation which sponsors issues of stock and shares, often a merchant bank.

JOBBERS Members and member firms who maintain the market in securities, buying and selling from fellow member firms but without contact with members of the general public.

KAFFIRS The colloquial term applied to shares of South African gold-mining companies.

LIMIT A restriction applied to the price at which an order may be executed.

LIMITED MARKET Descriptive of the fact that dealings in a particular stock or share may be restricted.

LINE A large amount, i.e. 'line of shares'.

LIQUID Having cash.

LIQUID ASSETS Generally, as opposed to fixed assets, cash or assets held for the purpose of conversion into cash during the normal course of trading.

LIQUIDATION (i) In connection with a company, the fact that it has been or is in the process of being wound up.

(ii) In connection with a line of shares, the fact that it has been or is being sold.

LIST BOOK Journal used in a stockbroker's office showing, in stock classification, purchases and sales of individual securities during an account.

LISTED A security 'listed' on a stock exchange is one which is included in the Official List of securities quoted on that exchange.

LISTS CLOSED At the time of making an issue, the sponsoring organisation closes the application list at a time after which no further applications will be considered. The advertised particulars or prospectus must state the time at which lists will open and, if the issue has been fully subscribed, it is normal to close them shortly after the opening time.

LONG (i) Having a 'bull' position. Particularly used of a jobber who has purchased more stock than he has sold.

(ii) In reference to a Government stock, having a life of more than about fifteen years.

MADE UP (MADE DOWN) Refers to the process of settling bargains following the 'hammering' of a member firm.

MARGIN An amount payable on a speculative order by a client, the broker financing the balance. Should the price of a security bought 'on margin' fall to such an extent that, if the purchase were reversed the loss would use up all the margin payment, the broker is normally at liberty to close the transaction to avoid involving his own capital in risk.

MARK The price at which a bargain has been executed, recorded for publication in the Daily Official List.

MARKET (i) The trading floor of The Stock Exchange.

(ii) A section of that floor, i.e. the 'oil market', the securities comprising that section, or the jobbers dealing in those securities.

(iii) The freedom of dealing in a particular security, i.e. 'enjoys a free market'.

(iv) The level of prices, as in 'the market is up today'.

MARKET PRICE The price of a security quoted in the market.

MARKET VALUE The amount of stock or shares multiplied by market price.

MARKETABILITY Freedom of dealing in a security.

MATCH (OR MARRY) A broker who receives orders from different clients both to buy and sell the same security is permited to match one against the other. In order to ensure, however, that the price is fair to both sides, he must first offer the business to the market. Usually the business is 'put through' a jobber at a very small price difference.

MEDIUM-DATED Normally used for fixed-interest securities with final redemption dates of between ten and fifteen years.

MERCHANT BANK A City banking house which engages in some or all of many activities such as acceptance credits, export finance, issue of securities, etc.

MIDDLE PRICE A price mid-way between the bid and offered price.

MONEY STOCKS Short-dated securities used as alternatives to deposits, i.e. short-dated Government securities, etc.

NAMES (i) Names and addresses of clients used in registration of securities.
(ii) The department concerned with tickets, which used to carry this information.

NAMES DAY The day on which tickets for purchases are received.

NEGOTIATION Dealings in securities which do not enjoy a free market are carried out 'by negotiation', which means that some delay will probably ensue before a jobber can find a buyer either to take the security or to make a bid for it.

NET (i) In dealing with brokers resident outside London, contracts for relatively small amounts may be rendered at a 'net' price, i.e. a price which takes account of the London broker's commission.
(ii) In connection with yields, the return after deducting tax.

NEW (i) In connection with stock or shares, this usually applies to a recent issue, particularly where securities are transferable on allotment letters or renounceable certificates free of *ad valorem* stamp duty.
(ii) In connection with the account (or 'new time'), this refers to the account just about to commence, not the current account.

NO PAR VALUE (N.P.V.) Shares having no nominal value.

NOMINAL (i) When referring to a share, the value printed on the share certificate, i.e. 'shares of 25p each'. This must be confused with the market price.
(ii) When referring to a quotation in the market, this indicates that it is impossible to deal in this security except by negotiation.

NOMINATION FUND Applicants for admission to membership of The Stock Exchange contribute towards a fund for repaying those members who purchased 'nominations' under earlier regulations.

NOT TO PRESS (N.T.P.) Where a security enjoys only a restricted market, a jobber may sell shares which he has not got on the understanding that the buying broker will not press for delivery.

ODD LOTS A broken or small number of shares, or amount of stock, which, in American markets, necessitates a wider price than 'round amounts'.

OFFER FOR SALE A public issue where securities are offered to the public for purchase.

OFFERED (i) Where shares are easily obtainable in the market they are said to be 'freely offered'.

(ii) 'Offered, not bid' indicates that there are only sellers, not buyers, of this particular security.

OFFICE (i) 'General office' applies to the departments in a stockbroking firm which are concerned with the accounts and the transfer of securities.

(ii) 'In the office' indicates that an initiating order has been given by one of the brokers' own clients and is not a market bid or offer.

OFFICIAL LIST The Stock Exchange Daily Official List of securities, closing prices and prices at which transactions have taken place (marks), published daily by The Stock Exchange.

OPEN-ENDED (i) An expression used in the U.S.A. to indicate that a fund is based on the unit-trust principle where its capital can fluctuate by the variation in the number of units in issue.

(ii) In referring to loan-stock issues, the trust deed provides for further issues of similar stock subject to certain carefully defined limits.

OPENING PRICE (i) The price at the opening of the market each day.

(ii) The first price quoted in dealings in a new issue.

OPTION The right to deal in a security at a fixed price over a specified period. A 'call option' gives the right to purchase a security at the 'striking price' over a period normally up to three months. A 'put option' gives a similar right to sell the security. A 'double option' gives the right up to the end of the period to buy or sell.

ORDER An instruction to buy or sell a security.

ORDINARY The most common title for the equity or capital of a company which is entitled to the residue of both profits and assets after the rights of the prior-change capital have been satisfied.

OVERSUBSCRIBED In the case of a new issue, where applications are received for a total in excess of the amount available, the issue is said to be 'oversubscribed'.

PAR The nominal or face value.

PARI PASSU Having equal rights.

PARTICIPATING (i) In connection with capital, usually preference shares, holders of which are entitled not only to the fixed-interest dividend, but also to an additional distribution as described in the particulars of the issue.

(ii) Participating partners in stockbroking firms are those who derive their remuneration from a share in the residual profits after the fixed charges have been met. It should be pointed out, however, that all partners whether participating or not are at risk as to the whole of their resources on behalf of the firm.

PARTLY PAID Securities on which a liability still exists which may be called in due course.

P/E RATIO The ratio of price as to earnings which is used in assessing relative values of shares in the market, since it indicates the number of years' purchase of latest earnings represented by the price.

PLACING Direct sale of securities by stockbrokers to their clients. This term is used either in the context of a new issue or in disposing of a large amount of an existing security which they are instructed to sell.

PORTFOLIO A list of holdings in securities.

POSITION The state of an operator's book, particularly a jobber's, showing whether he is 'long' or 'short' of a security.

POST TRADING System of operating a stock market where buying and selling of securities takes place at fixed points, known as 'trading posts'.

PREFERENCE CAPITAL Share capital whose holders are entitled to prior rights as far as dividends and assets are concerned.

PREMIUM (i) In the case of a new issue, the excess of the market price over the issue price.

(ii) This term is also used to indicate the excess over the nominal value of quoted stocks.

(iii) 'Dollar premium' is the excess over a specified rate of exchange which must be paid for investment dollars required to purchase overseas securities.

PROBATE PRICE The price of a security accepted by the Capital Taxes Office, which is normally the bid quotation from the Official List plus one-quarter of the difference between this and the offered quotation. It is also sometimes called the 'quarter up' price.

PROCEEDS The amount raised on a sale, having taken into account the expenses.

PROSPECTUS The document published in connection with the issue of securities, subject to both statutory requirements and the rules and regulations of The Stock Exchange.

PROTECT An offer, usually by a jobber, to maintain a 'firm' bid or offer while the stockbroker consults his principal or endeavours to obtain a better price elsewhere.

PUT OPTION The right to sell a security at the 'striking' price within some specified period.

PUT-THROUGH See Match.

QUOTATION (i) A dealing price in the market.

(ii) The price taken from the Official List.

(iii) In the case of securities previously unquoted, the Council of The Stock Exchange grants 'permission to deal' and 'official quotation' when they approve an application for listing.

REDEEMABLE With reference to a stock, one which is repayable at some future date.

REDEMPTION YIELD Used in connection with a stock which is repayable, the yield is calculated to include both the interest receivable and an annual increment to allow for the increase or decrease in capital value to redemption. In calculating the 'net redemption yield', allowance is made for income tax and capital-gains tax at the relevant rates.

REGISTRATION The process of including a holding of securities in the company's books or other appropriate register.

RENOUNCEABLE CERTIFICATES Documents of title which bear, usually on the reverse, facilities for the original allottee to renounce his holding in favour of someone else.

RENUNCIATION FORM That part of a renounceable certificate or an allotment letter which is completed by the allottee in renouncing his allotment.

RETURN (i) Income obtainable from an investment.

(ii) Return of commission is allowable by stockbrokers to certain agents on the relevant stock exchange register, namely banks and certain professional individuals such as chartered accountants, solicitors, etc.

RIGHTS Any entitlement. In the case of issues to existing shareholders on a proportionate basis, this is generally known as a 'rights issue'.

RULING PRICE The market price applicable at the time.

SCRIP (i) Any form of security, particularly those in bearer form.

(ii) 'Scrip issue' is a term often applied to a capitalisation issue.

SECURITY (i) A generic term used to describe all stock exchange investments.

(ii) A document of title.

(iii) Assets pledged as collateral for a loan.

SELLING-OUT DEPARTMENT The Stock Exchange department to which a seller resorts if he is unable to obtain satisfaction in the delivery of a security.

SERVICE COMPANY A company owned by a stock exchange partnership which carries out the essential servicing of the firm. Utilisation of a service company may have tax advantages.

SETTLEMENT (i) The seven-day period during which accounts between member firms are settled.

(ii) The date of payment for securities bought and sold.

SHAPE Where one purchase is satisfied by a number of sales, or vice versa, the part deliveries are known as 'shapes'.

SHORT (i) Having a 'bear' position. Particularly used of a jobber who has sold more stock than he has bought.

(ii) In reference to a Government stock, having a life of less than five years.

SINKING FUND A fund, normally established in connection with an issue of loan capital, to extinguish all or part of the liability over a period

SPECIALIST A stock exchange member (especially in New York) who arranges the matching of transactions at the trading post.

SPLIT The division of a ticket, or the loss involved in this division.

SPONSOR The issuing house or stockbroker arranging the details of a new issue.

SPREAD (i) A diversity of interest, usually to describe the consitution of an investment portfolio between different classes of security and holdings in different geographical and industrial areas.

(ii) The difference between a jobber's bid and offered price.

SQUEEZE Application of pressure. This term is applied both to Government pressures on restricted credit and also to operations by jobbers to force bears to buy back their stock or bulls to liquidate.

STAG A speculator who applies for a new issue with the object of selling his allotment when dealings commence and taking a profit.

STAMP See Ad Valorem and Contract.

STRIKING PRICE See Option.

SUBJECT An offer or bid from the market, which has been made to more than one broker, is designated 'subject' to denote that it is not 'firm' and may thus not be available unless accepted immediately.

SWITCH An exchange from one security to another.

TAKE-OVER A bid by one company to acquire another.

TAKE UP To pay for a security, normally one allotted at the time of a new issue.

TAKER (i) Someone who, in a contango transaction, having sold a security will accept a rate for not delivering it.

(ii) In an option transaction a 'taker' is one who acquires an option to sell.

TALISMAN (Transfer Accounting Lodgement for Investors, Stock MANagement for Jobbers). A pool system in process of development for settlement of transactions and delivery of securities.

TAP An expression applied to a security where consistent sales are coming from one source, in particular a Government issue where the departments are gradually liquidating their holdings to the public.

TAPE (i) Two services supply information reproduced in subscribers' offices the Exchange Telegraph Company and Reuters Ltd. Information received in this manner is known to be 'on the tape'.

(ii) In the U.S.A. the tape is a printed record of each transaction published as quickly as possible to give maximum visibility to the market.

TENDER A method of selling securities, particularly new issues, whereby applicants submit bids independently and the issue is either allocated to bidders from the highest price downwards (e.g. issues of water stocks) or an issue price is selected at which subscriptions fully cover the offer and the required spread of shareholders is established.

TICKET A slip, prepared by the centre, to identify a purchase and passed to the jobber or to the selling broker.

TICKET DAY The second day of the settlement and the day on which tickets are passed. This is also called Name Day.

TITLE Short for entitlement, denoting ownership.

TRACE The act of identifying, or the record of, the intermediaries between the seller of a security and the buyer.

TRADE To deal or do business.

TRANSACTION The name applied to any completed purchase or sale of securities.

TRANSFER (i) The act of exchanging a security from one owner to another.

(ii) The document recording the change of ownership which is signed by the vendor is the 'transfer deed', abbreviated to 'transfer'.

TURN (i) This term generally refers to the difference between the bid and offered price quoted by a jobber. The jobber's 'turn' is only the same as the gross profit he makes on a transaction in a security when he buys and sells equal quantities at the bid and offered prices.

(ii) any small profit may be called 'a turn'.

UNAUTHORISED CLERK An employee of a member firm who is admitted to the trading floor of The Stock Exchange but is not allowed to deal in securities. See also Blue Button.

UNDATED A security without final date of redemption is termed 'undated'.

UNDERWRITE To insure. Offers of securities to the public are in most cases underwritten as a form of insurance that the issue is fully subscribed.

UNFRANKED INCOME Revenue which has not already suffered U.K. corporation tax.

UNIT (i) A subdivision of capital quoted as 'stock', i.e. 25p. stock unit.

(ii) Unit trust. An investment fund formed under the terms of a trust deed. Unlike an investment trust, which is a company with a fixed capital, the capital of a unit trust fluctuates with the injection or withdrawal of funds by investors.

UNLISTED (UNQUOTED) Having no listing on a recognised stock exchange.

UNSECURED Usually descriptive of loan capital having no specific assets earmarked as security.

VOTING RIGHTS Rights attached to share capital which permit the owner to vote at general and other meetings of the company under circumstances laid down in the Memorandum of Association.

WAITER The uniformed attendants in The Stock Exchange. The name is derived from the origins of the stock market, which first operated in a City coffee-house.

WALL STREET The colloquial term used for the New York Stock Exchange.

WITHHOLDING TAX Tax deducted at source from dividend payments, especially in the case of overseas companies, where tax is deducted before dividends are remitted to non-residents.

YIELD The yield is the annual return from an investment. It is usually quoted per cent. In the case of dated securities see Redemption Yield.

Recommended Reading

H. D. Berman, *The Stock Exchange* (Pitman, 6th ed., 1971).
R. J. Briston, *The Stock Exchange and Investment Analysis* (Allen & Unwin, 1975).
J. G. Day and A. T. Jamieson, *Institutional Investment* (Institute of Actuaries and Faculty of Actuaries, 6 vols, 1975).
M. Firth, *Investment Analysis: The Techniques of Appraising the British Stock Market* (New York: Harper & Row, 1975).
Investors Chronicle, Beginners, Please! (Throgmorton Publications, rev. ed., 1973).
E. V. Morgan and W. A. Thomas, *The Stock Exchange: Its History and Functions* (Elek Books, 1970).
D. Weaver, *Investment Analysis* (Longman, 1971).

Index